DORA BRIGHT

Women in Music

Series Editor

Anna Beer

Oxford University

This book series creates a platform for ground-breaking studies which offer new insight into any and all aspects of women in music. Building on Equinox Publishing's established lists in popular music, film music and the wider industry, the series is of interest to the scholar, practitioner, and general reader.

Women in Music aims to be inclusive, seeking to publish historical and critical studies, cultural analyses, life-writing, traditional musicology and more. The series as a whole works to challenge some of the less helpful divisions in music scholarship – for example, between 'popular' and 'classical' – by welcoming submissions which range, where appropriate, across genres, eras, and disciplines. The common thread, however, remains women's lived experience, whether as individuals or groups, and/or cultural understandings of the category of 'woman'.

Almost all areas of the music industry are now waking up to women's under-representation, and not just as a historical phenomenon. Change nevertheless remains slow. Through the dissemination of the latest scholarship in the field, *Women in Music* not only celebrates and explores the often hidden contributions of specific individuals and groups, but by contributing to a richer, more complex, picture of women in music, provokes some important questions for the industry.

Dora Bright

Her Life and Works in the Public Eye

Anthony Bilton

eǫuinox

SHEFFIELD UK   BRISTOL CT

Published by Equinox Publishing Ltd

UK: Office 415, The Workstation, 15 Paternoster Row, Sheffield, South Yorkshire,
      S1 2BX
USA: ISD, 70 Enterprise Drive, Bristol, CT 06010

www.equinoxpub.com

First published 2023

British Library Cataloguing-in-Publication Data

A catalogue record for this book is available from the British Library.

ISBN-13 978 1 80050 280 2 (hardback)
         978 1 80050 281 9 (ePDF)
         978 1 80050 357 1 (ePub)

Library of Congress Cataloging-in-Publication Data

Names: Bilton, Anthony, author.
Title: Dora Bright : her life and works in the public eye / Anthony Bilton.

Description: Bristol, CT : Equinox Publishing Ltd, 2023. | Series: Women in
   music | Includes bibliographical references and index. | Summary: "This
   book offers the first full-length study of Bright's inspirational life
   and work. It takes the reader from the arrival of Dora Bright's
   grandfather in Sheffield in 1769 through to her death in 1951. Through a
   rich variety of archival materials, it provides a public perspective on
   the life of this important, but now little-known, musician and
   composer"-- Provided by publisher.
Identifiers: LCCN 2022049074 (print) | LCCN 2022049075 (ebook) | ISBN
   9781800502802 (hardback) | ISBN 9781800502819 (pdf) | ISBN 9781800503571
   (epub)
Subjects: LCSH: Bright, Dora. | Women composers--England--Biography. |
   Composers--England--Biography. | Music--England--19th century--History
   and criticism. | Music--England--20th century--History and criticism.
Classification: LCC ML410.B8505 B55 2023 (print) | LCC ML410.B8505
   (ebook) | DDC 780.92 [B]--dc23/eng/20221011
LC record available at https://lccn.loc.gov/2022049074
LC ebook record available at https://lccn.loc.gov/2022049075

Typeset by S.J.I. Services, New Delhi, India

Dedicated to my wonderful wife Maxine and son Alexander who provided me with encouragement and support throughout the development of this book.

Contents

Acknowledgements

Throughout the production of this book, I have been overwhelmed by the kindness of individuals and the level of interest shown by them of the works of a largely unknown composer. These individuals and organizations are listed below in no specific order. Many thanks to you all.

The Bright family – Cymone De-Lara Bond and Lister De-Lara Taylor

Chris Hobbs – chrishobbs.com – Sheffield historian

Valerie Langfield – Editor of the SOMM CD piano works

Robert Matthew-Walker – Editor of *Musical Opinion*

Paul Som – Librarian at the Library of Congress, Washington DC, USA

Dr David Coates – Warwick University

Catherine Wilmers – Cellist

Caroline Caldwell – Finder of Maurice Delara music and letters

Aiden Hailey – Chatsworth Archive

The Devonshire Collection, Chatsworth

Eleanor Fitzpatrick – Archives and Library Manager, Royal Academy of Dance

Louise Calf – PhD Scholar, University of York

The Honorable Andrew Joliffe and the St Margaret's Church Babington, Charitable Trust

Somerset Archives

Derbyshire Archives

Jacqueline and Susan Knatchbull

Chertsey Museum – Emma Warren, Curator and Doris Neville-Davies, Museum Assistant

Richard Ormond – Sargent Drawings Catalogue

The British Newspaper Archive

The Illustrated London News

The Chatsworth Settlement Trustees

Mirrorpix newspapers

The estate of Dora Bright for permission to quote from her *Memoir*

List of Illustrations

Preface

My home town, the City of Sheffield, is well known for its recent contributions to music, with famous artists such as the Arctic Monkeys, Joe Cocker and the Human League. It is also renowned for its popular venues including the Sheffield City Hall, the Leadmill and the Sheffield Arena. Even back in the nineteenth century the town could claim musical fame as the birthplace of the composer and principal of the Royal Academy of Music, William Sterndale Bennett, born there in 1816. The famous conductor, Sir Henry Coward, came to Sheffield as a cutler's apprentice, became a teacher instead, and in 1876 founded the choir that became the Sheffield Philharmonic Chorus, one of the most prestigious Yorkshire choirs still active.

Less well known are the Bright family, industrialists and entrepreneurs, who over the course of two hundred years had a considerable impact on the town as it grew into a city. They played an important part in the development of its heavy industry, which would make it internationally famous as The Steel City.

The Bright family were musical, as were many middle-class families of the time, but unlike most, had two composers who could claim to be well-known and well-regarded during their lifetime. The first, Maurice Delara Bright, was bandmaster of the local military rifles unit and wrote military band music, some of which was played at Buckingham Palace in the presence of Queen Victoria. The second composer was his niece, Dora Bright, the winner of many prizes at the Royal Academy of Music and the first woman composer to be invited to write a work for the Philharmonic Society in London. Regarded as one of the finest piano players of her time and throughout her career, she was well reviewed by the press with her music receiving considerable praise, and she was particularly noted for her 'grace and charm'.[1]

My own introduction to the world of women composers happened many years ago, when the only classical music by women to make it to the recording studios were from the likes of Fanny Mendelssohn Hensel and Clara Schumann. Such big names, associated with their male relatives, brother Felix and husband Robert, were inevitable recording choices, not only because of the family connection, but also because both women had their works published in their own lifetimes and remained, to some extent, part of the concert repertoire. The first CD that I came across including women composers was a special edition by the BBC with Fanny Mendelssohn Hensel, Clara Schumann, Louise Farrenc and Marie Grandval. I loved the music but finding many more recordings at the time proved difficult. Even in 2013, when I first did a Wikipedia search of classical composers, out of the hundreds on the list there were only three women, Hildegard of Bingen, Fanny Mendelssohn Hensel and Clara Schumann. A similar search today gives a whole page devoted to women composers and a very long list from composers who predate Hildegard through to those of today.

To me it seems clear, having listened to many works written by women composers, which have only recently been recorded, that a great deal of their music across the ages has always been as good as any of the most gifted men, and for us to distinguish on gender is a very narrow viewpoint, and no doubt led to the loss of some very fine works. A composer's status, gender, colour, or any other bias we can invent, should never prevent us from considering their music in its own right.

It was a chance snippet on the radio that eventually led me, somewhat circuitously, to Dora Bright. I didn't know at the time whose music I was listening to, but when I looked at the playlist and found it was by Fanny Mendelssohn Hensel, I knew I was missing something and needed to retrace my steps and listen to her music again. A CD including the piece from the radio was duly purchased and it was a new dawn – her music was captivating and despite being a fan of Felix Mendelssohn I couldn't help but be drawn to the fresh, clean and crisp sounds that were so familiar but yet so different. More Mendelssohn Hensel CDs were purchased and those led to others such as Cécile Chaminade, Dorothy Howell and Amy Beach; the Beach piano concerto being a particular favourite. I began to wonder what else I was missing and how many other wonderful pieces of music by other women composers still existed.

With a lifelong love of piano concertos, the question was – were there others to discover? By chance I came across a French website, 'PresenceCompositrice' and the 'que demander a Clara' search engine. My initial question was: were there any English women composers who wrote piano concertos? The answer was: many. The inevitable second question was: were any from Sheffield? A review of the list somewhat surprisingly identified just one – Dora Bright. Coincidence is an amazing thing and a very quick internet search found the newly issued 2019 SOMM CD of her two major orchestral works including the *Piano Concerto in A minor*. The CD was ordered and when it arrived the music was new, creative and wonderful. A comment in the CD literature suggested most of her works were lost or destroyed and further internet searches of her works suggested a second piano concerto existed. That was enough to start my quest to find the second piano concerto and draw up a catalogue of her works.

The search has been enlightening and led me to an understanding of the complexities and difficulties faced by women composers simply to have any works published at all. The prejudice of Victorian/Edwardian values kept women away from mainstream composition and large-scale performance as they had to put up with the critics in a way that men did not, being constrained in their writing and often only able to publish songs. What impressed me was that Dora Bright did not seem to bow to these restrictions and merely set out her stall to be as good as she could be, and through her own endeavours, made a real place for herself in the heart of the nation as one of the great women composers of her era.

It took many months scouring the archives in search of her works, with the obvious starting point being Wikipedia, which provided a short list of works. This list was merely replicated across numerous other sites with all its inaccuracies and shortcomings. Even the 'PresenceCompositrice' website, specifically set up to record women composers and their works, had only a small subset of the Wikipedia items. (I am pleased to say it now has a very fair representation after I shared the catalogue with them.) After a comprehensive search I am now happy to publish what is the most complete Catalogue Raisonné possible from the records which remain from the time of her life and works (see Appendix 1).

The catalogue is extensive and covers a wide range of types of music from large orchestral work to more intimate chamber pieces and songs. What is dramatic is the time span of the compositions, her first recorded work, the song *Whither?*, was in 1882, the year after she first joined the Royal Academy of Music. Her final work, a piano transcription of Arne's *Siciliano and Gigue from the Suite in D minor* was published in 1948, when Dora was seventy-six. Unfortunately, the second piano concerto turned out to be a red herring and its inclusion in her 1913 *Who's Who* entry was due to a misunderstanding over the use of the words 'condensed-concerto', to describe her Fantasias. Sadly, the Fantasias no longer exist either. (More about this issue in Chapter 5.)

The chapters ahead follow her life from the arrival in England of her great grandfather, through her early life and then on to her performance and composing career. The biography has been developed from searches of all the key archives and libraries around the globe, together with other recollections of her life from peers and acquaintances, along with reports of her life and works from the British and foreign press during her life, from her birth in 1862, until her death in 1951.

Author at Babington House

It may seem unreasonable, after such a passage of time, to conclude on who Dora Bright was as a person, as the historical records can only hint at the reasons for her actions, thought processes and beliefs. It is also difficult to ignore our own view of the period and clear our eyes of our own modern-day prejudices and beliefs. However, I have tried to find the real Dora Bright. But this is my perspective on her life from the research I have conducted and although I have made some interpretations and suggested some reasons for her choices, by and large the story unfolds through the reporting of her life by the newspapers and archival material. As is the case today, the papers then were full of bias against women, but somewhat surprisingly, they weren't afraid to write something positive about things they felt were well done, and as a result their overall verdict on Dora Bright is, by and large, more positive than one might expect.

Was she great? If we liken her to some of the acknowledged greats of all time, Beethoven or Mozart as examples, then the answer has to be no. But if we consider her against the other well-remembered and often-quoted leading women composers of the nineteenth/twentieth century, such as Rosalind Ellicott or Ethel Smyth, then she is as prolific as they were, more broad-ranging in output and had a greater impact on the population of music-goers and music players than those and many others. Her songs, such as those based on 'The Jungle Book', and her ballet music travelled across the Atlantic, and through her association with Adeline Genée she championed the renaissance of English ballet, which would lead to the establishment of the Royal Academy of Dance and the Royal Ballet. Dame Adeline Genée provided a fitting epitaph in a memorial piece in *The Times* shortly after Dora's death: 'Whatever she did, she made worth doing, and appreciated her friends, whom she never lost through a long life'.[2]

She has been sadly overlooked, in part because the quantity and availability of her printed works is quite small in comparison to her output, with only four of her works having ever been recorded (see Appendix 6), but also due to the lack of a definitive catalogue of her works and an understanding of her importance to the many strands of music in Victorian/Edwardian England. I think she deserves to be better recognized and this book is a small step in placing Dora Bright in her rightful place alongside the other great women composers. Hopefully, it ensures that both she and her works are remembered, and one day heard again.

Introduction

In 1905, an article in the *Sheffield Daily Telegraph* could assure its readers of the following truths:

Women as Composers

Mr Albert Visetti is writing a book on female composers and their music. The higher fields of composition have not been attained by women, who in musical art shine more as interpreters than as creators. Yet the role of gifted female composers is by no means an insignificant one. It is easy to recall such gifted writers as Ethel Smyth (whose opera, Der Wald, is a fine work), Augusta Holmes, Liza Lehmann, Dora Bright, Maude V. White, Rosalind Ellicott and C. Chaminade.[1]

One of the gifted composers mentioned here is the subject of this book: Dora Bright. Despite the apparent praise, the overall tone of the piece is disparaging about women as composers, who by their very nature, lack creativity. Even as late as 1944, the great conductor Sir Thomas Beecham, considering the importance of Ethel Smyth, wrote:

As a result of thirty years of women in music, it has been brought to a state of hopeless decadence. There are, he continued, no women composers, never have been and possibly never will be.[2]

Dora Bright's life, 1862 to 1951, was, of course, impacted by these views of women, but this book will demonstrate the ways in which, rather than being stifled by them, she established herself as a performer and composer. Bright worked with her society's understanding of women's roles rather than against them, whilst she championed women either through charitable works or through her part in upcoming women's movements such as the Forum Club, set up in 1919 to support women professionals.[3] She was not a feminist in any modern sense of the word and did not openly support the suffragette movement as did other women composers such as Ethel Smyth. However, her ability to identify the changing role of women, and the way in which she adapted her musical output to the changes in society at large, are some of the reasons for her long and successful career. These same changes, in her retirement and after her death, would leave her music behind and forgotten.

Bright's career began in the final decades of the nineteenth century, a period that saw a resurgence in English music, fuelled in part by the growth of the Empire. There was a marked improvement in the quality of music being composed, and musical culture began to assume a more significant role across the nation. These years, between 1880 and 1918, have been labelled the English Musical Renaissance (for English read British), and as early as 1902 John Fuller-Maitland, an influential music critic of the time, identified five key leaders of this renaissance along with eighty followers, including sixteen female composers, one of which was Dora Bright:

> They have shown remarkable gifts, gifts which are certainly enough to warrant us in doubting the general dictum that no woman has ever yet succeeded in the creative arts.[4]

The leaders of the renaissance were viewed differently depending on the critic, but Fuller-Maitland favoured his Oxford colleagues, Parry and Stanford, as the pre-eminent composers of the period, dismissing the likes of Delius, Sullivan and Elgar, as they were either of the wrong class, not English enough, or wrote too much operetta. Despite the differences of opinion, the period was one in which music was redefined and revived with a national voice.

Ethel Smyth, a contemporary of Dora Bright, was acknowledged at the time to be the greatest of the women composers of the renaissance. However, Dora Bright was at the heart of this movement from as early as her first years in the Royal Academy of Music when she championed English composers and the music of her own British friends. Throughout the period from 1885 to 1904, time and time again she would return to this idea of English music and a resurgence of a national music through her own concerts. Ralph Vaughan-Williams would champion the renaissance after the First World War with music harking back to Thomas Tallis, and would:

> cut the bonds that from the times of Handel and Mendelssohn had bound England hand and foot to the Continent. He found in the Elizabethans and folk-song the elements of a native English language that need no longer be spoken with a German accent, and from it he forged his own idiom. The emancipation he achieved thereby was so complete that the composers of succeeding

generations like Walton and Britten had no longer need of the conscious nationalism which was Vaughan Williams's own artistic creed. There is now an English music which can make its distinctive contribution to the comity [association] of nations.[5]

This second English musical renaissance can in one sense be considered to be the first women's English musical renaissance. Finally, the role of women composers as part of this movement were recognized by the critics. Their time in the spotlight was short and even the great Ethel Smyth, the first woman composer to be given a Damehood in 1922, ended her days as a critic, being regarded as an amusing eccentric. To a large extent the women composers of the renaissance, such as Frances Allitsen, Rosalind Ellicott and Adela Maddison, have been largely forgotten along with their music, in sharp contrast to the continued presence in our musical culture of Elgar and others.

The last twenty years have fortunately seen the beginning of a second English musical renaissance in women's music and it is time to revisit these women composers and their works. This will allow us to understand the role of women in music, but also to rediscover some of the music that is characteristic of the era, which should itself be viewed as a vital and defining element of the wider British Musical Renaissance.[6]

Bright was able to identify change as it occurred, and to live through it and make it her own. It is not only that she was successful, although she was certainly that. Bright was one of the first British women to receive a multitude of prizes during her time at the Royal Academy of Music; her high-profile concert engagements of her own and others' works at prestigious venues in London and the major musical cities of Germany were well-received. But Bright, unlike any other woman composer of her period, continued to compose before, during and after her marriage and continued as a concert pianist and a performer throughout her life. Her musical style did not alter greatly during her life, but she continued to give pleasure to millions of listeners over her fifty years as an artist. She embodies the spirit of women in music during the English Musical Renaissance:

> The spirit of this volatile society inevitably affected the position of women musicians, themselves a gloriously diverse group, ranging from performers working in seaside hotels and music halls, through aristocrats singing in society drawing rooms to soloists of international renown.[7]

This one sentence encapsulates Dora Bright's life, who started her career as a composer and concert pianist, wrote for and performed with aristocrats in society drawing rooms and in front of the King, created mimodrama and theatrical works for the music halls of the early 1900s, and was a soloist of high regard in Germany in the 1890s. Had she been asked to work in a seaside hotel, there is no doubt that had it furthered her career she would have said yes. As it was, her works were performed at the Bournemouth Winter Gardens a number of times, which although not quite a seaside hotel, is most certainly by the sea and a holiday venue.

This major force in English music is now largely forgotten. Her works were played little after her death and much of her music was destroyed. Dora Bright was a considerable woman, a fine pianist, a great composer, an excellent host and a good friend. She was no shrinking violet, but nor was she self-obsessed as she worked hard with charities and in championing other composers' work at home and on the Continent. Her ballet works with Adeline Genée set the scene for a resurgence in the English love of ballet and the establishment of the Royal Academy of Dance through Genée's Presidency from 1920. Bright's self-determination, tenacity and plain hard work, on her own behalf and also for her friends and through her charitable works, make her a force to be reckoned with, and should be a role model to all.

1 Contemporaries

Two composers, Adelina De Lara (1872–1961) and Dorothy Howell (1898–1982) offer contrasts and connections with Dora Bright, revealing the common challenges faced by women, but also the significant differences between them as individuals. There are similarities in their lives and stories, but their successes arise from different paths: De Lara reliant on patronage, Howell on social advantage, and Bright on ability and self-determination. Of the three, only Dorothy Howell's works are played today, although she is still not well-known.

Adelina De Lara (originally Lottie Adeline Preston)

Figure 1.1. Adelina De Lara (originally Lottie Adeline Preston)

De Lara was born into a musically gifted but financially precarious family, in a very similar vein to Dora Bright. Her mother was once a singer of promise, but had ruined her prospects by a disastrous first marriage. De Lara's father, an engraver and illuminator, travelled from town to town taking his family with him. He played several musical instruments and also sang. George, De Lara's half-brother, incurred the wrath of his father by leaving home to marry an actress; a curious similarity to the story of Dora Bright's Uncle Horatio (see Chapter 3).

De Lara's family moved home frequently, but at each new lodging her father always ensured access to a piano. De Lara did not attend school as her father had decided she was to play the piano professionally and so she was made to spend many hours a day playing, developing her musical talent. The family's income fluctuated so much that they would often go hungry and have to rely on emergency funds from a well-to-do aunt in London. Aged six and a half, De Lara played in front of a hotel owner where the family were staying, who seeing the potential of her early aptitude encouraged her to continue her studies. She went on to play at a children's musical competition in Liverpool, which she won. Her parents realized her potential as the breadwinner of the family and went on to direct their efforts in furthering her career. After a conversation between her father and the owner of a music shop, who advised that Adelina Preston would go nowhere with such an English name, she adopted her mother's maiden name and became Mademoiselle Adelina De Lara. Dora Bright's Uncle Maurice took the surname Delara, over his original, Bright, in respect of his own mother's maiden name (see Chapter 3) – there is a possible distant family connection.

For several years, De Lara supported the family playing at a Madame Tussaud-like waxworks gallery in Liverpool, where she played for £4 (£520 today) a week every afternoon from 3pm to 5.30pm and 3pm to 10pm. Her performances often drew crowds and the *Manchester Guardian* remarked on the considerable ability of this ten-year-old pianist that could play for several hours from memory. Unfortunately, in 1883 De Lara was orphaned, her father died of pneumonia, her mother of heart failure, her eldest sister committed suicide and she was left supporting her remaining sister by playing the piano until her second aunt invited them both to live with her in London, where she ran a boarding house.

One of the residents of the boarding house turned out to be very well connected and on hearing De Lara play, introduced the young pianist to some of his society friends. De Lara performed at Marlborough House, London, in front of the Prince and Princess of Wales and then visited Birmingham, playing for two wealthy families, who went on to provide considerable patronage in the form of introductions to famous musicians and financially supporting De Lara for many years to come.

De Lara wrote in her autobiography:

> When I was young, music was a far more social and personal affair than it is today, and it was very usual for eminent families to give their patronage to musicians of promise, to help and encourage, support them financially and give social functions at which an artist was introduced to their circle and played in the intimate surroundings of their homes.[1]

At a musical evening to which she was taken, De Lara heard the pianist Fanny Davies, just returned from Frankfurt, where Davies had been studying with Clara Schumann. The performance made the young De Lara aware of her limitations and stimulated her desire to improve. Sometime later, De Lara performed at another house party and no sooner had she finished playing than Fanny Davies rushed up to the piano, embraced De Lara and exclaimed, 'you must go to Madame Schumann'.

After a year of preparation with Fanny Davies, De Lara auditioned with Clara Schumann and spent the next five years studying in Germany, her expenses underwritten by several patrons. The years in Frankfurt were the happiest of her life, interspersed as they were with holidays in England, hosted by her patrons and their musical friends.

De Lara wrote about one of her lessons in her autobiography, where she was shown how to play Robert Schumann's Piano Concerto:

> Clara was very exacting. She insisted that 'thought, not technique' should guide performance. She would balance tone from both hands, accurate grading of diminuendos, no sentimentality, no misshaping of the rhythms. Above all she emphasized the need for calmness.[2]

Through De Lara's acquaintance with Clara Schumann and her English patrons, she met with many of the great composers of the age, Grieg, Dvorak, Parry, Stanford, Steiner and Sullivan, all of whom took time to talk and play piano with her. In her autobiography De Lara details numerous encounters with these great composers. One touching example is a recollection of a meeting with Dvorak, who was a regular visitor with her patrons in Birmingham:

> One morning when I was practising in the music room, the door quietly opened and to my surprise he strolled in thrusting his hands as usual deep inside his pockets. 'I give you a ha'penny if you play our Ballade', by which he meant Chopin's *A Flat Ballade*. It was one of my special pieces and a great favourite in those days. I was determined to have that ha'penny! Without more ado I started to play, whilst he listened intently. When I had finished he took my

hand, solemnly shook it, smiled his thanks and turned to go. 'Herr Dvorak', I called, and as he turned I faltered, 'my ha'penny?' 'Do you wish it Fraulein Adelina?' 'Oh yes, I shall keep it all my life'. But he turned again to the door, opened it, and I thought my ha'penny was lost forever. Then with a sudden smile he said, 'I come back with ha'penny', and was gone. I went on playing and after quite a long time he returned and held out my halfpenny. 'See what I wrote for you', he said, and I felt his eyes on me as I eagerly studied his inscription. On one side of the coin he had scratched ... 'Dvorak'; on the right-hand side of Britannia was written 'Birmingham' and by the Ship 'October '91'. On the other side across Queen Victoria's chest was scrawled 'Adelina' and in front of her majesty's nose he wrote 'Ballade'. I think I hugged him I was so pleased. Later I had it covered with a sovereign's worth of gold.[3]

In 1891 De Lara returned to England to launch her career with a crowd-pleasing debut at the Popular Promenade series, made possible through an introduction from Clara Schumann:

When I had finished there was a great ovation; I had won the coveted 'encore'. To crown my happiness came another 'call'. I knew that I had not failed Clara Schumann ... I knew that I was 'made', for the standard of the 'Pops' was so high, and the concerts famous throughout the world, that success or failure could be decided then and there.[4]

De Lara went on to have a very successful career as a pianist and composer. She mentions Dora Bright when they worked together as adjudicators for a piano examination at the Royal Academy of Music:

I found it rather trying having to listen to the same piece again and again. On one occasion it was the *Chopin Fantasie in F minor* and by the end of the day I wished he had never written it. I remember Dora Bright, who already was making her name as a composer, was my fellow examiner that day.[5]

Despite this moment working together they would not meet again until fifty years later, when, with typical hospitality, Dora Bright invited her fellow composer to a house party.

De Lara was a member of the Society of Women Musicians and her publications for 1940 are listed in the Society's annual report and comprise two piano concertos, *Suite for Orchestra – In the Forest* and *Schumann Suite*. Throughout the war De Lara continued to perform playing on many occasions with the BBC on the radio. As a last pupil of Clara Schumann, De Lara was called upon to perform Clara's works on many occasions and left recordings of the works, now in the British Library as a final link and musical reference to one of the most famous woman composers of the nineteenth century. Gaining favour from the Queen Mother, in 1951 the honour of Officer of the British Empire (OBE) was bestowed upon her at Buckingham Palace. A considerable number of her own works have survived and are part of the British Library collection along with recordings of her demonstrating Clara Schumann's piano technique.

Despite her success, Adelina De Lara is now another almost forgotten woman composer. Musical tastes in the decades after her death in 1961 moved away from the romantic music associated with her own works and those of her teacher, Clara Schumann. Orchestral performances focused on what audiences paid to hear, the larger works of Mozart, Beethoven, and the other great classical composers. As with so many other women composers, many of De Lara's works were not printed in her own lifetime, due to the difficulties associated with finding publishers willing to take on women's compositions as they were often deemed unsuitable for a wider audience. As a result her archive slipped out of public view and only as recently as 2005 has it been partially revived through the work of De Lara's family and the publisher Stainer and Bell. The increased interest in women composers and the 150th anniversary of De Lara's birth are also factors in a limited revival of interest in her life and works.

Dorothy Gertrude Howell

Figure 1.2. Dorothy Gertrude Howell

In contrast to De Lara's early years, Howell's family life was stable and solidly based on Christian principles, derived from her middle-class upbringing, with education at its heart. Howell's father had developed a lucrative business trading in iron, with money no object. Unlike De Lara, Howell was free to follow her own musical inclinations, rather than being forced down a specific path to keep the family financially afloat. The Howell family lived in a wealthy suburb of Birmingham and the local parish magazines and trade directories include numerous entries relating to the local Philharmonic orchestra and the many professional musicians and instrument builders in the area. Howell's father was the organist and Director of Music at the family's local Catholic church, a prestigious post for a part-time amateur musician and one that no doubt played a considerable influence on the whole family's musical activities.

Howell was taught piano, violin, musical theory and composition by her father, a hugely gifted amateur musician. Born in 1898, her early education was through a family nanny and her father, who she claimed in later life 'was her greatest musical influence'. After attending a convent school in Birmingham, at the age of eleven Howell's parents sent her to a convent in Flanders, Belgium, to complete what was viewed as an authentically Catholic education.

Aged thirteen, Howell produced a set of six works which her father published, becoming her Opus 1. As children's pieces they have titles such as 'Puddle Duck', 'Mouse Dance' and 'Will o' the Wisp', but they do give some small impression of her future style and playful approach, which would become part of her compositional design. Her father, who had identified the potential in his daughter, employed Sir Granville Bantock (composer and founder of the Birmingham City Orchestra) to teach her composition in the holidays, and promoted her works at dinner parties to which he was invited, hosted by local dignitaries and industrialists.

The family prospered and moved out of Birmingham to Stourbridge, where they acquired a large house and built their own private chapel, with its own two-manual organ. Now aged fifteen, Howell successfully applied to the Royal Academy of Music to study composition. Amongst the works she submitted, as part of her application, was a choral piece, *My Soul is Awakened*, which went on to win her the Academy's Hine Prize in 1914, only months after becoming a student. Her studies went well, and she won the Sterndale Bennett Prize in 1916, previously awarded to Dora Bright in 1887.

After graduating from the Royal Academy of Music, Dorothy returned home to her family in Stourbridge as was expected of an unmarried young lady, although in line with her own desire to continue her musical career from the West Midlands. However, almost immediately the family received numerous letters from influential musical figures in London begging her to return to London, where they suggested she had a great future as a composer and pianist. One such letter, from J. B. McEwen, Professor of Harmony and

Composition at the Royal Academy of Music, attempted to persuade Howell's father to allow her to return to London:

> I can quite understand the natural desire on your part, and on the part of her mother, to have her at home with you. I can also see that, from her point of view, Dorothy herself is anxious to get back to home life ... but I think that I should in some measure be failing of what is my artistic responsibility if I did not put the other side of the matter before you.[6]

Her father acceded to the requests and Dorothy returned to London, where she set about writing her first large-scale orchestral work, *Lamia*. The work, a tone poem based on John Keats' poem of the same name, was a huge success and brought her to public attention as a woman composer. The maturity of her music was noted, despite being considered relatively young aged twenty-one. The piece was such a public success that Henry Wood, father of the Proms, included it a further four times in the 1919 Promenade series. Henry Wood and Dorothy became good friends and he later promoted and conducted her other major works, a ballet *Koong Shee* and the *Piano Concerto in D minor*, as they premiered under his baton.

Such was Howell's new-found success that the newspapers reported her as the English Strauss, after comments by Henry Wood:

> Sir Henry Wood ... on the conclusion of the performance stood up and shook Howell warmly by the hand. It is declared that he described her as the finest composer since Strauss.[7]

The public also clearly took to Howell:

> Miss Dorothy Howell, who stepped into fame at the Queen's Hall on Wednesday night, is the very antithesis of what the general public imagine a musical genius to be. The positive public and critical reception naturally made her a much-sought after young lady by musical experts, interviewers and autograph hunters yesterday. But adulation does not appeal to her, and while many people haunted her hotel, Miss Howell, happy and unmolested, spent the morning with her youngest brother Alfred and the animals at the Zoo.[8]

However, after the acclaim given to *Lamia*, her subsequent works did not achieve such positive reviews and her orchestral compositions grew smaller in scale, most likely as a result of the critical reviews of her ballet and piano concerto. A final attempt to woo the audience with *The Rock*, another tone poem, failed. The *Musical Times* bemoaned the lack of substantial melodic material and lack of direction throughout the piece:

> Like much of Miss Howell's music, this overture opens with some
> effective material, and then loses its way among a number of frag-
> mentary ideas which are not co-ordinated into convincing design.
> It has, however, its picturesque moments; it is not over long and
> it does not make a great noise – and that's something to be thank-
> ful for.[9]

The work had only one performance, after which Howell moved away from
large-scale composition for some time.

There followed a successful period as a concert pianist and she established a close working friendship with a ballet dancer, Ivanava (real name
Nancy Hanley) experimenting in the simultaneous improvisation of music
and dance. The 1920s saw Howell move more towards teaching and examin-
ing, and she developed close relationships with a number of Catholic private
schools and associated with this period are a number of choral works for two-
part choir and organ. With the advent of radio, Howell became a favourite
with the BBC as a pianist and music broadcaster, with regular programmes
throughout the 1920s. This was a platform to continue her career as a pianist,
but also to play her own music to the nation, which she did frequently. During
the Second World War she took part in secret performances for the BBC
Overseas Music Department, and although she was offered a full-time post
in 1943, she turned it down in favour of other commitments and the need to
look after her ailing mother, as expected of a spinster daughter.

The BBC played a very important part in the inter-war years allowing many
women composers the opportunity to perform and display their own works.
De Lara, Howell, Bright, Hess and others were frequent players on what was
one of the few platforms open to women composers. Concert performances
remained largely in the hands of male conductors and profit-minded pro-
moters, whereas the BBC with its public broadcast duties were able to offer
smaller and more intimate opportunities to display the music of a wider
range of composers of both sexes. The other major opportunity for women
to perform and display their own works was through small local chamber
groups where women would get together to play each other's works. These
small chamber groups became a significant focus of the Society of Women
Musicians, founded in 1911, who actively collated chamber works for their
members to play.

The 1950s saw a decline in the popularity of Howell's work to the point that
the Oxford University Press pulped several of her works for piano, inform-
ing her that sales of the works had been disappointingly small for a number
of years and that it had concluded public interest had disappeared. At this
time Howell was suffering from cancer, leading to depression. She turned to
her religion, writing more liturgical works which she continued to compose
until the late 1970s. Her last years were spent living in a retirement home in
Malvern, during which time she composed her final piece, a piano work for

one hand for an amputee friend. At the age of eighty-three she passed away in January 1982 and was buried near to one of her heroes, Edward Elgar.

Unlike so many others, her name has lived on due in large part to her niece who established an archive of her letters, diaries and music catalogue. A short autobiography followed in 1992 and then in 1998 an exhibition at the Barbican Music Library in London. *Lamia* and the Piano Concerto have now been recorded and some of her works remain as part of the concert repertoire.

Howell's lasting legacy comes from what her story reveals about the nature of English music in the twentieth century. In many respects she was an outsider from the governing musical elite – being female and Roman Catholic – and yet she achieved rapid success at the Royal Academy of Music in an entirely meritocratic manner. Throughout her time at the Royal Academy of Music, she flourished, as did Dora Bright, in a way that challenges Ethel Smyth's declaration that women musicians had to struggle for the musical opportunities freely open to men.[10] Although the circumstances of the First World War provided a greater opportunity for female composers to be recognized, Howell's experience at the Royal Academy of Music is telling of the social reforms that were taking place at the beginning of the twentieth century in British musical life.

The unfulfilled promise of Howell's subsequent career as an orchestral composer provides an insight into the difficulty female composers often had in being taken seriously when composing in traditional forms, whilst also being viewed in the wider context of the decline of Late Romantic music during the 1920s.[11]

***

There are significant similarities with the career of Dora Bright in both the lives of Adelina De Lara and Dorothy Howell. Their stories illustrate very well how patronage and social advantage opened doors and helped to create careers and success. In spite of these advantages both De Lara and Howell remain largely unknown and forgotten. The privileges afforded them, and their own natural abilities and determination, were not enough to ensure their place in posterity, as has also been the case for many male composers whose names we know well, if not always their music.

Although from a comparatively wealthy middle-class background, Dora Bright enjoyed none of these advantages, and from her arrival in London in 1881 she had to work to pay for her place at the Royal Academy of Music. It was only through her own determination, and despite little support from anyone else in the musical world, that she achieved her hard-won success.

2 The Brights of Sheffield

The Brights were one of the earliest Jewish families to settle in Sheffield. Members of the family were influential in the city's development and were highly regarded and played important roles in its institutions throughout the eighteenth and nineteenth centuries. There are suggestions that the Bright brothers, Isaac and Philip, came to England from Biarritz in France,[1] but it seems more likely that they travelled from Bayreuth in Germany[2] and the name of Bright was an anglicization of the German town name. Whichever their direction of travel, with the general instability and wars across Europe, England must have seemed a much safer place, teetering on the brink of the Industrial Revolution and economic expansion – a country in which one could make a name and create a prosperous future to nurture a new family.

Originally Ashkenazi Jews, the brothers' later descendants took a liberal view of their religion and regardless of the general lack of intermarriages between sects in the early nineteenth century, there are marital ties to both the De Metz and the De Lara families, both being Noble Spanish Sephardi Jewish families. Over the course of the 1800s the family grew further from their Jewish ancestry and although some members of the family chose to return to their religion for their final burial rights and internment, many espoused their religion totally, being buried as Christians and living non-Jewish lives. During the early years of the Brights' integration into English life there remained a considerable prejudice against the Jewish population and it is probable that Isaac and his descendants wanted to amalgamate into English society. Census entries for the men of the family record them as Gentlemen and it is clear they wanted to be as much a part of the establishment as possible.

Dora Bright's father was born and buried in the Jewish faith, but lived his life as an English gentleman, marrying a Christian and raising his daughter in the Christian faith. Throughout her own life, Dora remained true to this Christian background, but also showed pride in her Spanish origins.[3]

The family trade was jewellery and silverwork, and their arrival in Sheffield coincided with the development of crucible steel and the industry most associated with Sheffield, cutlery and Sheffield plate. Within 100 years of the Brights' arrival, the population of Sheffield had grown tenfold and its economic success, and that of many members of the family, was well established. The family did not remain wholly in Sheffield, and as their success grew, they established jewellery and silversmith businesses in Leamington Spa, Brighton, Scarborough and Doncaster.[4]

(See simplified family tree in Appendix 2.)

Isaac Bright (Dora's great grandfather)

The first members of the Bright family arrived in Sheffield around 1786; Isaac at the age of twenty-three together with his two-year-old brother Philip. Isaac established himself as a watchmaker with his earliest surviving piece having a London hallmark of 1778, engraved 'Bright And Sons, Sheffield, No. 6790'.[5] By 1797 Bright and Sons had a workshop in the centre of Sheffield and Isaac was doing well enough to support local charities and his growing family. He was a regular donor to the Sheffield General Infirmary between 1799 and 1813 and, somewhat oddly, the treasurer of the Masonic Royal Brunswick Lodge in 1817.

At the time of Isaac's arrival there were only a few Jewish families in Sheffield and nothing that could be called a Jewish community. As a result, he had to be introduced to a family from Norfolk to find his wife to be. In 1796, Isaac married Ann, the daughter of Hirsch Nicholls of Dereham, Norfolk (also known as Henry Micholls).[6]

Married in a London synagogue they went on to have a large family of ten children and dozens of grandchildren, many of whom followed the family business and became jewellers. Isaac and his two eldest sons, Maurice and Selim, became partners in the Bright & Sons Company,[7] 'merchants, watchmakers, jewellers, silversmiths and cutlers', with premises at the Market Place in Sheffield.

Isaac was strongly involved in the creation of the first synagogue in Sheffield in 1790, although the family did marry into non-Jewish families in later years.[8] The intermarriages of Jew to non-Jew and Sephardic Jew to Ashkenazi Jew within the Bright family may have been a result of the small number of Jewish families in England at the end of the eighteenth century, but was certainly a reflection of the Bright family's wider wish to assimilate into English life more readily. Isaac became less interested in being part of the Jewish community in Sheffield and purchased land for future family burials, up on the moors above the town, completely separate to the new Jewish Cemetery being laid out in Sheffield itself.[9]

A receipt, initially dated 27 September 1814, from Isaac to Philip Gell for a timepiece, is the only remaining paperwork from his tenure of the Sheffield business. The document shows the final instalment of £1 16s being paid two years later on 13 September 1816. The reverse of the receipt has a number of calculation options for the purchaser with eighteen payments totalling the purchase price of £23 15s (£2,400). A handsome price even today.[10]

Around 1825, Isaac moved to Buxton in Derbyshire and established a new jewellery business, leaving his son Maurice to manage the Sheffield business as a partner. Times were not always easy and the partnership was dissolved in 1831, with Isaac buying back his son's debts. However, they partnered again, but only for a short period as once again the partnership was dissolved in 1847. Isaac moved to Leamington Spa in 1835, to establish a further outpost of the Bright jewellery business, leaving Selim, his second son, to run the Buxton business and Maurice running the re-established Sheffield business. Isaac died in 1849, at the grand old age of eighty-seven. His death certificate records him as a doyen of English society – Gentleman. His hard work had paid off and in future years the family would associate with aristocracy and even royalty. Isaac left £300 (£40,000 today) in his will and his final remains were transferred from Leamington Spa to be buried at Deane Road Jewish Cemetery in Liverpool.

Philip, Isaac's younger brother, moved to Doncaster in the early 1800s and established himself on the High Street as a jeweller. In 1830 he made the horse racing Doncaster Gold Cup, valued then at 150 guineas[11] (£18,000 today). His daughter, Maria, went on to marry her first cousin Henry, son of Selim, in the synagogue in Hull in 1844, before moving with him to his father's home in Buxton.

Great Uncle Maurice (eldest son of Isaac)

Maurice (Moses ben Isaac), born in 1796, was politically minded and active in local affairs. Appointed a Police Commissioner in 1827, he was a key player in obtaining Corporation status for the Town of Sheffield in 1843. As a Jew he was not allowed to stand for political office until the law changed in 1854, at which point he was immediately elected as a Representative on the Council by the Burgesses of St Peter's Ward. His overriding principle was documented as, 'to do unto others as he would be done unto'.[12]

The dissolution of the partnership with Isaac in 1847 came at a difficult time for Maurice who continued the business in Sheffield under his own name and finances. In March 1848 his eldest son Edmund died and his wife Anne fell ill. Along with a wider and more general depression in the economic climate, Maurice himself became increasingly troubled. So much so that on 30 August he committed suicide in the most horrific fashion:

Suicide

Great Excitement was on Wednesday excited in the town of Sheffield from a report having obtained circulation that Mr Maurice Bright, of High Street, a member of the town council of the borough, and the most extensive Jeweller in the locality, had, very early that morning, been found in his dressing-room, quite dead, with his throat cut in a fearful manner.[13]

His brothers were called for and there was an immediate suspicion of murder, but the attendant doctor dispelled the possibility and days later the inquest provided the detail behind the dreadful occurrence:

An inquest was held on Wednesday before the Coroner, at the Town Hall, Sheffield. It appeared that Mr Bright went to bed at about 10 o'clock; and about 2 o'clock on the following morning he got up and went in to his dressing-room. As he did not return, and in consequence of Mrs. Bright hearing a noise as if some-one falling down, she went to see what was the matter and found her husband stretched upon the floor, and covered with blood. Mr. Overend, Surgeon, was sent for, and found that Mr. Bright's throat was cut through all the arteries to the spine, a bloody razor was behind him, as though it had dropped from his hand as he was falling to the floor. There could not be the slightest doubt that the wound had been inflicted by his own hand. For some weeks past a variety of circumstances, such as the death of a son, the illness of his wife, and the general depression in trade, had combined to unsettle Mr. Bright's mind, and he laboured under a delusion that his affairs were not in a healthy state, although a statement of his accounts, which he made out last Saturday, showed that after all his liabilities had been met he would have a surplus of several thousand pounds. In consequence of the state of Mr. Bright's mind, his friends thought it right, on Monday, to send for his brothers, Mr. Selim Bright of Buxton, and Mr. Henry Bright of Leamington, jewellers, and, on Tuesday, Mr. Overend was called in to attend the deceased as a lunatic. The Jury were fully convinced that the deceased committed the act while labouring under temporary insanity, and a verdict to that effect was returned. Mr. Bright was fifty-one years of age and has left a large family. He was of the Jewish persuasion, and was much respected for his probity and for the interest, which he always manifested in the general affairs of the town.[14]

Maurice was interred in the Brights' private burial ground known as Rod Moor at Hollow Meadows, on the Manchester Road (A57), heading out of

Sheffield. The assets of his business, Bright & Sons, were advertised for sale in the *Sheffield Independent* in September 1848 and subsequently purchased from the executors by Maurice's widow Henrietta (née De Metz), and son Frederick. Regardless of Maurice's good reputation and patronage from the 6th Duke of Devonshire, the business fell into decline and nine years after his death, Henrietta and Frederick 'relinquished for prudential considerations of health'[15] the Sheffield business, and moved to Scarborough together with another son, Herbert. This business continues to trade today as Bright and Sons more than 230 years since Isaac, as founding father, first arrived in England.

Grandfather Selim (younger brother to Maurice)

Selim was born in Sheffield in 1799 and trained as a jeweller and silversmith in the family business under his father Isaac. In January 1825 he married Estella De Lara (Estherle bat Moses HaCohen de Lara), a Moorish princess, in the New Synagogue in London; no doubt an arranged marriage within the wider Jewish community. Together they had a large family including Dora Bright's father, Augustus. Clearly a wealthy family, the 1851 census documents them living with a governess, a nurse and three staff at The Crescent in Buxton. Selim appears in the Buxton business directories of 1822 as 'Bright and Sons, the Square'. By 1835 the business had moved to the 'Crescent, Buxton', a very prestigious location.

Figure 2.1. Location of the shop at 1 The Crescent, Buxton, 2021

White's Derbyshire Directory of 1857 lists the business as Bright & Co, still at the Crescent, with a jewellery shop and living quarters above. Selim also retained close ties with the business in Sheffield and was recorded as a manufacturer of cutlery, general and South American merchants.

As well as a jeweller, silversmith and clockmaker, Selim was a skilled craftsman and gained an honourable mention for his work, which was displayed at the 1851 Great Exhibition and subsequently purchased by the Marquess of Westminster. The vases he created stand nearly a metre high and two metres when stood on their plinths. They are made of Derbyshire black marble, which was greatly prized by the Victorians, being used in the manufacture of highly decorated and colourful items. The vases were included in an article in the *Illustrated London News*, 4 October 1851, and were originally designed to stand on a tripod base. The items sold in 2010 for just under £35,000; a label still attached to one of the vases reads:

> S. BRIGHT & CO.S. FANCY MARBLE AND SPAR MANUFACTORY CENTRE OF THE CRESCENT BUXTON. INLAID TABLES, VASE &c., &c. Of the Finest Workmanship and most Elegant Designs ADMIRABLY CARVED ANIMALS, In Great Variety

Figure 2.2. Vases made by Selim Bright and exhibited at the 1851 Great Exhibition

Selim became an important member of the community and in 1845 joined the Committee of the Leeds, Huddersfield & Sheffield Direct Railway, promoting the development of rail links to Buxton. He was a trustee of the Buxton Bank, a tenant farmer on the 6th Duke of Devonshire's land and a consummate businessman. A visit by the Prince of Wales to Buxton in 1853 included a visit to Selim's elegant showroom on The Crescent. Whether the Prince made a purchase is not recorded. Dora Bright recollects being told stories of her grandfather and his time at Buxton in her memoir:

> My grandfather was the ('artist') Duke of Devonshire's oldest tenant and the Duke being fond of music, used to invite himself to the family music evenings. I was told that he came in state from Chatsworth with postillions and outriders. Those were indeed, the good old days; and what an excitement for the neighbours! He maintained a private orchestra which included Lazarus (the famous clarinet player) and the conductor was Charles Coote of Coote and Tinney's famous Dance Band.[16]

Estella, Selim's wife, died in 1878, aged seventy-four, and in his elder years Selim 'became a fancier and breeder of canaries', some of which were let loose in the Spa Conservatory for the 'special delight of Queen Victoria', on her visit to Buxton in September 1887. Selim finally retired in January 1889, at the age of ninety, and went to live with family in Liverpool, where he died on 10 January 1891. His body was returned to Sheffield and interred at the family Rod Moor burial ground.

Selim's sons all went on to make names for themselves in one way or another. The eldest Horatio became a multi-millionaire, Dora's father, Augustus, travelled to Brazil and returned to take over Bright & Son in Sheffield, whilst the youngest, Octavius, led a slightly less respectable life.

Uncle Horatio

Figure 2.3. Carte de Visite Horatio Bright, 1881

Horatio was a very dramatic figure and the most successful of Selim's sons, accruing a huge fortune and a certain notoriety in nineteenth-century Sheffield. Born in 1828, he was surrounded by the success of the family and seemed to have been determined to be equally as successful, if not more so. Educated at a boarding school in Liverpool he was reported as of 'unusual intelligence, outstanding in personal appearance and gifted in many ways'.[17] As a young man he became a traveller for the steel manufacturer Turton Bros. and Mappin. In 1849 Horatio married Anne Turton, the daughter of his employer, Henry Turton, Master Cutler (1846) and Mayor of Sheffield (1850). He was given a partnership in the new firm of Turton, Bright & Co, manufacturers of high-quality dyes for the Royal Mint and other nations. The business was a huge and lucrative success and the name Turton remains associated with steel in Sheffield to this day.

At an early age he relinquished Judaism and was reputed to be 'a hard-nosed but fair employer, paying above average wage'.[18] He was most definitely an intrepid entrepreneur and in the 1851 census was reported as a 'wine agent' (with a German wine merchant as a visitor), and then later in 1853 as an 'insurance agent'.

In 1856 Horatio bought the Original Steel Warehouse, renaming it 'Horatio Bright & Co, manufacturers of bar cast and shear steel for the cutlery industry'.[19] Things may not have gone as planned, as the following year he had to sell the contents of his fine house, East View, on Western Bank in Sheffield.[20] At the same time he became an auctioneer and was declared insolvent. A further venture into steel manufacture ended in 1861 with the sale of goods and the house at Spring Hill, Crookes Moor, Sheffield,[21] and a declaration of bankruptcy.[22]

Along with the ups and downs of business life, there were difficulties with the law. In 1854 Horatio was before the bench in Leeds charged with 'cruelly beating, ill-treating, over-driving, abusing and torturing a horse', together with a charge of abusive and insulting language for which he was fined £3 and costs[23] (£350 today). Then in 1859, he was charged with pushing a young girl down the front steps of his house after she was, according to him, antisemitic in her behaviour and language. After a series of letters and threats to the young girl by Horatio, he was bound over for 12 months with £200 (£25,000 today) in guarantees to prevent him offending again. Initially, he was outraged by the judgement and refused to pay, but after a night in prison the monies were paid over.[24]

The 1860s brought an upturn in his fortunes and Horatio repurchased the Crookes Moor house and by 1874 had amassed enough to pay back all of his debtors from fourteen years earlier. He rented out the house a few years later after building his new home, Lydgate Hall, a grand manor on the hill above the city, and by 1876 was busy buying oil paintings to decorate its walls. The paintings were later loaned to the new Weston Park Museum in Sheffield in

1879, the Mappin Art Gallery, Sheffield in 1889 and The Guildhall London, as part of a commemoration of Queen Victoria's reign in 1890.[25]

In 1887, he took on the lease of two houses and the Iron Warehouse, with steel melting furnace, at a cost of £51 18s per annum (£7,000 today). Also, in the same year his business partner died leaving him the steel and Royal Mint business, his estate and £26,039 16s and 2d (£3,500,000 today). Horatio had jumped from bankrupt to millionaire in less than thirty years.

He lived up to his new-found wealth and indulged his life-long passion for horses and carriage driving:

> He had a strange passion for horses, and was a clever and fear-
> less whip. It was for many years his chief delight to drive a coach
> and four about the country roads, and even through the city. He
> betrayed a marked persistence in searching for well-matched
> teams, and would one day be seen driving four spanking bays and
> another day a different but equally fine set of animals. On special
> occasions he would increase his team to six and have outriders.
> Always he held the reins, firm on the box seat with a cigar in his
> mouth.[26]

Figure 2.4. Horatio Bright leaving Lydgate Hall, 1885

Horatio was also an avid theatre goer, owning a box at the Theatre Royal, Sheffield, and was a 'silver ticket' owner, which gave him access to all the shows. Despite this love of the theatrical world, when his son married an actress, he was hugely disappointed and 'would seize every opportunity for causing unpleasantness to his daughter-in-law'.[27]

Notwithstanding his wealth and success, he took no part in the life of Sheffield or the Jewish community. He built a spacious second home on the moors at Hollow Meadows above Sheffield, and within the grounds he erected a mausoleum for him and his family.

Unfortunately, in 1891 his wife Mary, whom he adored, died of influenza and then tragically three months later his son, Sam, died of tuberculosis. In his grief, he shunned all religious intervention, interring his family himself and performing the last rites in the mausoleum at Hollow Meadows. The mausoleum was sumptuously furnished with family portraits, jewelled ornaments, mosaics and oak panelling, and each of the coffins were housed in fine marble sarcophagi.

Following the deaths of his family, Horatio would ride to the mausoleum accompanied by a groom, whose duties were to dust and polish the furnishings, whilst Horatio played the small organ he had installed. Frequently, he would take his teenage grand-daughter Mary on these outings, but then later the same day would take her to the theatre in the evening, as if to ensure the day had a happy end.

In spite of his previous disappointment with his son on his marriage to an actress, Horatio hypocritically took a second wife – an actress, Minnie-Harl, who was a member of the cast playing at the Theatre Royal in Sheffield and who was only twenty-five years old. Together they had three children. However, Horatio's health was by now failing and he retired from business life, refusing to sell the goodwill to anyone and burning the books of the company that had secured his fortune. After a short illness 'he died peacefully in his favourite armchair in front of the fire'. Three days later his coffin was loaded into a black undertakers' cart; 'in secrecy in the early morning, and transported to the mausoleum where he was laid to rest between his wife and son'. There were no mourners, service or ceremony.[28]

Horatio left £136,220 16s and 10d (£16,700,000 today) after taxes, of which £100,000 (£12,000,000) was to be bequeathed to benevolent institutions, with one significant instruction, 'the trustees are specially directed to give nothing to Sheffield charities'.[29] The main beneficiaries were the Royal National Lifeboat Institution, the Buxton Bath Charity, Manchester Royal Infirmary, the Leeds Infirmary and Guy's Hospital. A sale of his paintings in 1906 raised a further £125,000 at today's rates.

As a final adjunct to this branch of the family, Horatio had a son with his second wife named Horatio Harle Bright, born in 1898, a cousin of Dora Bright. He was left well looked after financially by his father and was educated privately at Sherbourne School and Marlborough College.[30]

At the start of the First World War Harle signed up to join the Royal Flying Corps (RFC), having been an early member of the Sheffield Aero Club. He was posted to Netheravon, where the RFC soon realized he was only fourteen. Some correspondence ensued and his then legal guardian agreed he could continue to fly if the RFC agreed, and there would be no blame upon the government if any injuries occurred. The War Office declined, but in 1917 Harle gained his ticket as an Air Mechanic 2nd Class, through the Sheffield Aero Club. He was posted to France, but came down with influenza and left the RFC taking up a post as a test pilot for the Aeronautical Inspection Department in Bristol a few months later. There were complaints of dangerous flying and he was court martialled for showing photographs of use to the enemy to unauthorized individuals. Sentenced to a year in prison, his term was remitted due to his young age and lack of treacherous intention. Now old enough he immediately re-enlisted into the RFC and was posted to France on 6 September 1917. He took his first practice flight in the morning of 22 September. The next morning he went out on a five-plane sortie and never returned; no one saw what happened and the Germans claimed no kill. An unfortunate end to this arm of the family.

Uncle Octavius

Born in 1833, Michael Octavius lived with his father, Selim, at The Crescent in Buxton as an assistant in the family business. As with many of the Bright family he and his children were musical and happy to use their skills charitably to advance good works. Octavius and his family first appeared in the newspapers in September 1858, when they were to be the singers in a vocal and instrumental concert in aid of the building fund for the Buxton Spa Hospital. According to the advertisement in the *Buxton Herald*, the Bright family:

> Knowing how anxious his grace (The Duke of Devonshire) was to have this charitable building completed and aware how great would be the expense of professional singers, have most readily and kindly offered, with the willing consent of the Misses Bright, their powerful assistance in the vocal department, by which liberal offer nearly the whole of the proceeds will be devoted to the purpose above stated.[31]

The late Duke of Devonshire's private band accompanied the Bright family in an extensive programme of Verdi, Rossini, Mozart and others. The Misses Bright sang together, and individually, and were 'applauded so that neither could refrain from providing the encores, which were enthusiastically called for by the audience'.[32] But the undoubted star of the evening was Octavius playing the solo *By Particular Desire*:

> The extraordinary performance of Mr. Octavius Bright on the Flauto Magico, a mere piece of cardboard rolled-up in the form of a Flute was quite wonderful, those who heard it could scarcely believe that such rapid passages so perfectly in tune could be

produced by such means. Mr. Bright must have a perfect ear and a good knowledge of music, he received, as he richly deserved rounds of applause. The takings, after expenses, amounted to £60 (£7,500 today), donated to the Hospital fund.[33]

Ostensibly, Octavius appeared to be a pillar of the Buxton and Derbyshire scene, being a Captain in the Peak Rifle Corps and an important merchant together with his father. However, his favours changed and after his wife died, a few years later in 1864, he courted a Miss Thorpe of Northampton and after a short time asked her to marry him. His father Selim did not approve of the marriage and Octavius was forced to write to Miss Thorpe telling her that he had not intended to ask for her hand and that he would no longer marry her. Miss Thorpe, described as 'under age and an orphan', having been slighted and publicly embarrassed, was enraged and took Octavius, her to-be suitor, to court and was granted £500 in damages for 'breach of promise of marriage'. This was reported nationally as a huge scandal, with the question on everyone's lips being, 'how could a gentleman deny the hand of a good lady?'

Unlike his brother Horatio, who returned from bankruptcy to pay his debts and become a millionaire, Octavius simply ran away to London and took a new name because, as he said to the courts, 'he was in fear of arrest by the Sherriff'.[34] He took up residence in the Crown Court public house in Cheapside in June 1865 and registered under the name of Ferguson. In that same month he petitioned to be declared a bankrupt in an attempt to evade paying the costs to Miss Thorpe. During his time at the Crown Court pub, he amassed £75 (£9,600 today) in debts, met with friends and was accused of 'giving champagne breakfasts'. In June 1866, Octavius, having petitioned for bankruptcy, was granted protection from arrest with debts of £1,038 4s 7d (£124,500 today).

The first bankruptcy hearing was heard in November 1866.[35] Octavius declared he never intended to defraud or deceive anybody and that he was the victim of a vicious verdict (alluding to the breach of promise). The court requested accounts and found that he was spending £300 a year (£36,000 today) and that his father must have been sending him money in support. Selim was requested to attend the court and the case adjourned until Octavius could prepare accounts. The case resumed in February 1867, with Selim having been brought from Buxton to attend the court in London and being cross examined as to their business/partnership arrangements. Due to Octavius' failure to pay the previous costs relating to the breach of promise, the case was once again adjourned pending full accounts being produced.[36] Finally, in November 1867, Octavius returned to court having paid his fine to Miss Thorpe and was allowed to amend his final accounts and be discharged as a bankrupt.[37]

Octavius returned to Buxton and was accepted back into the family, and irrespective of his moment in the limelight and notoriety, assumed the gentleman's lifestyle once more. He did not remain out of the news, as in August 1871 he was once again in court, summoned for assaulting a taxi driver. From the details of the news report it appears that Octavius had travelled by train from Buxton to Sheffield Midland Station, where he took a cab to Broomhill, the residence of his brother Augustus:

> At Broomhill some dispute occurred about the fare, which ended in the defendant paying 6d. (£6 today) less than the fare demanded, and striking the complainant three times in the face and kicking him. The result of the blows in the face was that for three days the complainant had a black eye, and suffered much pain ... Evidence having been called in support of this statement the defendant admitted having committed the assault, but said the complainant was impudent, and that the blows he gave him would not have caused a black eye. The bench told the defendant they had considered whether to commit him to prison without the option of a fine, but they had at length decided to fine him 50s. (£300 today) and costs.[38]

Although remaining employed by his father, Octavius clearly thought his pay insufficient as in 1874 he was remanded for the 'alleged forgery of a cheque'.[39] Owing £5 to a hatter in Manchester, Octavius presented a cheque for £20 to the hatter to pay the debt; the hatter obliged with change in cash of £15 expecting the cheque to be valid. On presentation at the bank the cheque was dishonoured as both signatures were in the hand of Octavius. Selim was reported 'as stating he had never given his son authority to sign a cheque in his name'. Octavius was sent to Belle Vue prison in Manchester and given twelve calendar months' hard labour.[40]

A final news report in 1882 found Octavius on the wrong side of the law once again, charged with obtaining items from an India rubber manufacturer on the High Street, Sheffield, by means of 'false pretence' and being brought up on remand. The court were informed that friends of the prisoner had come to an arrangement with the manufacturer who now wished to withdraw the complaint. At this point in time Octavius was of no occupation; the friends were most probably other members of the family maintaining the integrity of the Bright name.[41]

Leaving Sheffield, Octavius took a second wife in October 1883, Catherine McKay, and fathered four children, Basil, Rosen, Minnie and John. He became a merchant and in the 1891 census was reported living in St Pauls, London. The following year in December 1892, Octavius died and his remains were returned to Sheffield to be interred in the family burial ground at Rod Moor. His grave relates only his first name and year of death – Octavius 1892.

Uncle Maurice Delara

Maurice Delara Bright was a well-known composer of military band music. His music became a staple part of Victorian life, being heard in parks across the country at the weekend and at special gala events. Born in 1825, he was a son of Selim and Estella and carried on his mother's maiden name, Delara, instead of Bright, most likely because of her noble background.

Figure 2.5. Photograph of Maurice Delara Bright, October 1894

Maurice ran his own steel business, 'The Hallamshire Iron and Steel Warehouse' and was Quartermaster and Honorary Bandmaster of the Hallamshire Rifles, alongside his brother Augustus who played violin in the band. Passionate about the funding, structure and role of musicians in the volunteer rifle movement and the wider British military, he visited France to learn how the French Army managed military bands and was so impressed that he wrote a number of works for the French army, dedicated to the Emperor Napoléon.[42]

His music for military bands consists mostly of quadrilles and marches, one such being:

> the *Emperor Fountain*, dedicated, by express permission, to his Grace the 6th Duke of Devonshire, and embellished with his Grace's Arms and Orders, elegantly emblazoned. These quadrilles are now being played by Coote's celebrated Quadrille Band, with great success, at Chatsworth.[43]

Perhaps his greatest accolade was the publishing of the work *Napoléon et Eugénie, a Grande Quadrille Militaire*. Maurice sent the score to the War Ministry in Paris as a present to the Emperor hoping it would be admitted into the repertoire of the French military. On 28 June 1856, the Minister of State for War responded to Maurice in a handwritten letter accepting the work for distribution throughout the French Army.

Figure 2.6. Front page of 'Napoléon et Eugénie', a Grande Quadrille Militaire

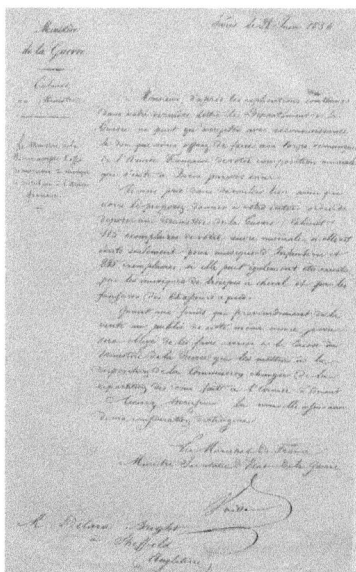

Figure 2.7. Letter to Delara from the French Minister of War

Figure 2.8. First bars of the quadrille 'Napoléon et Eugénie'

The *Sheffield Daily Telegraph*[44] wrote in response to the letter: 'This is a great honour, as it is well known to be exceedingly difficult to get new music admitted in to the repertoire of the military bands in France'. A few months later the work had been officially published in France and was reported by the *Sheffield Independent*:

> The work has been published in a very handsome form. It is surmounted by the French Crown and Eagle, and also ornamented by portraits of the Emperor and Empress, and by military emblems. It is entitled Napoléon et Eugénie. Grand Quadrille Militaire, précédé d'une Marche introduction, joué à location de la visite Impériale en Angleterre par la Musique de Coldstream Guards, composé par M. Delara Bright, de Sheffield et dédié avec permission de S. E. Mr. le Maréchal Vaillant, Ministre de la Guerre, à l'armée Française. Pour être vendu au profit des blessés de L'armée d'Orient.[45]

> [... Napoléon et Eugénie. Grand Quadrille Militaire, preceded by an introductory March, played by the Coldstream Guards band on the occasion of the Imperial visit to England, composed by Mr. Delara Bright of Sheffield and dedicated with permission of H.E. Mr. Marshal Vaillant, Minister of War, to the French Army. To be sold for the benefit of the wounded of the Army of the Orient.]

It is difficult to know how many works he composed as there are few references to his work in concert listings. Appendix 3 outlines his known works as available in the British Library, Bibliotèque National de France, and those reported in the newspapers of the time.

Whilst researching the background to Maurice, I came across the news reports in the Sheffield papers regarding the work written for Napoléon and Eugénie. It occurred to me at the time how incredible it would be if these letters and even the music itself still existed, and if they did how fantastic it would be to find them. As my researches continued and only a few weeks later, while I was looking into Horatio's background I discovered a website on Sheffield history belonging to Chris Hobbs.[46] I emailed him and he sent me details of others who had shown interest in Horatio and the Bright family. One of the emails was from a person in France who had acquired a chest in an auction in Sheffield a few years earlier containing letters and drawings. One of the letters mentioned Maurice Delara Bright. I was intrigued and sent a prospective email and a few days later a reply arrived with a picture. It was the letter from the Ministry of War in perfect condition and even more glorious than I could have imagined. The owner agreed to send more photos: I thought they would add some colour to this book and the Maurice Delara section. Some months later, a further email arrived: 'I have found some music...' was the opening sentence. I wondered if it might be by Maurice or perhaps a new quadrille or something simple from another composer. When the photograph of the front page arrived, I couldn't believe my eyes, it was the Napoléon et Eugénie quadrille – in colour – just as it had been detailed in the press of 1856. It seemed totally impossible that suddenly I had not only found the letter but also now had the music dangled in front of me from across the channel in a Covid-19 lockdown. Discussions on value ensued and after the then owner failing to find a French antique house sufficiently interested, the items were purchased by myself and duly arrived in Sheffield where they had been created over 170 years earlier. The photographs in this book pay homage to the work of the man himself and the adulation of the French military. It turned out the music was the proof copy sent with the letters to Maurice in 1856 and stored in a drawer that eventually ended up at auction and taken to France. The letters and music are now with Maurice Delara's family and will be loved and cherished for many more years to come. Had I not written this book they would still be languishing in a drawer in France or, worse still, discarded and lost forever. Maurice is buried in All Saint's Church, Ecclesall, a mere ten-minute walk from my home.

Cousin Ada

Ada, born in 1852, was a second cousin to Dora Bright, with Isaac as their common great-grandfather. A pianist of some note, she was engaged regularly as an accompanist at concerts around the Brighton area. In line with the changing role of women, Ada, in typically determined Bright family fashion, organized her own series of Matinée musicale, in which she would play piano, accompanying her friends.

Also performing in Brighton at this time was Mr John Toplady Carrodus, eminent violinist (and owner of an expensive Guarnerius[47] violin[48]), who attended the Royal Academy of Music at the same time as Dora Bright and headed an orchestra in which Dora Bright was a regular performer in London and across the country. It seems very likely that Dora Bright staged an introduction for her cousin to Mr Carrodus; as a result they became good friends and played together frequently. The first of their concerts together was in May 1885 when Ada accompanied Mr Carrodus in a Grand Violin concert at the Royal Pavilion, Brighton. This and the other concerts were a huge success, and Mr Carrodus received excellent reviews. However, Ada was only ever described as the accompanist – her place as support was noted but not worthy of further mention.

After the death of his wife Mr Carrodus asked Ada to marry him and, on 14 October 1890, they tied the knot, but unfortunately for Ada the marriage only lasted five years, as on 13 July 1895:

> Mr. Carrodus after returning shortly after one o'clock in the morning, complained of extreme pain and fatigue. For some time after he seemed to be in great agony, but this condition ceased, and sinking rapidly, he passed away at a quarter past eight. His relatives are unable to account for the death.[49]

The musical freedoms and changes to society that Dora Bright would exploit so well had been taken away from Ada and there are no further reports of her, either as Ada Bright or as Mrs Carrodus.

***

Why Isaac and Philip chose to establish their new lives in Sheffield can only be surmised, but it is most likely because of the emerging silversmith and steel industry and the opportunities it provided. The family made the most of those opportunities and within two generations had established themselves in the community within Sheffield and across Yorkshire and the Midlands.

The family were clearly musical and fine musicians, something Dora Bright would inherit, cultivate and take to a far wider audience. The family enjoyed relatively privileged lives and her uncles Horatio and Maurice Delara, who she would have known well by reason of living only a short distance apart, knew how to enjoy life and the wealth they had amassed. It was into this comfortable and prosperous heritage that Dora Bright was born on 18 August 1862.

3 The Bright Family

After a brief courtship and much to the disapproval of her father, Kate Pitt married Augustus Bright at St John's Church, Cardiff in 1861. Augustus, an entrepreneur, was involved in Sheffield's developing steel industry and Kate, also born in Sheffield, was an actress in her father's touring theatrical company. Initially, the couple lodged in a recently built terraced house in Stanton Broom which today is overshadowed by the Royal Hallamshire Hospital. The following year, 1862, the first of their two daughters, Dora, was born on 18 August, and then eleven years later, a second daughter Georgiana, on 5 March 1873.

Figure 3.1. Stanton Broom today – Dora Bright's first home (although the numbering has changed, it is most likely that the house with the car in front was where they lived)

Augustus

Augustus, along with his brothers, received a good education. In the 1841 census, aged eleven, he was recorded living with the Deekens family in Liverpool, together with two other boarders. These may have been relatives and, like his brother Horatio, Augustus had been sent to school in Liverpool and these were his lodgings. Liverpool held a strong family link, with his father Selim retiring to live with relatives in the city and his grandfather being buried in the Jewish Cemetery.

From Liverpool, Augustus travelled to Rio de Janeiro, Brazil, to develop trade connections for his father's business. In a letter to the local Sheffield newspaper supporting emigration to Brazil, he reports himself as 'visiting a coffee plantation near Sao Paulo'[1] and in another letter on a different subject, reports his time in Pernambuco, when in 1849 it was 'overrun by insurgents'.[2] These towns are some considerable distance from each other and he must have travelled under extreme circumstances across Brazil, with what was a real threat of death at the hands of bandits.

Throughout his life he was a fervent supporter of Brazil, and on his return to Sheffield set up his own business selling Brazilian cigars,[3] and as a cutlery manufacturer and merchant. The links with Brazil remained strong and in April 1865 Augustus was instructed by the British Government in London to meet and assist the Princess Imperial of Brazil and other dignitaries, in a visit to a number of steel works around the city.[4] A grand dinner was held at the Victoria Railway Station Hotel and a few weeks later, 'as a gesture of gratitude and thanks to Augustus', the Brazilian Ambassador passed a letter expressing 'the great pleasure which her Imperial Highness experienced during the late visit to Sheffield'. The letter was accompanied by a very beautiful scarf pin in the shape of a horse-shoe, set with diamonds.[5] A few years later in 1871, Augustus was again honoured with an interview with His Imperial Majesty the Emperor of Brazil,[6] resulting in his appointment, initially as consular agent to Brazil and then as Vice-Consul to Brazil.[7]

His business manufactured fine pocket knives and in 1866 one of his bespoke knives was stolen by a letter sorter in London. The quality of workmanship becomes apparent after the thief's apprehension and discovery of the knife by the police. Augustus identified the piece:

> It was so peculiar in many respects that he did not believe a precisely similar knife had ever been produced. It was a four bladed pocket knife with a mother-of-pearl handle. The fittings were of 18 carat gold, engraved upon a peculiar design, according to the directions of the purchaser. It bore the inscription S. L. S.[8]

Perhaps as a result of witnessing the troubles in Brazil, Augustus was one of the founders of the Hallamshire Rifles, a volunteer military unit, many of which had been in existence across the country since the fear of French invasion in the late 1700s. Augustus took the rifles unit very seriously and there are long letters to the newspapers about the dress codes, skill requirements and the importance of their defensive capability in support of the regular forces.[9] During his time in the rifles, he rose through the ranks to become Captain in 1871.[10] Although he and his brother Maurice served in the same rifles unit and played in the associated military band, they did not see eye to eye on the purpose of the unit and there are letters between them in the local press arguing the case. Augustus's response is certainly to the point and supportive of the rifles:

> Sir, I have perused in your columns this morning a letter written by my brother, Mr. De Lara Bright, on the subject of volunteer rifle corps. With all the due deference to his general opinions on military and naval matters, in the present instance, as regards volunteer riflemen, I consider that the notions expressed by him are of a most erroneous character. What right has he to stigmatize with the offensive term, humbug, a demonstration so universally popular and so patriotically national as is the present rifle corps movement.[11]

It is clear that both were in favour of Britain's military might and defending the nation from overseas threat, yet both had interests in other countries that seemed equally as pressing to them; Augustus with Brazil and Maurice with the French military. This sense of national pride is something that would influence the young Dora throughout her life.

Augustus was a fine musician and played the violin as part of the Hallamshire Rifles military band. His violin was reported to be a Guarnerius and had been exhibited at the South Kensington Museum and stated to be highly recommended by the Duke of Edinburgh.[12] His playing was of a high standard and in March 1861, the celebrated 'BAND of the HALLAMSHIRE VOLUNTEER CORP' kindly ventured their support in a 'Grand Amateur Performance at the Theatre Royal', Sheffield.[13]

Also performing was the actor Miss Kate Pitt, recently arrived back in Sheffield with her father's company. She had already received very good reviews for her theatrical roles in the news reports and no doubt Augustus, along with the other young gentlemen of Sheffield, were very aware of the new theatrical presence. Indeed, he may even have attended a show at the theatre and seen her on stage.

The performance was a great success for Augustus, drawing public attention to his playing: 'Ensign Augustus Bright played a violin solo from *Lurline*, and at its close elicited an encore'.[14] Within three months of the performance, Augustus and Kate were married in Cardiff.

Bright & Co prospered and the Brights moved into a new stone-built villa on Ashdell Road, Broomhill. The house was well furnished and accommodated Augustus's new collection of fine paintings. In the 1871 census they were recorded living with Kate's two brothers and had a servant.

Figure 3.2. Olanda Cottage, Ashdell Road

Kate

Katherine Coveney-Pitt was born in 1843. Both her mother, Ellen Coveney, and her father, Charles Pitt, came from well-known and established theatrical families. Kate was well educated and sent abroad at an early age to a boarding school in France; it was reported she could speak two or three languages.[15] She made her debut on the boards at the Queen's Theatre, Manchester, on 7 May 1860, playing the part of Elvira in *The Muleteer of Toledo*, a comic drama in two acts. Her mother and father played other roles in the play and together, over the next three weeks, they took the play to Derby, Accrington and Hanley, with her first press notice suggesting 'herself competent to sustain the highest parts within the range of comedy of modern French extraction'.[16]

The following month the family arrived in Sheffield to take over the lease of the Theatre Royal. The theatre was 'cleaned, polished and painted', with the first show on 20 October 1860 opening a week of tragedies: *Macbeth*, *Othello*, *The Man in the Iron Mask*, *King Lear* and *Katherine Howard* – Kate playing none of the major roles and only getting a mention as part of the cast.[17] However, the following week she played the heroine in a short comedy to a little more acclaim: 'She is a young lady of considerable promise. She showed much natural power; her playful precocity and cheerful manner, so fully sustained throughout, did her great credit'.[18]

Then in 1861, came the Grand Performance with the Hallamshire Volunteer Corps Band in which Augustus Bright played his violin solo. A news report some years later provides a small insight into how Kate was viewed and also gives a nod to her relationship with Augustus:

> Miss Pitt's youth, her beauty (she was a lovely girl), her accomplishments (she spoke two or three languages, danced like a fairy and sang like a bird) combined to make her a popular idol, and the *Jeuness Doree* [fashionable wealthy young people] of Sheffield went mad about her. She could have flung her handkerchief and married whom she pleased; but Mr. Augustus Bright, a young merchant, to the chagrin of his rivals, the disappointment of the public, and the indignation of the maternal and paternal Pitts, carried off the prize. The girl was married at eighteen and her career (which promised to be a brilliant one) was over almost before it happened.[19]

On 10 May 1861 Kate took half the proceeds of the show in a benefit performance with her brother and then travelled to perform at the Cardiff Theatre in mid-June. The *Cardiff Times* reported: 'she is an exceeding clever young lady, possessing also natural advantages, which used as the handmaid to intelligence, will prove an adornment to her professional efforts'.[20] Despite this glowing acclamation, the following week she married Augustus in St John's Church on 22 June. It seems highly likely that Augustus followed her to Cardiff, unbeknownst to her father, and the pair married in secret resulting in Kate not acting again until after the death of her father.

Marriage at this time was often the end of a woman's freedom, with her new husband expecting her to be a dutiful wife running the home and providing children. Had she married another actor Kate would most likely have continued in her profession, but marrying a businessman and burning her bridges with her father, who didn't speak to her again, left her limited to a life as wife and mother. The following year Dora Estella Bright was born on 16 August 1862 and Kate's life was determined for the immediate future.

Dora's childhood

By all accounts, Augustus and Kate were a very happily married couple[21] and Dora was most likely taught at home by her talented mother and enterprising father. Certainly, both parents were musical and well educated as were many other members of both families. Uncles Horatio and Maurice lived locally and may also have had some impact on the young Dora's education and musical upbringing. A composer as celebrated as Uncle Maurice and his military band music couldn't have gone unnoticed, and there are instances in her compositions, decades later, that include military drums not usually associated with orchestral music.

In 1868, aged five, Dora had her first introduction to the wider world of music, when she attended the Freemason's Ball in Sheffield with her parents. 'Dancing commenced at 10pm and the programme included quadrilles, polkas, waltzes, Lancers and Galops, and much dancing.'[22] This must have been an incredible sight for a young girl and quite an introduction to the world of music and partying.

Only three years later, at the age of eight, she was recorded on the 1871 census as a pupil at Highfield School in Wath-upon-Dearne. The school opened in the 1820s as a seminary for young ladies and focused on the arts and music. Boarding was available for up to twenty young girls and the census showed they ranged in age from Dora, the youngest, at eight, to the eldest at nineteen, and coming from homes as far away as Manchester, but mostly from Sheffield and the immediate locality.

In this same year, Dora's mother was recorded in the 1871 census as living with her sister Lottie Pitt in Bloomsbury, London. It is possible that she was helping her younger sibling to find work as an actress; her aunts, Harriet and Jane Coveney, had long-term relationships with many London venues and had well-established acting careers.[23] It does suggest that Kate having already made a limited return to acting in 1866 wasn't the usual stay-at-home mum and with no young child to prevent her as Dora was away at boarding school, she had ventured back into society.

Out of school term, Dora returned home to Olanda Cottage and was involved in daily family life and events. Her memoir gives a small glance into this Sheffield life and her closeness to her father, Augustus:

> We lived in Yorkshire near Sheffield until my beloved father died. His family were all really musical and constituted a tiny orchestra amongst themselves in the old house at Buxton, where they used to play the symphonies of Mozart and Haydn before I was born. The family taste was very sound and I imbibed the great masters from a very early age. My father was an excellent amateur violinist and I have often regretted the boredom when accompanying him – in holiday time – in the operatic duets for violin and piano of de Bériot.[24]

Figure 3.3. Highfield School building, Wath-upon-Dearne (Author's own collection)

Dora talks lovingly and at length about her father's time in South America in her memoir and the quote above shows a slight melancholy and longing over his memory.

The Hallamshire Rifles gave another military concert in 1873 to raise funds for the band's sick fund. The local papers reported the event:

> There was a moderate attendance, but the audience was not by any means as large as the concert deserved … The entertainment was thoroughly enjoyable … included in the programme was a duet on violin and piano by Captain A. Bright and his daughter with a selection from Lucia by Donizetti. The concert was the means of introducing a very young pianist, Miss Dora Estella Bright, who acquitted herself with a proficiency that was really remarkable. The duet which she played with her father somewhat prepared the audience for performance; but she fairly took them by surprise when she gave a sonata (Beethoven) entirely from memory. This was played with very good taste and with a brilliancy of execution and lightness of touch that gave promise of future excellence. She was encored. A like compliment was paid to Captain Bright at the

conclusion of the duet. The latter showed himself no mean per-former on the violin.[25]

December 1876 saw the return of the Grand Military Amateur Theatricals (as per 1871 when Augustus and Kate starred together before their marriage). This was Kate's return to the boards in a performance of the charming comedy *Perfection*, with Kate being 'very well received by the audience'.[26] Dora by now aged fourteen and her sister, Georgiana aged three, may have been in the audience to applaud. It gives some indication that for Kate she had the theatre in her blood and that displaying these talents was not an issue for either her or Augustus.

The following December, 1877, Augustus organized an entertainment in aid of the Brazilian famine fund, which again was an amateur musical and dramatic entertainment.[27] Those partaking in the event included Mrs Augustus Bright (Miss Kate Pitt), Miss Fanny Pitt and Dora Bright, with a programme of songs, duets, pianoforte solos, readings and dramatic sketches. There is no specific mention of the part played by Dora, but her mother and aunt performed a comedietta, adapted from the French which was very well received.

Over the next few years Kate made a limited return to the stage in benefit events, but also started writing plays, dramas and novels. This must have exerted a huge influence on the young Dora, with an artistic mother who was breaking the norms of Victorian family life by her obviously deeply rooted desire to be part of the theatre and the wider dramatic community.

On 1 November 1880, Augustus died suddenly of a heart attack. 'He had been taken some years before with rheumatic fever, which attacked his heart and finally caused his untimely death at the age of fifty'.[28] He was interred in the family's private burial ground on the moors above Sheffield, at Rod Moor, together with his father, mother and brother Octavius. The rites were performed by a Rabbi from Manchester in the presence of the family.

Figure 3.4. Burial plaque at the Rod Moor burial site

A further indication of her closeness to her father was a gold locket containing his portrait and a lock of hair which she retained throughout her life, bequeathing it, in her 1918 will, to her sister Georgiana.[29]

Within only a few months of her father's death Dora, now aged eighteen, had moved to London. She is recorded on the April 1881 census living in a Kensington boarding house, with a number of other young women. She had been recommended by the music publisher Stanley Lucas to the Royal Academy of Music, which she entered in the Lent term of 1881.[30] This was a real opportunity and one that she embraced fully and wholeheartedly.

Prior to enrolling, Dora returned to Sheffield to take part in her mother's newly written play *Dane's Dyke* at the theatre in Sheffield. Kate played the leading role and Dora played her daughter Lily. This was Dora's first true acting role, but also gave her another opportunity to showcase her musical talents. *The Sheffield Independent* was evidently more impressed with her playing than her acting. The critic reported that 'although she was very nervous ... she was thoroughly at home at the piano, and played a nocturne with no little ability'.[31] After this stage baptism, Dora left for London, only to find some months later that her mother's dream of returning to her stage career had brought about the untimely end of all her father's hard work in establishing the good name of A. Bright & Co. It would have impacted Dora financially, finding her without funds to fall back on and as a result she turned away from her mother for good. The memoir in which she talks warmly of her father makes no mention of her mother or her maternal relations. Over the next few years piano performance would dominate her life, and only somewhat later in life would she return to the theatre.

Sister Georgiana

Georgiana Delara Bright was born on 5 March 1873, named in part after her grandmother Estella Delara. She preferred to be called Georgie, and unlike Dora there are no references to her childhood. It must have been similar to Dora's, but with no obvious musical talent she was not sent away to boarding school and her schooling was completed at home or more locally. Aged only seven when her father died, her mother Kate continued to look after her and they stayed at Olanda Villa in Sheffield until mid-1882.

Her mother returned to the stage in 1882 and the following year Georgie, at the age of nine, was working beside her mother and aunt, Miss Lottie Pitt, at the New Queens Theatre in Oxford, playing Lo-Spi, a Chinese detective in *Success! Success! Success!*, a play by Mrs Augustus Bright.[32] Georgie continued to work with her mother and they advertised for work together in *The Stage* in 1886.[33] Some years later in 1895, Georgie was working with a new band of actors led by Mr John Kennedy Allen, to whom she was married.[34]

Figure 3.5. Miss Georgie De Lara Bright in 'Yellow Sands', *Hull Daily Mail*, 28 September 1928

The Allens were a successful company and played across England in all the major towns and cities, their specialty being comedy, Georgie being referred to as a 'Dame Comedian'.[35] Unlike her mother, Georgie never received rave reviews and was frequently upstaged by others in the company, but despite this the company played without a break until 1928. The newspaper image of Georgie from 1928 shows her in one of her comedic roles and was from a handout supplied to the newspaper by herself, rather than by the theatre or the company. The paragraph on the play, *Yellow Sands*, goes on to describe the upcoming play but makes no mention of Georgie as part of the cast. It seems her only way to claim any fame was to do it herself, not unlike her sister's approach.

During the winter of 1929, Georgie was unemployed and forced to advertise in *The Stage* for work. As an actor, it seems that she did not have a family home to share with her husband and the advert shows her living in London with her address as Lexham Gardens, the home of her sister Dora.[36] Although there are no records to suggest how close the sisters remained, Dora was happy to help in an emergency and her 1918 will went on to leave the income from Dora's trust fund to Georgia. With the success of Dora's career at the time this would have been a very substantial annual allowance.[37]

After a successful summer in Morecambe and Plymouth, she did no further work until a final performance at the Palladium in 1931, where she was referred to as 'assisting in the sketch'.[38] Her final mention in the press was in 1934, when she appeared on stage with her husband Kennedy and the rest of the company.[39] The final mention of Kennedy on stage was in 1937 at the Brighton Hippodrome.[40] Only a few years later Kennedy died on 26 January 1940. Georgie placed an In Memoriam in *The Stage*, which read: 'in tender memory of my beloved husband, a fellow of infinite jest – of most excellent fancy'.[41] Georgie outlived her husband by twenty-one years and died in London on 8 July 1961.[42] How much contact there was with her sister is unrecorded but they must have remained close as Dora's final will of 1951 included her as a beneficiary, leaving her a pansy ruby and diamond ring.

Mrs Augustus Bright (née Kate Pitt)

The death of Kate's father, Charles, in 1866 seemed to have been a turning point for Kate, as she made her reappearance on the stage in Sheffield in a benefit concert at the Theatre Royal. Her mother, now the lessee of the theatre after her husband Charles's death, had a bad season in 1867 with a poor return,[43] which tempted Kate back to the boards to help her mother increase the popularity of the theatre and their income. The play wasn't a success and although they took it further afield with the Sheridan London Company to Ryde,[44] it did not capture the imagination of the audience. Kate was only mentioned as a part of the cast and perhaps due to this lack of acclaim, she turned her attention instead to writing and in 1874 published her first work, a one-act comedy-drama titled *Not False, but Fickle*. The work was well received to an unusually crowded house and although the critic reported the piece as 'not brilliantly written and the first part rather dull, the audience gave hearty applause with loud cries for the author, who bowed from the dress circle to loud applause'.[45]

Within only a few months Kate produced a second work, *Noblesse Oblige*, which premiered at the Theatre Royal, Exeter in October 1878,[46] followed by *Bracken Hollow* at the Alexandra Theatre, Sheffield in November 1878,[47] *Naomi's Sin; or where are you going to, my pretty maid*, again at the Alexandra in May 1879,[48] a novel *Unto the Third and Fourth Generation* in 1880,[49] and a further drama *Danes Dyke* in 1881.[50] Each was a success and played at a number of theatres across the country. Kate, as a married woman, was now far from the norms of polite female behaviour for the times in which women were still very much seen and not heard. Augustus, until his untimely death, was clearly a modern man, allowing his wife such a lifestyle and not worrying about bringing shame upon the family, and for the teenage Dora, it was a strong role model to follow.

One of Kate's works provides an almost autobiographical impression of her earlier life, as she depicts the conflict between a theatrical career and a desire for security and respectability in a short story which appeared in the Era Almanack of 1879. *Grandfather's Little Actress* is the tale of talented juvenile performer Miss Maggie Stewart, who is performing with her relative in an unnamed provincial town at the beginning of the narrative. Like her mother before her, Maggie struggles to reconcile her desire for wealth and status with her life in the profession and although she knows that it will deeply upset her grandfather, she runs away and secretly marries Lord Penwether, who had admired her from the audience. When she finally returns to make peace with her aged relative, dressed in silk and fur, velvet and diamonds, she is too late, he has already died. Life becomes drama, reflecting very much her marriage to Augustus and early life.[51]

Kate's career as a writer and playwright seemed to have taken off, but the finances for the venture had to come from somewhere and it was Augustus who provided the backing. At the time of his death in November 1880, the company of A. Bright & Co. was found to be only just solvent with £1 of debt. Kate, who took over as executor, 'lacked the ability to carry on the business and trade soon fell off'.[52] Although the business was failing, Mr William Erskine Mawhood, the business manager, was left to run the company; he continued to manage the business to the best of his ability, but without Augustus in charge it fell into terminal decline.

Meanwhile and unbeknownst to anyone, as the business failed Kate took the life insurance money from Augustus's death and sold furniture and other items from the family home, to continue the pursuit of her own theatrical aspirations, funding the performance of her own plays from this illicit stash.[53]

In September 1881, Kate sold the Villa in Ashdell Road by auction; the advert in the *Sheffield Independent* gives some insight into how well Augustus, Kate and their daughters had been living:

> The house is replete with every convenience and exquisitely fitted up, having recently been papered and decorated regardless of expense and entails capital Dining and Drawing Rooms, Entrance Hall, Kitchen on the ground floor; Three bedrooms (formerly four), Bathroom and W.C., on the second floor; Three large Attics and Four excellent Cellars.[54]

An indoor bathroom and toilet, converted from a fourth bedroom, must have been a costly exercise, but clearly showed the aspirations of the Bright family. December 1881 also brought the completion of the sale of Augustus's painting collection and violin with a handsome income of over £150 (around £20,000 today). With her plays doing well and the proceeds from the insurance, house and paintings, Kate seemed to be a wealthy woman.

On 3 December 1881, Kate married Mr Mawhood, keeping her name of Mrs Augustus Bright for 'professional and literary purposes'. It seems that in keeping the business going as requested by Augustus, William had become more than an employee, or perhaps Kate was ensuring her financial future as the business of A. Bright & Co. continued to fail.[55]

Only eight months after the wedding, Kate's new husband appeared in the Sheffield Courts as a debtor in the liquidation of A. Bright & Co. The receivers' report found that 'Mr. Mawhood was unaware of the debts at the time of his marriage to Kate, who had incurred a large number of these debts for her own personal use'. The receivers discovered what Kate had done with the life insurance and 'items from the family home',[56] placing the business in further debt, but as she was a married woman she could not be made bankrupt and Mr Mawhood could not be held to account due to his youth and ignorance of Kate's behaviour. The business was liquidated and both Kate and William left Sheffield to pursue Kate's future in the theatre.

Initially, Kate returned to the theatre through local amateur dramatic performances, but very quickly returned to full-scale performance appearing with her sister, Fanny, in Rugby, in December 1882.[57] Mr Mawhood became her business manager and over the next few years Kate was in and out of work with many short tours alongside some extended periods of illness. In December 1885, Kate's sister Lottie died after a tragic accident falling down an open trap on the stage leading to 'a broken back and entire mental aberration'.[58] For the next fifteen years Kate worked across Britain and Ireland with varying degrees of success, at times a lessee of a theatre with a touring group, and at others as a lone actress seeking employment. Her final years echo the demise of her sister Lottie:

> At the end of a disastrous tour in May 1901, I had been out of work two months in London, and being short of means, was induced to take an engagement at a small town in Kent, where on my arrival, I found, to my dismay, the theatre was a mere canvas pavilion of the poorest order. On the opening night during one of my waits, I sought a seat and fell down a death-trap, twelve feet deep upon a bed of cut stones and dirty mould, and shattered my left arm, the bone being broken in three places.[59]

She goes on to describe the ill effects of the work of a local physician and the repairs to her shoulder by a London surgeon. The fall finished her career and despite 'great-kindness' from her family, it was through the involvement of the Authors Club and requests to her fellow actors that a fund was set up to aid her in her final years.[60]

Kate's final newspaper entry was the record of her death on 4 January 1906, as mother of Mrs Kennedy Allen (the married name of daughter Georgie Delara)[61] with no mention of daughter Dora.

In sharp contrast to her mother's demise over the twenty years from 1881, Dora Bright's life took completely the opposite direction as she learnt her musical trade and found ways to assimilate herself into the upper echelons of society, finding her own financial stability. She had learnt a lot from both her parents about self-belief and the determination to succeed, which would be her driving force, and of particular importance given the lack of financial or moral support she had been left after the death of her father.

***

The Bright family were very much a product of the spirit of the Victorian age – entrepreneurial, aspiring and focused on their own personal advancement. For Dora this must have been a great influence and together with music and theatre in the family's domestic and public lives, her path was set. However, despite this appearance of success, things were not always as they seemed; Augustus's ill health and early death, the failing steel business, Kate's underhand approach to the execution of Augustus's will and her apparent calculating marriage to Mr Mawhood. The sisters did well to find their own success from this maelstrom, and of the pair, Dora's move to London to take a place at the Royal Academy of Music was the bravest, but also most in line with the family spirit brought to Sheffield by her great grandfather Isaac.

4 The Early Years, 1880–1891

The move from Sheffield, a small provincial city, to London, capital of the British Empire, represented a huge change in lifestyle for the young Dora Bright. Living as a lodger in a boarding house for ladies in Kensington gave her some initial security and potentially like-minded acquaintances with whom to explore the new city. Dora embraced the change, reached out for new opportunities, excelled in her studies and rapidly established herself as a rising star in the musical world.

The Royal Academy

Music had always been a vital part of a young middle-class lady's skill set, with a proficiency in piano playing being regarded as an indispensable skill to improve their family's domestic life. Musical training was focused on playing and lacked any in-depth consideration of elements such as composition and harmony, and with the high prices of sheet music women would learn to write their own songs and parlour music for use at home. Women were largely excluded from serious music and although the 1870 Education Act included the mandatory teaching of music, even as late as the 1880s teaching of any kind was still regarded as diverting women from their true destiny:

> So far as cleverness, learning and knowledge are conducive to women's moral excellence, they are … desirable, and no further. All that would occupy her mind to the exclusion of better things, all that would involve her in the mazes of flattery and admiration, all that would tend to draw her thoughts from others and fix them on herself, ought to be avoided as an evil to her, however brilliant or attractive it may be in itself.[1]

Throughout the nineteenth century, there was a proliferation of music schools, academies and colleges, which arose because of societal change leading to the loss of chaperonage, increased leisure time for young women and the Victorian ethos of worthwhile pursuits, either charitable or philanthropic. These music schools were largely populated by women (piano, violin or voice students), who regardless of the views that women should not perform in public, were now actively following their own career choices.

The Royal Academy of Music was one of the first of the early nineteenth-century institutions which rallied against the opinion that women should stick to the home, and was set up in 1822 with the express purpose of teaching music to both men and women in equal measure. The college was co-educational from the beginning and all students were able to study music theory, harmony and composition. Through regular student concerts they were all encouraged to compose and perform on stage.

Aged eighteen, Dora joined the college in the winter of 1881, shortly after her father's death and her move to London. She was fortunate to receive teaching in piano technique with the composer Walter Macfarren, and composition with the renowned Ebenezer Prout, whose books on musical theory are still in use today. As well as receiving teaching in the college, Dora also attended piano lessons with Julian Adams, a student of Moscheles, a celebrated pianist of his day. Julian Adams also taught violin to J. T. Carrodus, who had joined the Academy a few years before Dora and with whom she would work closely over the coming years.

Her studies were extremely successful and in the first three years she achieved the Bronze Medal (1882), Silver Medal (1883) and the Certificate of Merit (1884). On 15 December 1884, Dora received the coveted piano scholarship Cipriani Potter Exhibitioner, giving her £12 (about £1,500 today) towards further study.[2] (Details of the Royal College prizes are outlined in Appendix 4.)

In 1886 Dora was awarded the Lady Goldsmid Scholarship, awarded to those with a talent for composition, and giving her a further two years of free tuition.[3] In May 1887 she was awarded the Sterndale Bennett Scholarship, which required the student to pass an exam in general education including Geography, English Grammar, English History, Arithmetic and a language.[4] Dora already spoke French learnt from her mother and it seems probable that she also spoke German, a language that would become very useful over the coming years.

Dora continued to excel and the icing on the cake came in July 1888, when against nine other candidates, she became the first woman to be awarded the prestigious Charles Lucas Silver Medal for her *Air and Variations for String Quartet*.[5] The competition required each of the entrants to write a piece of music in a specific genre, in this instance chamber music, which the judges announced only two months before the completion date.

Figure 4.1. RAM Potter Prize Board

Throughout this period Dora performed in Royal College student concerts, performing her own works and accompanying others, establishing herself as a concert pianist of some note. Outside of the Academy she was a prolific concert performer and in the early days of her attendance used these performances to fund her studies and living requirements.

The Party

Dora was surrounded by very talented students at the Academy, some of whom became life-long friends and with whom she continued to both perform and compose. The rules of the Academy kept men and women apart except for musical discussion, but inevitably social groups sprang up and Dora soon formed a close-knit friendship group with four other students: J. A. Greenway, Ethel Boyce, J. Moir-Clark and Edward German.

As a group they would refer to themselves as The Party: 'The group were assiduous in attending public concerts and listening to each other's works, finding that slender territory which exists between frankness and encouragement.'[6] An example of their support for each other is provided by Edward German at the premiere of his first symphony in 1886: 'All the members of the party attended the rehearsal in the morning, refreshed by fruit, which Ethel Boyce had brought from her Orchard home in Chertsey. In the afternoon they attended a performance of *Ruddigore* at the Savoy Theatre.'[7]

Dora and Ethel Boyce formed a very strong friendship and performed together at many Academy concerts. Ethel was herself a talented composer and won a similar set of prizes to Dora, including the Lucas Medal in 1889. She was by all accounts somewhat emancipated:

> Please send some tobacco – I'm running short … She lived the open life of a student at a time when many young ladies were sequestered in the home. In 1885, she travelled abroad with Dora Bright and A. J.[8]

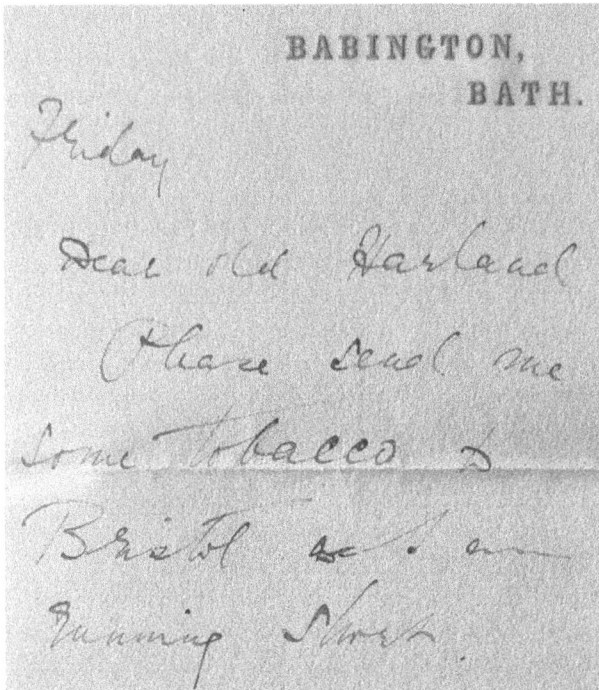

Figure 4.2. Letter from Ethel Boyce whilst staying at Babington House for Christmas

Ethel wrote many letters with reference to Dora. One such letter written to Edward German on their trip to Bohemia in 1888 provides some insight into Dora's character: 'Dora is very trying; I believe that she would like to do nothing better than to get up late – dawdle about all day – and go to the Opera at night.'[9] Perhaps that doesn't sound so different to many young holiday-goers today, if you swap opera for nightclub.

Ethel and Edward formed a strong friendship and after a few years they were engaged. Their relationship ended around 1886 'and neither young lover married, though Ethel maintained a long, tentatively romantic acquaintance with a Chertsey Solicitor, Harland Chaldicott'.[10] Ethel's freedom as a student came to an end quite quickly and after graduating from the Academy, she was required to return to Chertsey to look after her elderly parents. As a woman the burden of care fell to her as it did for all unmarried daughters in the late nineteenth century, a practice that has changed little today regardless of the changes in health systems. After the death of her parents, she continued to live at the Orchard home and went on to have a comparatively successful career, writing at least three cantatas, numerous songs for female choirs and many books of songs.

Along with so many composers of her time Ethel faced considerable difficulties having works published and in 1907 could only have her *Concertstück for Violin and Orchestra* printed in piano reduction. Whilst publication would not have been easy for any but the best-known composers of either sex, the presumption of inferiority that greeted women's more ambitious compositions constituted a serious obstacle beyond those faced by male peers.[11]

Ethel remained good friends with Dora and over the ensuing years they played in public many times together and shared authorship of some children's works. Throughout her life Ethel was a very regular guest at Babington House, until her death in 1939.

Edward German was ostensibly the most successful of the party and became a household name in Edwardian England through his links with Gilbert and Sullivan and the D'Oyly Carte company. He wrote many theatrical works as well as a number of more serious works including symphonies, choral works, songs, chamber and organ music. German was the first composer to write music for a British film, composing a mere 16 bars for the coronation scene in *Henry VIII* and receiving 50 guineas as a fee (£6,000 today). He became a great friend of Sir Edward Elgar and was knighted for service to music in 1928. German's output was significant, although not so different in many respects to that of Dora Bright – light opera, theatre, orchestral and chamber works. Perhaps in a more enlightened world where women composers were regarded as equals, Dora might have been honoured and remembered in the same way as Sir Edward German.

J. A. Greenway was a cornetist, and a professional brass band conductor winning forty-two national championships between 1904 and 1952. His virtuoso trombone showpiece *The Acrobat* is well known to British brass band players; he is also the composer of *The British Legion March*. Of J. Moir-Clark there seems to be little information remaining and he is recorded merely as a composer, showing that men can also be forgotten regardless of their success in their own lifetime.[12]

From student to concert pianist and composer

Applying herself diligently to her studies and college life, 1881 was a year of consolidation for Dora. Her first recorded public appearance was in January 1882 at the Hornet Cricket Club in Islington, when she opened the concert with 'a skillfully played piano solo, which was applauded'.[13] An inauspicious start to her career, but only three weeks later Dora played her own work, and first recorded composition, *Whither?*, in front of HRH the Princess Louise at an Academy concert. The Princess expressed herself 'much pleased with the performances of the students'.[14] That same year she won her first medal, the bronze, and went on to play W. Macfarren's *Concertstück* at the October Promenade Concert in Covent Garden, under the leadership of Mr Carrodus.[15] This was her first major concert and together with Mr Carrodus this was the start of great things and a flourishing career as a concert player. Throughout 1883 Dora played at a further four Royal Academy concerts, at three of which she performed her own works.[16]

That Dora actively chose to compose and play her own compositions was not unusual. One of the expectations of the Academy was that students would compose and play their own works in concert. All her close friends, members of The Party, did exactly the same to some degree. The rise of the virtuoso composer such as Beethoven, Chopin and Liszt, paved the way for such an expectation and it was only in the latter part of the nineteenth century with the rise of virtuoso players such as Vladimir Horowitz and Arthur Rubenstein, who themselves became almost greater than the composers whose music they played, that the composer/performer became a less frequently encountered individual. The double financial gain was also a consideration for Dora, who largely unsupported could finance her lifestyle from concerts, alongside the revenue from sales of her published works. No doubt this was one reason she chose to write songs initially, as they were more easily published, and readily available to a public desperate for new works. She was to become a composer of some note and in her later life performance would take a back seat.

Dora's playing was already beginning to attract positive comment as reported in July 1883: 'and to Miss Dora Bright, who played the Andante and Rondo from Chopin's Concerto in E minor so well as to make us almost forget that it was the performance of a student'.[17]

'Second appearance of the solo pianist DORA BRIGHT, winner of the Gold and Silver medal, RAM' was how the Bijous Opera House introduced her to one of their 'Popular Orchestral Concerts' with the Buxton Pavilion

Band.[18] The band was led by a Buxton resident and composer, Karl Meyder, and perhaps an acquaintance of Dora's grandfather Selim, who may well have managed an introduction in support of her career as a concert pianist. Her association with the Buxton Band and the town itself was to become a regular part of life over the next few years as her career developed, as were visits to Liverpool, possibly including visits to family.

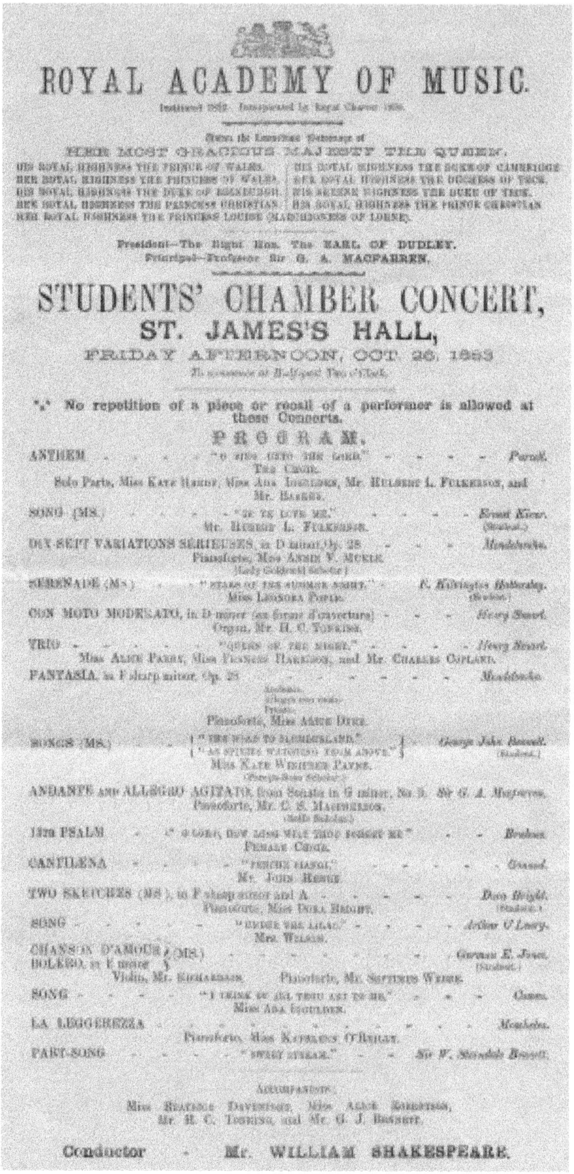

Figure 4.3. Royal Academy programme for 26 October 1883 with *Two Sketches in F# minor and A* by Dora Bright

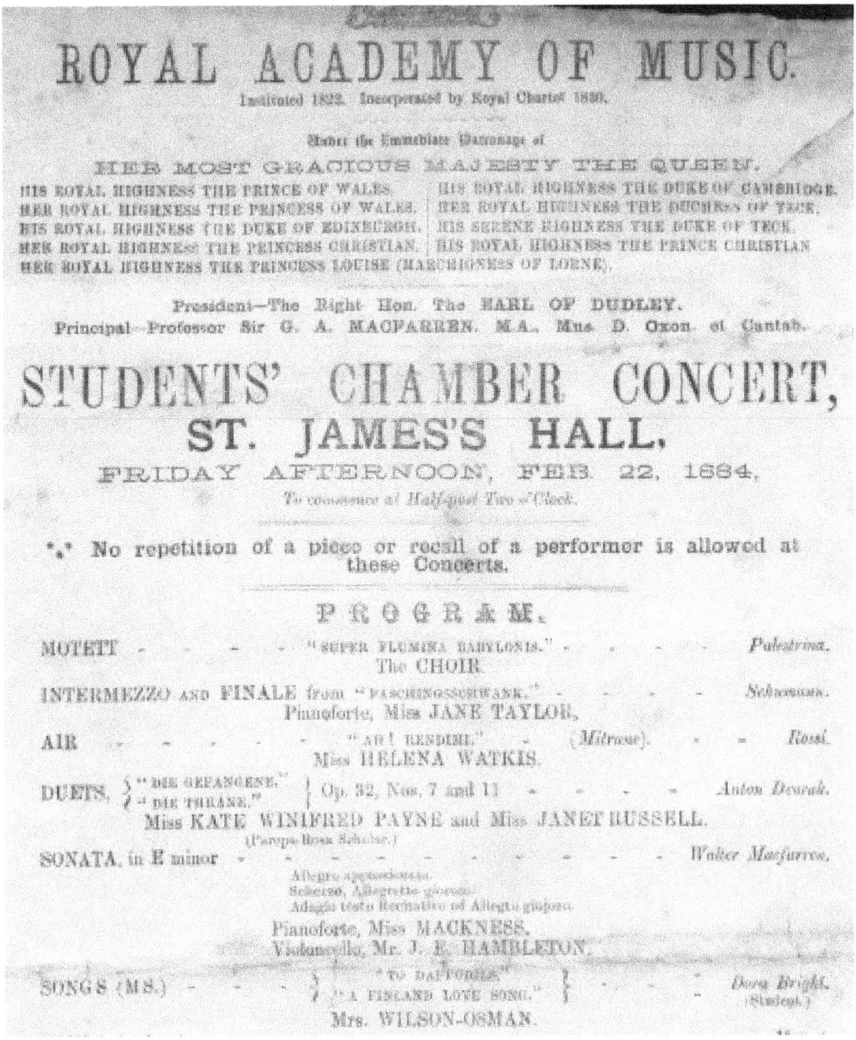

ROYAL ACADEMY OF MUSIC.

Instituted 1822. Incorporated by Royal Charter 1830.

Under the Immediate Patronage of

HER MOST GRACIOUS MAJESTY THE QUEEN.

HIS ROYAL HIGHNESS THE PRINCE OF WALES. | HIS ROYAL HIGHNESS THE DUKE OF CAMBRIDGE.
HER ROYAL HIGHNESS THE PRINCESS OF WALES. | HER ROYAL HIGHNESS THE DUCHESS OF TECK.
HIS ROYAL HIGHNESS THE DUKE OF EDINBURGH. | HIS SERENE HIGHNESS THE DUKE OF TECK.
HER ROYAL HIGHNESS THE PRINCESS CHRISTIAN. | HIS ROYAL HIGHNESS THE PRINCE CHRISTIAN.
HER ROYAL HIGHNESS THE PRINCESS LOUISE (MARCHIONESS OF LORNE).

President—The Right Hon. The EARL OF DUDLEY.
Principal—Professor Sir G. A. MACFARREN, M.A., Mus. D. Oxon. et Cantab.

STUDENTS' CHAMBER CONCERT,
ST. JAMES'S HALL,
FRIDAY AFTERNOON, FEB. 22, 1884,
To commence at Half-past Two o'Clock.

*** No repetition of a piece or recall of a performer is allowed at these Concerts.

PROGRAM.

MOTETT - - - - "SUPER FLUMINA BABYLONIS." - - - - *Palestrina.*
The CHOIR.

INTERMEZZO AND FINALE from "FASCHINGSSCHWANK." - - - - *Schumann.*
Pianoforte, Miss JANE TAYLOR,

AIR - - - - - "AH! RENDIMI." - (*Mitrane*). - - *Rossi.*
Miss HELENA WATKIS.

DUETS, { "DIE GEFANGENE." "DIE THRÄNE." } Op. 32, Nos. 7 and 11 - - - - *Anton Dvorak.*
Miss KATE WINIFRED PAYNE and Miss JANET RUSSELL.
(Parepa-Rosa Scholar.)

SONATA, in E minor - - - - - - - - - - *Walter Macfarren.*
Allegro appassionato.
Scherzo, Allegretto giocoso.
Adagio lento Recitativo ed Allegro giojoso.
Pianoforte, Miss MACKNESS.
Violoncello, Mr. J. E. HAMBLETON.

SONGS (MS.) - - - { "TO DAFFODILS." "A FINLAND LOVE SONG." } - - - *Dora Bright.* (Student.)
Mrs. WILSON-OSMAN.

Figure 4.4. Fragment from Royal Academy of Music student programme – *To Daffodils* and *A Finland Love Song*

The year 1884 saw the introduction of two new songs at the Royal Academy concerts, *To Daffodils* and *A Finland Love Song.*[19]

In July later that year, Dora visited Buxton once more:

> Special Grand Concert at the Pavilion
>
> Miss Dora Bright, the solo pianist, was most brilliant in her manipulation of the instrument, and her performances were loudly applauded, calling forth most hearty encores to which she

graciously bowed her acknowledgments ... Miss Dora Bright next made her appearance and gave as a pianoforte solo, Mendelssohn's Concerto in G minor. The manipulation of the splendid instrument was superb, and her execution of the solo exceedingly brilliant, delighting the audience, who accorded her a deafening encore, which she graciously acknowledged.[20]

On being awarded the silver medal and certificate of honourable mention, 'for her diligent application to studies', the *Buxton Advertiser* goes on to applaud her success: 'We heartily congratulate Miss Bright on her success, and feel assured from what we have heard of her playing at the Pavilion, and the high enconiums [eulogy] that have been bestowed upon her, that she has a bright future before her'.[21] The extent to which family contacts played a part in these tributes is impossible to know, but it most certainly had the desired effect of raising Dora's profile outside of London and giving her concert experience, which she used to great advantage over the next few years.

Back in London Dora introduced a new work at an Academy concert in July 1885. She performed her first large-scale work, *Concertstück for Piano and Orchestra in C# minor*, with one critic writing: 'In every respect this piece reflects the utmost credit upon the youthful artist, and the applause with which it was received will, we trust, nerve her to increased exertion'.[22] A slightly less positive critic suggested the work 'promising, but somewhat too ambitious'.[23]

The April of 1886 was a very hectic month as she played in front of, and met, the great Franz Liszt at an Academy performance,[24] won the Royal Academy Lady Goldsmid Scholarship, performed again in Buxton, then in Nottingham and London, and in the last week of the month, at the Covent Garden Proms.[25] The *Buxton Herald*, demonstrating the importance to the town of the Bright name, couldn't refrain from a moment of adulation:

> I am delighted to say that Miss Dora Bright, the grand-daughter of our venerable townsman, Mr. Selim Bright (and who delighted many of our visitors and residents at Mr Karl Meyder's Pavilion concerts last season), had the honour of playing before the great master of the pianoforte – Herr Liszt ... Miss Dora Bright played Sterndale Bennett's Caprice in E with great elegance and finish and ... descended to receive the master's encouraging word of approval as he rose and shook her warmly by the hand. So you see the fame of Buxton is getting greater and greater, for we may class Miss Bright as one of the bright particular stars of the musical universe. May it not be long ere she delights Buxton with her pristine brilliancy, which is undoubtedly Bright.[26]

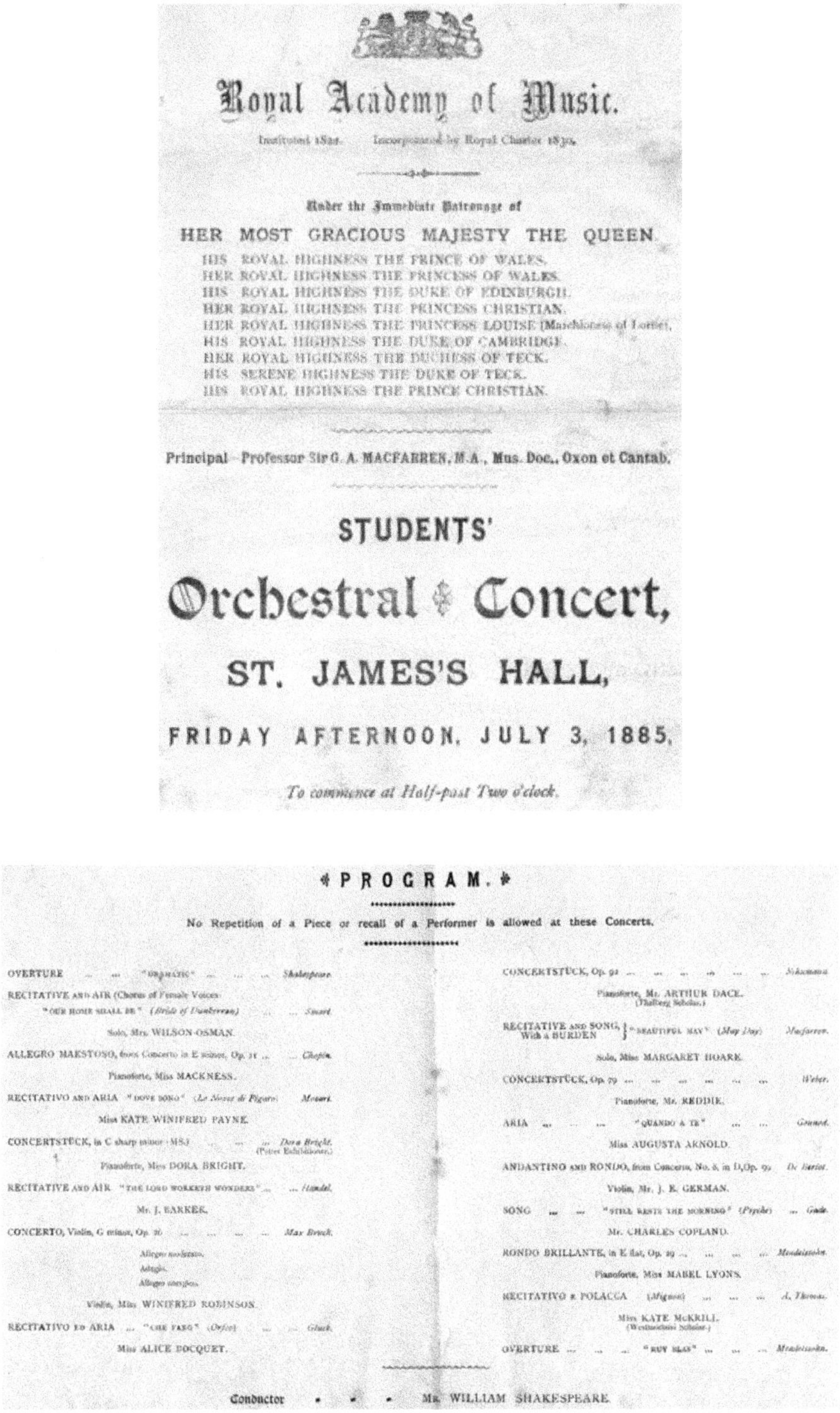

Royal Academy of Music.

Instituted 1822. Incorporated by Royal Charter 1830.

Under the Immediate Patronage of

HER MOST GRACIOUS MAJESTY THE QUEEN.

HIS ROYAL HIGHNESS THE PRINCE OF WALES.
HER ROYAL HIGHNESS THE PRINCESS OF WALES.
HIS ROYAL HIGHNESS THE DUKE OF EDINBURGH.
HER ROYAL HIGHNESS THE PRINCESS CHRISTIAN.
HER ROYAL HIGHNESS THE PRINCESS LOUISE (Marchioness of Lorne).
HIS ROYAL HIGHNESS THE DUKE OF CAMBRIDGE.
HER ROYAL HIGHNESS THE DUCHESS OF TECK.
HIS SERENE HIGHNESS THE DUKE OF TECK.
HIS ROYAL HIGHNESS THE PRINCE CHRISTIAN.

Principal—Professor Sir G. A. MACFARREN, M.A., Mus. Doc., Oxon et Cantab.

STUDENTS'

Orchestral Concert,

ST. JAMES'S HALL,

FRIDAY AFTERNOON, JULY 3, 1885,

To commence at Half-past Two o'clock.

PROGRAM.

No Repetition of a Piece or recall of a Performer is allowed at these Concerts.

OVERTURE ... ... "DRAMATIC" ... ... *Shakespeare.*

RECITATIVE AND AIR (Chorus of Female Voices) "OUR HOME SHALL BE" (*Bride of Dunkerron*) ... ... *Smart.*

Solo, Mrs. WILSON-OSMAN.

ALLEGRO MAESTOSO, from Concerto in E minor, Op. 11 ... ... *Chopin.*

Pianoforte, Miss MACKNESS.

RECITATIVO AND ARIA "DOVE SONO" (*Le Nozze di Figaro*) *Mozart.*

Miss KATE WINIFRED PAYNE.

CONCERTSTÜCK, in C sharp minor (MS.) ... ... *Dora Bright.*

Pianoforte, Miss DORA BRIGHT.

RECITATIVE AND AIR "THE LORD WORKETH WONDERS" ... ... *Handel.*

Mr. J. BARKER.

CONCERTO, Violin, G minor, Op. 26 ... ... *Max Bruch.*

Allegro moderato.
Adagio.
Allegro energico.

Violin, Miss WINIFRED ROBINSON.

RECITATIVO ED ARIA ... "CHE FARÒ" (*Orfeo*) ... ... *Gluck.*

Miss ALICE BOCQUET.

CONCERTSTÜCK, Op. 92 ... ... *Schumann.*

Pianoforte, Mr. ARTHUR DACE.

RECITATIVE AND SONG, With a BURDEN } "BEAUTIFUL MAY" (*May Day*) *Macfarren.*

Solo, Miss MARGARET HOARE.

CONCERTSTÜCK, Op. 79 ... ... *Weber.*

Pianoforte, Mr. REDDIE.

ARIA ... ... "QUANDO A TE" ... ... *Gounod.*

Miss AUGUSTA ARNOLD.

ANDANTINO AND RONDO, from Concerto, No. 8, in D, Op. 99 *De Beriot.*

Violin, Mr. J. E. GERMAN.

SONG ... ... "STILL RESTS THE MORNING" (*Psyche*) ... *Gade.*

Mr. CHARLES COPLAND.

RONDO BRILLANTE, in E flat, Op. 29 ... ... *Mendelssohn.*

Pianoforte, Miss MABEL LYONS.

RECITATIVO E POLACCA (*Mignon*) ... ... *A. Thomas.*

Miss KATE McKRILL.

OVERTURE ... ... "RUY BLAS" ... ... *Mendelssohn.*

Conductor - - - Mr. WILLIAM SHAKESPEARE.

Figure 4.5. Royal Academy of Music student programme – *Concertstück in C# minor*

The frequency of Dora's return to the North may reflect the bond between her and the Buxton arm of the family after the death of her father and the misbehaviour of her mother. Selim, the rich merchant, may well have taken Dora under his wing and helped her financially to continue her studies, but he was also able to help her with introductions and would have been highly satisfied with the prestige her accomplishments brought to the Bright name.

Alongside her concert performances, Dora continued to compose albeit with a change of direction from songs to larger works – the *Suite in G minor* and her second large-scale piano work the *Theme and Variation in F# minor for two pianofortes*, which she played with Ethel Boyce at the Willis Rooms in London. The latter work was described as being 'a composition of noticeable points of musicianship'.[27]

At the age of twenty-five Dora was elected by the Academy to become a sub-professor to her mentor and teacher Walter Macfarren.[28] She was now a tutor as well as a student and after winning the Sterndale Bennett prize in May 1887, against a field of 31 other students, secured a further two years of free tuition at the Academy.[29] The *St James's Gazette* went on to proclaim her 'one of the very best pianists that the Royal Academy has yet produced',[30] and the *Sheffield Evening Telegraph* proudly went on, 'her career at the Academy has been a most gratifying success and judging by the criticism of many leading metropolitan journals she seems destined to attain a high rank as a pianist'.[31] In characteristic style the papers are happy to comment upon her academic success, ignoring her recent compositions and foreseeing her future as a pianist and performer rather than a composer.

Finally, in October 1887, Dora returned to Sheffield for the first time since leaving for London:

> At the Parish Rooms, Psalter Lane, Sharrow … Miss Dora Bright, who is Sub-professor, Royal Academy of Music, will include in her selections a composition of her own. The concert is exciting so much interest that very few reserved seats are left for disposal.[32]

The excitement only went so far and although a success, Dora's return to her home town did not meet with quite the same level of adulation as that afforded in Buxton:

CONCERT AT SHARROW

> Although there was room for a larger audience, it was said that had all the ticket holders been present, the place would have been filled to overflowing. The event, musically speaking, was an interesting one in as much as it introduced to her townsfolk Miss Dora Bright, the young pianist whose work at RAM is so highly spoken of. Her first public appearance in her native town was hailed with much

criticality, and everyone at the concert was impressed by her playing, which was remarkable for its thought and poetry, the mastery she had over her instrument, and the perfection with which everything was accomplished ... She has a beautiful touch; her tone is rich, and altogether there is unity of effect about her performances. Miss Bright played her own Suite in G minor ... this and a few other musicianly compositions have established her reputation as a writer as well as a pianist.[33]

Dora continued to compose and produced two separate sets of variations and more songs. Her *Variations on an original theme by Sir G. A. Macfarren for Piano and Orchestra* was well received and reviewed in *The Era*:

We must award Miss Dora Bright hearty recommendation for the ingenuity she has displayed in a piece which, although the work of a student, deserves to be more widely known. Perhaps Miss Bright may have been influenced to some extent by the success achieved by M. Saint-Saens, but there is no trace of imitation in her ideas, which are fresh and attractive while also thoroughly effective.[34]

However, the crowning glory of 1888 was her new *Piano Concerto in A minor*, first played at the Academy concert on 24 July and subsequently at two Covent Garden Promenade Concerts on 19 and 26 September. The work was received with considerable praise and reviewed in detail across the press (see Chapter 11 for detail on the work itself).

The Royal Academy of Music has seldom given so important a concert ... Indeed matters are most promising for the future ... and there is an ambitious spirit on the side of the students which, properly controlled cannot fail to bring fruit. Striking evidence of this was afforded in the production by Miss Dora Bright of a new concerto for the pianoforte, which the young lady played with remarkable skill ... for it contains many fresh and charming ideas and some very effective passages, calculated to display the talents of the executants. It is in A minor, and in its general framework and character shows that the composer has been attracted by the genius of Mendelssohn. But there is nothing slavish in Miss Bright's leaning towards Mendelssohn. There are fresh and graceful ideas belonging unquestionably to herself, and the instrumentation, although not strong, is picturesque and well blended with the solo instrument ... Miss Bright has gained much from her professors, and they gain honour in return from a pupil so talented. Miss Bright was called to the platform again at the close of the work and applauded enthusiastically.[35]

This was a significant moment in Dora's career and raised her cachet considerably, as both a pianist and a composer of note.

Prince's Hall concerts 1889

Very focused on her career as a concert pianist, in 1889 Dora organized a series of three concerts at the Prince's Hall in London. These were a way to show her breadth of abilities and to perform not only her own works but those of her friends. They were a huge success and raised her profile even further, the concerts being reported widely around the country.

The reports of these concerts provide an interesting perspective on how Dora was considered by the press, her style as a pianist and her commitment to her friends and mentors. 'It cannot be complained that Miss Dora Bright is premature in coming forward on her own account to claim the attention and the verdict of amateurs,'[36] was how one paper reported the announcement of the series of concerts.

The first of the series, on 30 January 1889, included some old favourites: Bach, Schumann, Chopin, Liszt and Greig. She also included a piece by her friend, some variations by Moir-Clark and a new work by her tutor Walter Macfarren. Dora included her own *Romanza and Scherzetto*: 'a piece that should be on every amateur's pianoforte.'[37] 'She showed an excellent technique, a firm, elastic touch and considerable charm and tenderness of expression in her playing and there was hearty and spontaneous applause.'[38] Not all the reports were as positive: 'Miss Dora Bright, a young English pianist, and formerly a student at the Royal Academy of Music, gave the first of three recitals at Prince's Hall … The programme was well diversified, but as might be expected, the lady was heard to less advantage in Schumann's music than in works of a lighter character.'[39]

The second of the series, a month later on 27 February, had a similar lineup of Beethoven and Bach. Again, she took the opportunity to introduce her friends' work with Edward German's *Mazurka and Impromptu*.[40]

The final concert was played before a very large audience, when 'her technical proficiency and keen artistic perception were very satisfactorily displayed.'[41] The concert was noteworthy not only on account of its general interest, but because of the prominence given to English music in particular. Works included Mendelssohn and Bach but also W. Macfarren's new studies 5, 6, 7 and 8. Dora went on to play two pieces by Ethel Boyce, who then assisted her in Dora's two-piano version of her *Variation on an original theme by Sir G. A. Macfarren*.[42] In this finale of the series, the *Pall Mall Gazette* considers her playing:

> The fact is Miss Bright is a very gifted pianist. She will always draw
> a large audience. Her playing is full of natural sensibility, her touch

is delicious, and her technique is as remarkable as her memory. Her rendering, without book, of Grieg's incoherent *Ballade* was quite a feat, while W. Macfarren's wickedly difficult *Studies in Octaves* were thrown off with quite a saucy ease.[43]

Also, from the pages of the *Monthly Musical Record*:

Miss Bright's playing combines the genuine tenderness and warmth of womanly feeling with masculine vigour and energy; hence the singular charm of her performance ... the concert giver's own composition, to wit, a set of *Variations for Two Pianofortes on a theme in G Minor* by G. A. Macfarren, which breathe the spirit of modern romanticism, and present, like her playing, a most elegant combination of alternate grace and power. This fine work should, in the estimation of the genuine connoisseur, quickly supersede Saint-Saens' familiar piece among the very few available original compositions of this class. Miss Bright likewise introduced from her own pen a sweet and dreamy *Romanza and Scherzetto*, distinguished by piquancy and excellent musicianship within a small frame.[44]

Organized by Dora and showcasing her very great talents, these concerts are also an excellent example of how she wanted to introduce English music to the public, in particular the English music of her friends and colleagues, fresh from their pens and indicative of the times in which they were living. Overall, the series had been a huge success, the news coverage was generally positive and was even reported in Australia, with a full biopic in the Sydney press.[45]

Figure 4.6. Dora Bright, 1889 as displayed in *The Sydney Mail and New South Wales Advertiser*

The German tours

In 1888, Dora was granted her application for a passport,[46] which was for her first trip to Germany with Ethel Boyce and J. A. Greenway. The passport got a good deal of use over the coming years, as she returned on tour to Germany for at least three more years, even after she had become a married woman.

> The talented young English pianist, Miss Dora Bright, has just been playing with marked success in Dresden. The artist was heard there at a concert given under her auspices, on the 27th September, and on Tuesday next she is engaged for the opening concert of the Dresden Philharmonic Society, when she will appear in the double capacity of executant and composer, and play the principal part in her own Concerto for Pianoforte and Orchestra.[47]

This first visit to Germany was a success and resulted in a return in the autumn of 1890 and 1892. To undertake such European trips in the 1890s, for a single woman, would have been a daunting and formidable task. The organization of boats across the channel, trains across France and Germany, accommodation along the route and in Germany, and the trunks full of clothes and musical parts, must have been an enormous undertaking in the days before even the telephone had been invented. These tours are a true testament to Dora's drive and ambition and her determination to bring her music to as diverse an audience as possible.

Her second trip in 1890 was an opportunity to showcase a new Fantasia:

> The accomplished English pianist and composer, Miss Dora Bright, played her new Fantasia for Pianoforte and Orchestra at Dresden, at one of the Philharmonic Society's concerts in that town on the 8th of October and was announced to perform the same work at one of the Orchester Concerts at Cologne today (Saturday).[48]

The piece was a newly composed *Fantasia in G minor*, but reports in the German and English press described it, somewhat inaccurately, as more of a concerto. The misconception may have arisen from the report quoted from *Die Zeitung*: 'a pianoforte concerto, full of original and beautiful ideas, excellent workmanship, and very praiseworthy instrumentation, was received in the warmest manner.'[49] Only *The Queen* newspaper, reporting more extensively on the rise of Dora Bright in 1891, included the work as part of a list of her compositions: 'works include *Concerto in A minor, Fantasia in G minor*.'[50] Further evidence of the arising confusion can be found in another London newspaper:

English musical talent still receives – perhaps the word should be exhorts – recognition in Germany. As latest proof comes news that Miss Dora Bright recently played her Fantasia for Pianoforte at a Philharmonic Concert in Dresden, and that she repeated the performance at Coln last Saturday. The new work thus introduced is really a concerto freely constructed.[51]

Considering the success of the 1890 tour, the *Sheffield Daily Telegraph* was now happy to claim Dora as their own: 'All things considered we have before us a rarely gifted musician, whose brilliant future seems a certainty. Other German journals speak in the same strain ... Miss Bright is a native musician of whom Sheffield may be well proud.'[52]

There is no direct evidence that Dora returned to Germany in autumn 1891, but there are no reports of her playing in any concerts by the English press between June and December. However, she did return in 1892 playing once again in Dresden, Cologne and Hanover. A report in *The Gentlewoman* precedes the visit, but also suggests that there may have been a visit in 1891:

in 1889 she made her first Continental tour, visiting all the principal musical towns in Germany, where she was most favourably received by the German press. She played her first *Concerto in A minor*, at most of these places, always with success, and she has made a return visit each year since, and Miss Bright is under engagement to play the Fantasia composed with the Philharmonic for the Musikalische Gesellschaft in Cologne (the oldest musical society there) in October.[53]

Once again, the tour was a success and Dora also played her newly composed *Piano Quartet* in Hanover, her new *Fantasia No. 2* in Cologne and devoted a whole concert in Dresden to the work of her friend Moir-Clark – 'An Aberdeen Composer in Dresden.'[54] Dora would return again to Europe in the years to come, but it would be her work that appeared and not her as a performer, and it would be the theatre as well as the concert hall where her music was to be heard.

A rising star

'A new star is to arise,'[55] is how one newspaper referred to Dora Bright, and with the success of the Prince's Hall concerts and the *Piano Concerto in A minor*, there is no doubt that she was firmly established in her career and was also in considerable demand around the country.

Whilst in general Dora's playing was reviewed in glowing terms and her proficiency and sense of touch commended, there are rare occasions when her personality can be glimpsed, which are not always reported in the same vein:

> Her style has gained considerably in refinement, and her execution leaves scarcely anything to be desired. It is a pity that the effect of her performances was interfered with by the bad habit she has of exchanging recognitions with her friends in the audience whilst she is playing. This may seem a small matter to notice, but such a habit, though it may not interfere with the artist's playing, must produce the impression that undivided attention is not being bestowed upon the work being performed. In the case of a less promising artist it might be passed over, but Miss Bright is so clever that it would be mistaken kindness not to mention whatever distracts from her success.[56]

Her qualities as a great performer are acknowledged, but she is given a sharp rebuke for placing her friends and acquaintances above those of the audience. Friends were clearly the centre of her world and the ability to create and maintain such close relationships would be central to her continuing success. Dora's friendship was genuine and long-lasting and she would acquire a level of devotion from her closest friends which would see them unhesitatingly offer their services to many good causes to aid her in charitable works. She was also assiduous in acquiring friends in high places, who provided a level of soft patronage which was almost unnoticeable, other than to the outside observer.

In the latter part of the 1880s, Dora continued her association with Mr Carrodus and his players, touring England and giving concerts, including her own works and those of her friends, as well as those of the more established classical composers. In one three-day period, 14–16 October 1889, she played at five separate concerts in Halifax, Huddersfield, Leicester and Market Harborough.[57]

More composition followed throughout the next few years with a number of songs (1888/1889/1890), a song cycle *Twelve Songs* (1889) and a *Suite for Piano and Violin* (1891). The song cycle was only her third work to be published and despite the obvious importance of her larger works, publishers were not willing to publish orchestral works. Such an occurrence was the norm in Victorian England: one of Dora's predecessors, the prolific composer Alice Mary Smith (1839–1884), who wrote several symphonies, cantatas, a clarinet concerto and many other large works, was only able to find a publisher willing to print her songs and piano music, which were seen as the sole genres suitable for female talents.[58]

Dora's song cycle went down well:

> these songs ... and their musical setting show a commendable amount of constructive talent and thoughtfulness. There is also an apparent endeavour to avoid the tendency exhibited by some young composers to write their songs more in the form of pianoforte solos with vocal accompaniment, than to adopt the reverse process ... it would be as well if all who write songs were to follow, and if possible, improve upon the model these twelve songs offer.[59]

Despite the publishing constraints mentioned above, the demand for her music remained and in December 1891 the *St James's Gazette* announced: 'Among new works written specially for the Philharmonic Society may be mentioned a fantasia for pianoforte and orchestra by Miss Dora Bright, who will herself play the solo part'.[60]

An auspicious end to 1891, as this commission was a real honour and the first time a woman had been invited to write for the Philharmonic concert season.

***

The ten years from 1881 to 1891 took Dora Bright from being an unknown provincial student to an established and recognized composer and pianist, whose works and playing were in considerable demand. In the Royal Academy she had found a home in which to flourish, one that nurtured her abilities and helped her to hone her considerable skills. However, it is her own quite obvious drive and determination that are the compelling factors in her ascendancy. She was not from a wealthy family, unlike others in her sphere; her father had died all but penniless and her mother had, in a sense, sold the remaining family silver to establish her own theatrical career. Dora had to work hard to achieve success and she did this with considerable conviction and fortitude, travelling the length and breadth of the country, and Europe, to make her name and fortune. The next ten years would see an even more dramatic change in her circumstances, which would lead to financial stability for the remainder of her life.

5 Mrs Knatchbull, 1892–1900

The 1880s had been a whirl for Dora. She had moved from provincial Sheffield to cosmopolitan London, started to train as a professional musician and within a short time became one of the most talked-about women pianists and composers of her generation. She was set on advancing her own career and those of her friends and colleagues, with tours of England and Germany to show the quality of her own playing and music, but also to show the appeal of English music as it had begun to develop and blossom towards the end of the century. Amongst those concerts, parties and trips about town, she had met a gentleman of some means and substance, married him and moved to Babington, Somerset.

Wyndham Knatchbull

Born in 1829, Wyndham[1] was the eldest son of Rev. Wadham Knatchbull, Vicar of Fritwell, Oxfordshire. In 1838, his father was made Prebendary of Wells (Prebendary is an honorary post given to a senior parish priest and has a stipend attached that is paid from Cathedral income) and the family acquired Chadderton Lodge in Hampshire, with its land and farming tenancies. The new estate brought the family prosperity and three of the sons bought commissions in the army and the fourth attended Christchurch College, Cambridge, becoming a vicar and following in his father's footsteps.

Aged eighteen, Wyndham joined the army and purchased the rank of Cornet (2nd Lieutenant) in the 3rd Prince of Wales Regiment of the Dragoon Guards.[2] By 1851, he had risen to the rank of Lieutenant and was posted to Manchester Barracks and then on to Dublin in 1854, to oversee the interred prisoners of war from the Irish rebellion of 1848. He enjoyed a varied and notable career in the cavalry and in 1854 volunteered for service in the Crimea, followed by a decade in India fighting at the battle of Lucknow, during the Indian Mutiny, and then in 1867 as part of the British Abyssinian Expedition.

In June 1871 Wyndham's uncle died, leaving an estate of £25,000 (£3 million today) and the Manor house at Babington to his wife, who after only nine days also died. As there was no issue from the marriage the estate passed down to Wyndham as next of kin, where he assumed the role of generous host, country landlord and justice of the peace:

> On Thursday, a party of gentlemen … were invited by Captain Knatchbull to a day's shooting … More than 500 pheasant , besides other game, were bagged; the gamekeeper thus provided the best day's sport to be met within a circuit of ten miles.[3] Captain Knatchbull gave a garden party at Babington House on Saturday, at which upwards of a hundred people were present.[4]

The Captain, as he was widely referred to, split his time between town and country and is listed on the London electoral register, living in Kensington between 1885 and 1892.[5] During his stays in town, as a gentleman of leisure he enjoyed coaching which involved driving horses and carriage at speed around the streets of London and on long overnight journeys.[6] Echoes abound of Dora's Uncle Horatio and his coaching exploits around Sheffield and environs; these were the petrol-heads and boy racers of their time.

It is highly likely that he attended numerous exhibitions, concerts and parties with his army colleagues and upper-crust friends. Dora's successful and blossoming career as pianist and composer must have drawn his attention and at one of the parties in the late 1880s the pair met and were drawn to each other, despite the age gap:

> As a young student in London, Mrs. Knatchbull [Dora's married name] had helped to finance her studies by playing popular music at parties given by a hostess whose reputation was slightly suspect. Captain Wyndham Knatchbull, late Third Dragoons, would come up from Somerset and attend these evenings. Dora Estella Bright would play the piano, and it must be added that there was no shadow on Miss Bright's reputation. Nevertheless, Captain Knatchbull's family were taken aback when, at the age of sixty-three, he married Miss Bright, about forty years his junior.[7]

On 22 March 1892, Wyndham and Dora were married:

> At St. Andrew's West Kensington, the wedding took place very quietly of Captain Wyndham Knatchbull and Miss Dora Estella Bright, daughter of the late Augustus Bright, Esq., of Sheffield. The Rev. John Halford the vicar of Brixworth, officiated at the service.

She looked extremely well in a gown of brown and gold corduroy velvet trimmed with golden cock's feathers and gold bonnet. The bridegroom's gift to her was a bangle with the wearer's name in diamonds. The wedding being quite quiet and private, there was no reception. Later in the day the newly wedded pair left for Torquay, where they are spending the honeymoon, the bride wearing a navy-blue costume with gold embroidered vest and long fawn fur-lined cloak trimmed with beaver and a blue silk hat. The presents included diamond pendant, ear-rings, star ring, diamond and sapphire ring, diamond solitaire ear-rings, pearl necklace and ear-rings, diamond and ruby ring, grand pianoforte, dressing bag with ivory and silver mounts, tortoiseshell and silver mirror, Indian gold embroidered piano cover, silver salt cellars, etc.[8]

Photo. by] *[J. Bown, Manchester.*
Captain Wyndham Knatchbull.

Figure 5.1. Photograph of Captain Wyndham Knatchbull, *The Gentlewoman*, 2 April 1892

Despite the wedding being a quiet affair, Dora's outfits are designed to make a statement. She is announcing she has arrived and is going to tell the world that she is now officially part of high society.

Babington life

On return from honeymoon, the newly-weds moved back to Wyndham's estate in Babington. The house had been in the Knatchbull family for five generations prior to being inherited by Wyndham. The Queen Anne mansion sits in a park of over 80 acres with stables, ice-house, orangery, a walled garden and is now listed by English Heritage as a Grade II listed building, together with Grade II listed grounds. The original village of Babington may have been depleted by the Black Death, but what remained was cleared to make way for the house, completed around 1700. Adjacent to the house is the Grade I listed Church of St Margaret, commissioned by Mrs Long, a previous owner of Babington prior to the Knatchbulls. The house remains largely unchanged with only the addition of bow windows on the east side in 1790, creating a drawing room and dining room. The drawing room became Dora's music room.

When the newly-weds took up residence, the house retained furniture and fittings from the original build; it was claimed one of the bedrooms had been slept in by King James II. The hall retained stained glass from the original church and the drawing-room curtains from the 1833 refurbishment. The furniture and fittings, featured in an article in the magazine *Country Life* in 1943 commissioned by Dora, remained this way until the mid-1950s.

Figure 5.2. Babington House

Dora, now Mrs Knatchbull, seemed very happy to take on the role of country lady and she became involved in charitable works and activities around Babington and the South West. She quickly settled and soon made an impact:

> As one eminent countryman put it, we were dull dogs until this merry little lady came among us. The merry little lady ruled us all with a rod of iron, but she fed her subjects, and housed many of them with a lavish hospitality. Babington became and always remained a centre of good music and good company.[9]

There are many reports of the hospitality laid on by the couple, and invitations were not only for the well-to-do of the county, but also for the staff and locals:

> Captain and Mrs. Knatchbull gave a servant's and invitation ball on the 28th February, which was largely attended. Dancing commenced at nine p.m., and was kept up with much spirit until six o'clock the following morning to the strains of the Colford Quadrille Band ... At midnight the company sat down to an excellent spread, and the health of Captain and Mrs. Knatchbull was cordially drunk.[10]

The couple were well suited, despite the age gap, and lived a happy life together. As observed by one friend, theirs was 'a most unexpected but successful union'.[11]

> On Twelfth Night a very brilliant Fancy Dress Ball was given by Captain and Mrs. Knatchbull, at Babington. The house being of such ancient date, is particularly suited for this form of entertainment, and was certainly upon this occasion seen at its best. The fancy dresses showed up well against the old staircase and in the quaint hall, where the host and hostess received their guests. Captain Knatchbull made a noble figure dressed as Santa Claus, in a long robe of red silk, edged with white fur, his head surmounted by a wreath of holly and mistletoe entwined – he carried a large Christmas tree. Mrs. Knatchbull made a happy choice in the costume of Carmen, the Spanish gipsy, suggested, no doubt, by her Spanish origin, the little Bolero velvet jacket being in the deep shade of pink so becoming to a brunette.[12]

Ethel Boyce was also a visitor that same evening and described the ball as 'quite the prettiest and nicest party I've ever seen ... Dora, as Carmen looked awfully handsome, but I thought the dress, a bright cherry colour, and short skirts, rather too daring'.[13]

Charity was an important part of the role of the country lady, which in typical Dora fashion she took on with a vengeance. Previously, in London, Dora had played at charity concerts, but in her new life charity was very much a way of life, with requests to open fêtes, jumble sales, perform at local events, organize concerts in aid of good works and giving to the needy.

> The annual Christmas gifts, consisting of serge for those with large families, and flannel for those with small ones, have been distributed to all the cottages in Babington parish, at Babington House, by Mrs. Knatchbull. The Christmas joint was also provided as usual for all households in the parish.[14]

At some of these events Dora invited her good friend Ethel Boyce to assist her on the piano:

Opening of a new parish room – A successful inauguration

> A large and distinguished audience assembled in the new parish room ... on the occasion of a miscellaneous entertainment ... for the purpose of meeting the expense incurred in converting what was once an old and dilapidated barn ... into a parish room. At 7.30 the programme was commenced with ... Schumann, played by Mrs. Knatchbull ... A duet for two pianofortes – Dora Bright – *On a theme* (by Sir George Macfarren), the performers being Mrs. Knatchbull and Miss Boyce, both of whom played with great taste and precision.[15]

Despite all the frivolity of entertaining, running an estate and undertaking charitable works, Dora did not, as some biographies suggest, dramatically curtail her own career in music. In 1892 and 1893 alone, she played at over fifteen concerts, toured Germany in the autumn of 1892, organized another of her series of three concerts at the Prince's Hall in London and began to publish some of her works. Indeed, her new-found freedom empowered her to take on larger-scale projects and allowed her to pursue her own writing and publication.

The Philharmonic Society – Fantasia No. 2 in G

Due to the success of the performance of the revised *A Minor Piano Concerto* at the Crystal Palace in March 1891, Francesco Berger, Director of the

Philharmonic Society and Professor of piano at the Royal Academy of Music, asked that one of Dora's new works should be part of the 1892 Philharmonic season. Her recently written *Suite* had been requested, but Dora would not allow such a possibility, writing to Berger that she would prefer to write a new composition, 'as although the suite was well constructed, the Spanish Dance makes it a little light for a Philharmonic audience'. Dora went on to explain that her preference for a new work would allow her to take part in the performance and that the work would be written with a 'critical audience well in mind'. The letter further outlined that she would start to write the work in August, and 'it would be completed by the end of November or beginning of December'.[16]

This interchange between Dora and Berger gives some suggestion that the attitude towards women as composers was changing, even though the initial request was for a much lighter work than Dora intended to produce. It also shows the strength of her own self-belief that she felt able to tell such a prestigious institute as the Philharmonic Society what she would produce for them and not be browbeaten to provide a lesser work.

There are no reports of Dora performing in England during the autumn of 1891 and perhaps she was absorbed in producing the new work, which was completed by December as the newspapers reported, shortly after Christmas 1891.[17] It seems that regardless of the looming commission, Dora returned once again to Germany for her season of concerts. The *Pall Mall Gazette* reported:

> Miss Dora Bright's Fantasia, which will be one of the novelties of the forthcoming season of the Philharmonic Society, is in the key of G, and in one movement, although practically the form of it is that of a condensed concerto. It was written on the return of Miss Bright from Germany last October, so that this is the young composer-pianist's latest work.[18]

Clearly, leaks to the newspapers are not new and *The Queen* magazine went on:

> Miss Dora Bright...who is to play a new Fantasia for Piano and Orchestra which she has composed for the Philharmonic Society, was engaged by the Musikalische Gesellschafts, to play one of her own works in Cologne on Saturday last.[19]

It may be that, as with the Piano Concerto in A minor and the Fantasia in G minor, Dora tried out her large works on a German audience before committing to an English one and so this new Fantasia was outed in Germany ahead of its premiere in London.

It is at this point that confusion over the key of the work begins to creep in. The *Pall Mall Gazette* correctly reported the work as in G,[20] but *The Queen* reports G minor[21] and the Philharmonic Society advertisement including the programme reports G minor,[22] and even the Philharmonic Concert programme itself reports G minor.

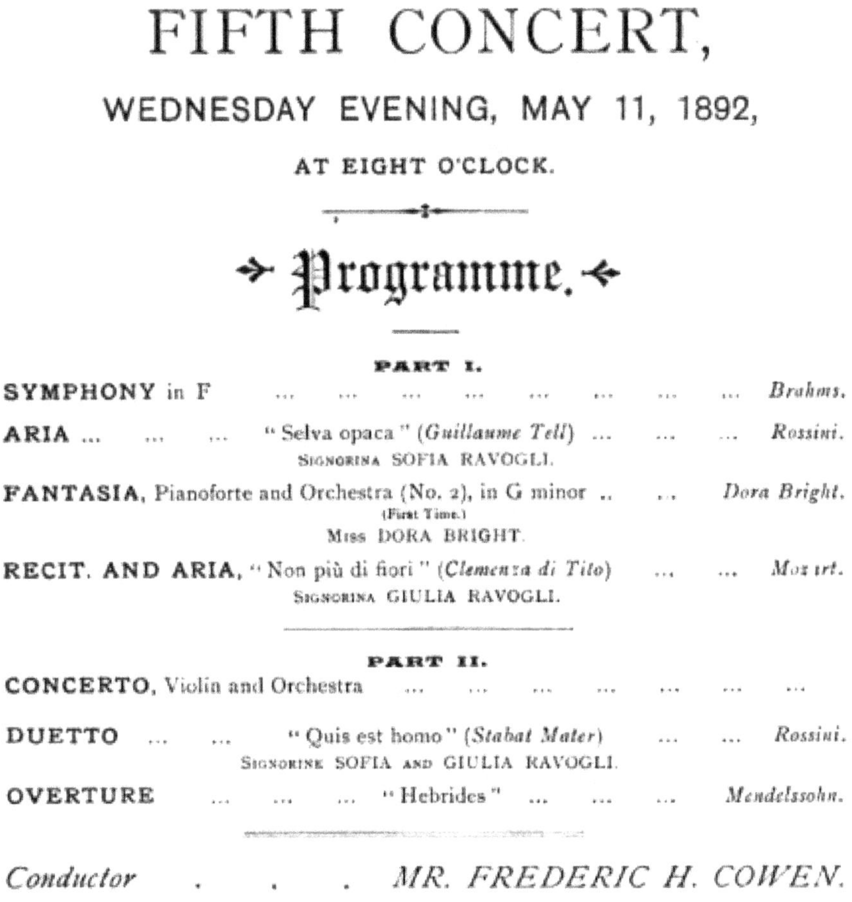

FIFTH CONCERT,

WEDNESDAY EVENING, MAY 11, 1892,

AT EIGHT O'CLOCK.

⇥ Programme. ⇤

PART I.

SYMPHONY in F ... ... *Brahms.*

ARIA ... ... " Selva opaca " (*Guillaume Tell*) ... ... *Rossini.*
SIGNORINA SOFIA RAVOGLI.

FANTASIA, Pianoforte and Orchestra (No. 2), in G minor .. .. *Dora Bright.*
(First Time.)
MISS DORA BRIGHT.

RECIT. AND ARIA, " Non più di fiori " (*Clemenza di Tito*) ... ... *Mozart.*
SIGNORINA GIULIA RAVOGLI.

PART II.

CONCERTO, Violin and Orchestra ... ...

DUETTO ... ... " Quis est homo " (*Stabat Mater*) ... ... *Rossini.*
SIGNORINE SOFIA AND GIULIA RAVOGLI.

OVERTURE ... ... " Hebrides " ... ... *Mendelssohn.*

Conductor . . . *MR. FREDERIC H. COWEN.*

Figure 5.3. Page 3 of Philharmonic Society concert programme

The programme (recently discovered by the author and previously unreported) includes a review of each of the works played and small printed snippets of the music with commentary on the key elements of the work. The programme for 11 May 1892 includes the following page:

FANTASIA, Pianoforte* and Orchestra (No. 2), in G   ...   ...   *Dora Bright.*

(First Time.)

Miss DORA BRIGHT.

THE Fantasia is written in the form of a condensed Concerto; the first section being the most important and worked out precisely in first-movement form :—

No. 1.

No. 2.

No. 3.

also—

After the recapitulation of first and second subjects, the cadenza occurs, when, instead of leading to a *Coda*, it prefaces the little Serenata which is the middle episode of the work in the tonic minor—

No. 4.

At its conclusion a slight pause is made before entering upon the last section of the work—a Rondo in 2·4 time in the original key of G—

No. 5.

This tiny Rondo contains one short episode in the key of E—

No. 6.

and after a return of the Rondo subject, the whole work is knit together by the re-introduction of the original theme.

Figure 5.4. Page 17 of Philharmonic Society concert programme

The heading of the work is correct and the key signature of the opening theme is clearly in G and not G minor, although the work does then move to G minor for the short Serenata, before again returning to G for the Rondo.

The concert and the Fantasia were a great success:

> *Fantasia No. 2* ... composed by Miss Dora Bright for pianoforte and orchestra, was played for the first time. It is unpretentious but clever; ably orchestrated, and brightened by strikingly original themes. The pianoforte part was played by the composer, whose merits were acknowledged by a triple recall.[23]

Other papers again reported the work in G minor until finally *The Times* and *The Queen* report correctly and positively:

> A new *Fantasia for Piano and Orchestra in G Major*, by Miss Dora Bright, was well played by the composer, who may be congratulated on the adroitness with which her piece is constructed. It is short and fairly concise, yet effective and grateful to the soloist.[24]

> The Fantasia performed last week is the second work of its kind which has proceeded from her pen. It is in the key of G, and is written in the form of a condensed Concerto, the most important movement being the first, which is very skilfully worked out, and is followed by a charming and melodious Serenata in the tonic minor, the work concluding with a brief but effective Rondo in the original key. The orchestration is skilful and happy, and the pianoforte part is brilliant and striking, and, on the whole, the Fantasia will worthily maintain the reputation of the composer.[25]

Reported in the programme and other newspapers as a condensed Concerto, it is very likely that this work was misreported not only as in G minor, but in future years as the Piano Concerto No. 2. Although included in lists of works as the Fantasia in G minor, no manuscripts remained after Dora's death and this work was presumed lost completely. Thankfully, the diligence of the Philharmonic programming team of 1892 has given a glimpse of another of Dora Bright's fine orchestral works and enabled the record, and catalogue, to be corrected with the Fantasia in G minor No. 1 and the Fantasia in G No. 2.

The Babington Strollers

Dora's musical career was now well-established and her own compositions were being acclaimed by the press and audiences across Europe. Marriage and a move to the country would not prevent her from continuing to compose and despite reducing her own concert performances she still needed an outlet for her musical nature. 1893 saw the first of her works specifically written for the theatre, *Uncle Silas* played at the Shaftesbury Theatre, London and subsequently, in 1895, on tour in Folkestone and Lincoln.[26]

Dora had been versed in the theatre and amateur dramatics from an early age and it was inevitable in those early years of marriage, with less time on the concert platform, that she would turn to creating music in this new environment:

When as a young bride, Dora descended on the County, she swept us all off our feet and startled its inhabitants in to musical and dramatic activity. Thus in 1893, the Babington Strollers came to life and for several years at Christmas time produced Gilbert and Sullivan operas at a high level of amateur performance, to a surprised and delighted neighbourhood.[27]

Such amateur groups were hugely popular and gave a platform to those with musical leanings to take an active role, where otherwise their talents might have lain undiscovered. The Strollers were a huge success locally and their concerts always fully subscribed. Described as Mrs. Horner's Company, the Strollers were made up of some of the wealthy landowners of the vicinity who strutted their parts in aid of charity for the local community. Some of the key players included Lady Horner of Mells Park and the Pagets of Cranmore Hall, who became great friends of Dora's.

Gilbert and Sullivan was an obvious choice with its many small parts, catchy tunes and its established place in the Victorian repertoire. 1895 saw a production of *The Mikado*, which commenced with a private performance at Babington in front of over 600 guests, including many of the great and good in the county, and followed by a dance. Much of the cast comprised members of local wealthy families and included Colonel Norton Knatchbull, Wyndham's brother, and at least six other younger members of the Knatchbull family. Ethel Boyce was in attendance and played the harmonium, with Dora on the piano.[28] The *Somerset Standard* reported:

> Whilst speaking of the music, mention must not be omitted of the accompanists, to whom belongs a not inconsiderable share of the credit due to the musical portion of the performance. Mrs. Knatchbull accompanied on the pianoforte in conjunction with Miss Boyce upon the harmonium, and these ladies carried out their duties in a masterly manner, and thoroughly earned the high encomiums bestowed upon their accompaniment.[29]

The opera was then sent on tour around the county playing in Midsomer Norton, Cranmore, Mells and Shepton Mallet over the course of a week. Dora had pulled some strings from her London network and brought Miss Angela Vanbrugh, an eminent London dancer, to be included in the cast and the costumes were supplied by Liberty of London. All the Strollers events were for charity and in this instance, 'the sum of £29 5s [£4,000 today] was realized for the benefit of the Memorial Hospital at Paulton'.[30]

Over the following years, the troupe now described as Mrs Knatchbull's and Mrs Horner's Company, introduced more Gilbert and Sullivan with *Trial by Jury*, *The Pirates of Penzance* and *H.M.S. Pinafore*, all with similar casts and in aid of charity. The charities took the form of the organ fund at East

Cranmore[31] and 'the wives and families of our Soldiers and Sailors in South Africa'.[32] Dora took on more than simply the piano accompaniment:

> Mrs. Knatchbull, who is at the head of the party, whose great his-trionic ability is well-known, and is exercised on these occasions as acting manager, and in the general training of the company, must be thoroughly and sincerely congratulated on the success with which she coped.[33]

Dora became active over the next twenty years with amateur dramatics and the theatre, and it became a very useful way of introducing new works to her audience, as well as raising monies for charities close to her heart.

Prince's Hall concerts

The year 1893 saw a rerun of the successful Prince's Hall concerts, which Dora had first sponsored in the winter of 1889. These concerts were once again an opportunity to display her own prowess as a performer and composer, but also a chance to display the music of England and that of some of her own friends. Alongside some of the greats, such as Mozart and Beethoven, was the music of Erskine Allen, Edward German, Moir-Clark and Dora Bright herself. The concerts were announced as musical evenings and were viewed as a means of widening the public's understanding of the growth of English music:

> We are glad to note that this clever native pianist and composer is not satisfied with producing music of the regulation type ... the feature to which we desire to draw special attention is that a num-ber of important works by English composers are to be accorded a hearing ... There is little chance for British authors at the Popular Concerts; but native composers and players are learning to take care of themselves. The aims of *entrepreneurs* are not always identi-cal with purely art purposes, and the public who patronise concerts are slow to learn of the changes that have come over English music within the last few years.[34]

The evenings attracted 'a fair if not crowded audience',[35] and in true style Dora played the piano for all the works in each of the three concerts. Even *The Times*, who had rarely covered Dora's concerts, printed a column for each concert at some length. Although the overall tone was comparatively positive, they did not always approve of Dora's playing:

> a little more refinement in the performance of the sonata might have been desired ... Miss Bright played with considerable care,

though her execution of the scale passages was wanting in clearness … Miss Bright gave a careful if not very poetical rendering.[36]

Interestingly, in the third of the concerts, Dora introduced her own *Quartet for Piano and Strings in D*, which was reported by *The Times*[37] as new, although it had already been played in Germany in October 1892.[38] This piece was again reported as specially written for a subscription concert in Norwich in 1894;[39] perhaps recycling was in vogue even in the 1890s.

Whether Dora considered these concerts a success or not, they had accomplished their objective and once again promoted her name, and those of her friends, bringing new English music and composers to a wider audience.

The National Concerts

After the success of the 1893 Prince's Hall concerts and a very busy year, 1894 was comparatively quiet, with only six performances and a number of local charitable events. However, in 1895 Dora proposed a series of National Pianoforte Recitals; a series of performances of music from the countries of Europe – Germany, France, Austria, Bohemia, Hungary, Italy, Norway, Spain, Holland, Belgium and England. The venue would be the Queen's Hall (Small Hall) in London and would be organized by Dora, with herself and Mr David Bispham (tenor) as the two recitalists. The scheme was very well received by the press, who considered this to be an excellent opportunity for students and musicians to learn more about music across the continent. There were to be four series of concerts and the first series commenced in November 1894.

Whilst musically a success, with Dora and Mr Bispham receiving accolades on their performances, the concerts were not well attended and there was considerable consternation at the quality of the programme and the accompanying notes. The first concert dealt with Early Germany and comprised works by Handel, Bach and Beethoven on the piano and some fifteenth-century songs. Overall, the works were regarded as 'admirably chosen'[40] and 'the playing having irreproachable technique.'[41] However, given the educational purpose of the concerts, errors in the programme set the scene for the concert series as a whole:

> It is a pity that, since it was apparently deemed advisable to give the dates of birth and death of the various composers, some care was not exercised in stating them correctly. Handel, for example, was not 110 years old when he died; nor is it likely that Hassler, at the age of three, was a pupil of Bach.[42]

The second concert focused on Modern Germany, and although there were some positive comments about Mr Bispham's singing, Dora's playing 'left a great deal to be desired'.[43] Programme issues remained, being described as 'somewhat meagre and unsatisfying', since Schubert was simply described as a 'pupil of his father, who was a schoolmaster', and Mendelssohn as 'a conductor of the famous Gewendhaus concert's' (instead of 'the Gewandhaus Concerts').[44]

The third concert dealing with French composers was largely a success, mostly for its efforts to provide works that were not mainstream, and provided a fresh insight into the music of Saint-Saens and Bizet. Dora also took the opportunity to introduce the works of another woman, Cécile Chaminade.

The final concert considered the music of Scandinavia and, 'as at the previous recitals, Miss Bright's playing was most enjoyable, and Mr Bispham's selection of songs most attractive'. However, the programme issues remained: 'Last evening the mis-spelling of the composers' names and the wrong dates must have been bewildering to students'.[45]

The remaining three series were never performed and the National Concerts faded away, seemingly a good idea, badly executed. The concerts mark a point in Dora's career, where she moved away from large-scale performance to one of composing and charitable works, settling more into her role as wife and country lady.

Dora Bright (Mrs Knatchbull)

Throughout the 1890s Dora played the dual role of performer/composer and dutiful wife to Captain Knatchbull. The frequency of concerts reduced slowly over the years but Dora continued to play, performing in over thirty concerts across the breadth of England from local charity concerts in Frome, Mells and Wells, to the Proms in London and subscription concerts in Bristol, Norwich and Manchester.

Although now a married lady, she continued to play under the name of Dora Bright when away from Somerset and her stature continued to grow, unlike so many other women who had to give away their independence as part of the marriage contract. Such an example arises in 1895 in a concert of Mozart's music:

> The solo performer on this occasion was Dora Bright, whose artistic style is heard to great advantage in music of this kind depending for its effect on grace, refinement, and melodious charm. Miss Bright, herself a composer of distinguished talent, interpreted music now over a century old with so much freedom, freshness and brilliancy that it sounded as if written yesterday. Her excellent playing was greeted with the enthusiasm it merited ... the solo player, who must also be credited with charming skill in playing her own cadenzas as well as ample technical ability in playing them.[46]

Even as late as the 1960s women were required to give up their jobs/careers upon marriage, to allow them to fulfil their role as wife and mother. Dora was not one to follow such norms and she had already witnessed the emancipated life her own mother had led, returning to the stage and forging her writing and stage career some twenty years earlier. Society women in similar circumstances to Dora, would, by and large, have followed the expectation that their first duty was to their husband and would not have considered that performing publicly other than for charity, through the auspices of amateur dramatics, was acceptable. Yet, Dora's success as a performer of note preceded her and for Dora, pursuing her career was the only way to continue. Most certainly, Wyndham supported Dora in her pursuits, and although seemingly happy their marriage did not bear children for whatever reason, the most likely being that Dora had found the stability she needed to lead life at her own pace and to her tune. Anything else was unnecessary. Dora Bright's own memoir gives no indication of how happy or otherwise she was in this period and makes virtually no mention of her husband or marriage, only that:

> My husband stood six feet four inches in his socks and was broad and muscular in proportion. He had great charm of manner (I have heard it called the Wyndham charm). His friends were many and steadfast, his brothers devoted and young men would go far to gain his kindly word and smile.[47]

She threw herself into country life and gave her society friends a new perspective. One of her good friends Lady Horner sums it up very well:

> Mrs. Knatchbull had first appeared amongst them before the days of electricity, wireless and cinemas, but that Mrs. Knatchbull had become their wireless and their cinema, and with her personality she had electrified their lives without charging them a penny. It had been a sleepy quiet neighbourhood where lived squires, parsons, and doctors with their wives and daughters and, within seven years, Mrs. Knatchbull had turned them into a first-rate theatrical company ... In these days people were tired of subscriptions, but Mrs. Knatchbull had hit upon a very happy plan. She had provided them with very good tea and sherry and then very good music in very comfortable surroundings.[48]

Life at Babington allowed time for composition, with six new works being written and more importantly printed for a wider audience. Some older works were also printed, the most important of these was the *Variations on an original theme of Sir G. A. Macfarren for 2 pianos in G minor*. This work had been a firm favourite with herself and Ethel Boyce, which they played at many concerts since its inception in 1888; the theme itself has a special interest from the circumstance that it was dictated to Miss Dora Bright by the late Sir G. A. Macfarren within a few weeks of his passing away, and was, 'as we are given to understand, the very last musical thought to which he gave birth'.[49] The orchestral version no longer survives, but the two-handed piano version remains in print.

After only eight years of marriage Captain Knatchbull died on 3 February 1900, at the age of seventy, after several months of illness and failing health:

> The announcement of the death of Capt. Knatchbull, J.P., of Babington House, occasioned widespread feelings of regret … A typical Somerset squire of the old school and a fine old English gentleman has gone to his long rest … The Captain, as he was called within a wide radius of Babington, was not a man who courted publicity, and beyond taking his place on the magisterial bench at Kilmersdon, preferred the quiet enjoyment of country life … social life will miss a cheery and hospitable host … Much sympathy will be extended to his widow (nee Miss Dora Bright) whose brilliancy as a pianist has delighted many audiences at Bath Quartette Society's concerts … Amid manifestations of the deepest sorrow and regret the mortal remains of the late Captain Wyndham Knatchbull were laid to rest in the family vault in Babington Churchyard.[50]

The Captain left an estate of £51,610 (£6.5 million today), bequeathing the Babington estate to Dora for the remainder of her life, at which point the entire estate would refer to his nephew and the Knatchbull family. The contents of the house became heirlooms for the family and Dora received only £100 (£12,000 today) annual allowance and the income from the estate. Whilst this secured Dora's residence, it would most likely not have maintained her in the lifestyle of a country lady to which she had become accustomed.

Dora went into mourning and in accordance with the requirements of the time largely withdrew from society, and other than a previously arranged charitable performance in April 1900, there is little mention of her in the newspapers. 1901 would be the start of a new chapter in Dora Bright's career, a change of direction, but also a return to her mother's roots – the theatre.

***

In eight short years Dora's life had changed dramatically. She had married, become a member of Somerset society and with the death of her husband attained some limited financial stability, enabling her to continue her career and life as she saw fit. The house at Babington would be hers as long as she lived and with a convenient base in London, she was now set to blossom once again as a composer and musician.

6 The Dancing Girl, 1900–1907

Dora's marriage to Wyndham had been short but as his wife she had become a respected member of the local community. Although financially independent, the monies from her husband's will and the estate were not sufficient to maintain her current standard of living. She needed a new direction and turned to a world she knew well of old, the theatre.

Now aged thirty-seven, Dora was in the prime of her life and had maintained her reputation as a performer and become a well-respected composer. She still had her country estate and her society life was waiting in the wings for her return from mourning.

As one acquaintance wrote:

> Eight years later, he [Captain Knatchbull] died and his widow [Dora] came into possession of Babington House, where she reigned for the next half-century. Her musical entertainments were of a quality far superior to many to be found in big cities and her neighbours recognised how lucky they were.[1]

The next twenty years was going to be a very productive period, taking her name across Europe and the Atlantic.

A new century

After the New Year celebrations, and the death of her husband in early February 1900, the new century must have seemed a daunting prospect. There are only two references to Mrs Knatchbull in 1900, one being a new song, *The Splendid Tattered Flag*, in aid 'of the war fund',[2] published in March 1900, having been written in conjunction with the Duchess of Somerset in 1899 and expressing Dora's ever present national pride.

The other concerned her financial situation and in an unusually uncharitable act she took steps to reduce the outgoings of the estate, ending the payments to the needy in Babington:

THE BABINGTON CHARITY

> The question concerning this charity … was explained by the following … The occupants of these houses receive 1s. (£6 today) each week under the Knatchbull charity. The late Captain Knatchbull, who was a trustee of the charity, used to see to the payment of that amount and added 2s for each occupant every week from his own pocket. Mrs. Knatchbull, having nothing to do with the charity, has discontinued this.[3]

It is not recorded how many beneficiaries there were to the charity, but with her own weekly allowance of only £2, she was not in a position to give away nearly 4 per cent of that sum to each household seeking assistance. This was the first and only time Dora was recorded acting uncharitably, and over the years to come she would make up for this with many charitable works and events.

Since Dora's initial entry into the world of music, twenty years previously, there had been a dramatic increase in popular music, fuelled in part by the newly wealthy middle classes eager for entertainment. Across the nation music was becoming an important part of daily life with an increase in London and provincial orchestras, and the ever-present Regimental band in the park at the weekend. This rising sense of Empire and nationalism led to many patriotic pieces, such as Dora Bright's own work, *The Splendid Tattered Flag*, to raise funds for the war in the Transvaal, South Africa fund.[4] The advent of more printed sheet music, which Dora had already contributed to, made playing music at home more accessible and with music hall becoming more respectable, the lower and working classes had the opportunity to be party to a more discerning quality of music and variety show. Music hall was having a renaissance.

Some of the first recorded music hall events were at the Canterbury Hall in Lambeth, where women were actively encouraged to attend, as they had a civilizing influence on the menfolk. However, many men did not take their wives as the theatres became notorious for prostitutes openly parading up and down the aisles touting for business and as a result the music halls developed a vulgar reputation. There was also a generally accepted view that acting was less than an appropriate profession and that women actors in particular were women of easy virtue. Despite this reputation, music halls prospered across England, as did theatres, with the newly affluent middle classes seeking entertainment. Gradually, women returned to the halls and the on-stage women performers began to achieve some semblance of stardom and could earn a very decent living. The Empire Theatre on Leicester Square was one of the most famous and largest, and remains one of the major London venues to this day, with a cinema and casino now taking the place of the auditorium and stage.

As music hall grew in popularity, the acts became the attraction and by the end of the nineteenth century performers were contracted to a theatre and would provide twice-nightly programmes including a variety of acts, although singing remained at the heart of music hall. The early twentieth century saw an explosion in new purpose-built theatres across Britain – the Empire, Palace, Coliseum and Hippodrome still part of many city centres today. They were the antithesis of the old music halls and ushered in a new audience who were actively discouraged from participating in the show. The new theatres were resplendent with chandeliers, gold leaf decoration and red plush velvet seats with armrests and provided: 'Frothy glittering magical music that wafted from the musical comedy ... these comedies usually had the word "Girl" in the title, featured light music tunes sung by glamorous leading ladies and gentlemen'.[5]

The London Coliseum was the largest and most luxurious Variety Theatre of its era, opening in 1904 and the only theatre in Europe to have lifts for customer use. It had a marble staircase and tea-rooms on each floor and was a teetotal establishment. The Coliseum led the way in a new style of musical entertainment, providing four performances a day of traditional music hall acts, but also new musical spectaculars, short dramatic plays and ballet.

Dora's return came in September 1901 with a new work, the incidental music to a new drama, *The Dream of Scrooge*, to be produced at the Vaudeville Theatre the following month. Dora had found a new challenge and was responding to the changes she witnessed.

The drama was very well reported:

> The piece is in one act, the successive Christmases which convert Scrooge, being shown behind a transparency. The element of music is largely and effectively utilised. It is contributed by Miss Dora Bright, who has furnished a prelude full of good melodic ideas, and accompanying melodrama, which insensibly assists the action. Both are well worth study, for Miss Dora Bright exhibits in her work ingenuity of idea and variety of treatment.[6]

The piece attracted the attention of King Edward VII, who requested the work be played at a command performance at Sandringham in honour of HRH Princess Charles of Denmark.[7] Dora took good advantage of this event and invited the photographer and reporter from *The Sketch* to Babington, to cover the new work. The report included a fine photograph of Dora at her desk, composing:

orchestrating the Overture to *Scrooge*, performed at Sandringham before the King and Queen ... The music to *Scrooge* is the first theatrical composition that Miss Bright has brought before the public, and there is no doubt that the performance was greatly strengthened by her music.[8]

Figure 6.1. Dora Bright at Babington, *The Sketch*, 11 December 1901

The report is not strictly accurate as the incidental music to *Uncle Silas*, presented in 1893, was Dora's first theatrical composition. But in the art of re-invention the past can, perhaps, be brushed over. Certainly, Dora had identified her new future, although before making a success of the theatre, there were still other ideas on the horizon.

One of Dora's best friends was Dorothy Paget who lived a few miles away from Babington at Cranmore Hall. In November 1901, Miss Paget married Mr Herbert Gladstone, the eldest son of a former Prime Minister and, who himself, would become Home Secretary. The ceremony and wedding breakfast was a huge social occasion and attended by Lords and Ladies from across the nation. Dora's wedding present was a *Dedication Song*, no doubt as brilliant as some of the silver and other finery offered as gifts.[9]

Moving in such circles, it may well be that she met or was introduced to Miss Muriel Wilson, daughter of the shipping magnate, Arthur Wilson of

Tranby Croft, Hull. Certainly, Dora's good friends the Pagets and the Horners were friends with Muriel, whose sister, the Countess of Chesterfield, also became acquainted with Dora through her playing at a number of concerts in aid of the Ladies Association of the Mission to Seamen, for which the Countess was President.

Miss Muriel Wilson was reputed to be one of the most beautiful and accomplished, as well as one of the most eccentric girls, in British high society. She had a reputation as a clever amateur actress and was a key player in a group of socialites who performed around the country mansions of England under the name of Lord Rosslyn's Players. Muriel was central to the group in creating the annual performances at Chatsworth House in Derbyshire, seat of the Duke of Devonshire. Back in 1899, Dora had created a mime-drama, *The Dancing Girl*, which was presented by the famous actor Violet Vanbrugh, who most undoubtedly would have been a heroine of Muriel Wilson. The work become a favourite of Miss Wilson and she played the central role of Namouna many times over the coming years, Dora accompanying her on the piano.

With the success of the music to *Scrooge*, Dora turned her attention to an opera and in 1902 presented the completed work to the Dresden Opera House. The opera, titled *Tuong Lung's Shadow*, comprised three acts and was set in the Chinese quarter of San Francisco.[10] The *Dresden Neueste Nachrichten* newspaper reported:

> Up to the present date we have always entertained the opinion that the composition of music was a gift denied to the female sex, elegant trifles (as exceptions) only confirming our doubts. And now an English lady appears on the scene, amazing the musical world of Dresden. She was as a young girl already a distinguished artist, a virtuoso on the piano, and played as Miss Bright a piano concerto of her own composition with extraordinary success. Her marriage separated her from her art for several years. Now (after the death of her husband) the young widow, Mrs. Knatchbull, has composed an opera – text, music and instrumentation all being her own work – and she has brought it with her to Dresden. The music is so captivating and, above all, holds on so strongly, that one exclaims in astonishment: can this be the work of a woman?[11]

Even the French newspaper, *Le Monde*, took up the story, which was reported in Paris on 11 October 1903.[12] The opera was produced in Dresden, but never made the transition back across the Channel, as had many of her other works which she had trialled first on German audiences.

The Dancing Girl, Chatsworth and the King

Amateur dramatics took off in England from the early 1860s with the rise of local drama clubs. At the same time it became popular for owners of large country houses to put on shows for their guests with many of them creating small theatres where visiting companies would entertain. These companies were made up of talented socialites with a desire to act and sing, but who could not take up the profession because of their social status – real actors being seen as somewhat wayward.

Muriel Wilson was one such actress who had a close relationship with the 8th Duke and Duchess of Devonshire, who in 1896 opened their own ballroom theatre at Chatsworth House. The ballroom was never used for its named purpose, but as the setting for theatrical events, the largest being the Winter show held each January, frequently attended by royalty as well as aristocratic friends and invited locals. Muriel was involved in these productions from the start and every year together with the cast would develop a programme to entertain the invited house party.[13]

The Dancing Girl and the Idol was written by another friend of Dora, the Honourable Edith Lyttleton, and in 1899 Dora wrote the music to accompany the play. At the time it didn't seem to have been a particular success, although it had clearly entered the imagination of Muriel Wilson. It is unlikely that Dora could ever have anticipated what a stir the work would make in the upper echelons of society, but it became a perfect vessel for her to raise her standing once more. (See Chapter 11 for details of the piece.)

In essence, the story tells of Namouna, a dancing girl in the temple of the God Siva, who is in great distress as she fears that her betrothed, Sundrum, is deserting her, for a girl with mocking eyes. Namouna dances and prays to Siva to help her and to give her love back to her. The god remains deaf to her, so she stops dancing and in great anger picks up the offerings of rice and flings them in the face of the idol, then in terror of what she has done she offers him her necklace and dances again to conciliate him. Then she begs of him a sign that he will send three cranes across the light of the moon. She listens until she hears the whirring of their wings, and then she dances in wild ecstasy until Sundrum's voice is heard in the distance. The three cranes fly across the moon, one, he comes not; two, he comes, yet loves me not; three he loves me; and the lover comes to Namouna, singing.

In 1903, *The Dancing Girl* was added to the Chatsworth winter programme and King Edward VII and Queen Alexandra were invited to attend. The build-up to the event led to considerable reporting in the papers as the King came down with a cold, the Palace reported the King would still attend the event and then on the morning of the day they were due to catch the Royal Train north, the advice changed and he was no longer allowed to travel. The event went ahead without him.

Figure 6.2. The Ballroom Theatre at Chatsworth House

Theatricals at Chatsworth – A Brilliant Scene

The amateur theatricals arranged to be given in honour of the visit of the King and Queen took place last night, in the theatre at Chatsworth House. The only disappointing feature that tended to mar the otherwise brilliantly successful entertainment was the generally deplored absence of their majesties. The performance took place in the gorgeously-decorated theatre, into which the ballroom has been converted ... In response to the invitations issued by the Duke and Duchess of Devonshire about 150 of the leading county families were present, and at the conclusion of the performance were entertained to supper served in the dining-room ... The curtain rose to a farcical comedy, entitled 'C'etait Gertrude' ... Miss Muriel Wilson, wore a yellow gown and played Madame Dolores ... Then followed a cinematograph exhibition, in which appeared magnificent pictures of Chatsworth House, and incidents which had occurred yesterday. The latter experiment created unbounded amusement. The concluding item was an oriental fantasy *The Dancing Girl and Idol* composed by Dora Bright ... Namouna a dancing girl played by Miss Muriel Wilson ... Thus concluded perhaps the most successful entertainment of the many the Duchess of Devonshire has arranged for her guests.[14]

Dora was present at the evening and played the piano accompaniment. The Chatsworth financial accounts for the year 1903 show that Dora was provided accommodation at a nearby hotel, costing around £500 today, and was merely a performer and not a member of the house party. However, anticipating the success of the work, Dora proclaimed to the press, the week before the event, that she would 'take her little work to Paris'.[15]

During October of 1903, Muriel, Dora and the cast travelled north to Alloa in Scotland, at the invitation of the Earl of Mar and Kellie and his countess. The play was presented to the public in aid of:

St. John's Episcopal Church

in the Town Hall last night, and were repeated this afternoon. The public thoroughly appreciated the opportunity of seeing blue bloods on the boards. Almost every seat was occupied. The first part of the programme consisted of what might be termed a tableau ... *The Dancing Girl and the Idol* ... music by Miss Dora Bright who herself played the accompaniments ... Miss Muriel Wilson, well known for her talent for acting was Namouna and appeared in the habit of the Oriental dancing girl, and gave a display of that interesting young lady's art which was hugely relished.[16]

On this occasion Dora and the performers were reported as forming the house party at Alloa House, seat of the Lord of Mar and Kellie.[17]

Figure 6.3. 1920s postcard of Tranby Croft, home of the Wilson Family

The little play certainly seemed to be moving Dora in ever grander circles and only two weeks later, in November 1903, she was part of the performance of *The Dancing Girl* at Muriel's home in Anlaby near Hull. Tranby Croft was built by Arthur Wilson in 1874, who when he died in 1909 left an estate worth over £3 million (£350 million today) and his shipping company The Wilson Line. He was a generous benefactor and very well connected and played cards with the then Prince of Wales (King Edward VII).

The visit to Hull was reported in the local paper:

Theatrical Performance at Tranby Croft

A large company of friends and acquaintances of Miss Muriel Wilson gaze with delight as she presented the love-lorn Namouna and danced to the propitiation [appeasement] of the stern Indian idol. The large party were assembled at Tranby Croft ... at the invitation of Mr and Mrs Arthur Wilson were afforded excellent and uncommon entertainment. His Imperial Highness the Grand Duke Michael and his Countess had left earlier in the day, but there remained a brilliant company of guests, forming the house party. The theatricals commenced at half-past nine o'clock. Throughout the programme the burden of the work was born by Miss Muriel Wilson ... The piece de resistance of the evening was Miss Muriel as the girl Namouna ... music composed by Miss Dora Bright, who was now present to furnish the accompaniment.[18]

Once more, the following year in January 1904, the performers attended Chatsworth House. However, this year the King and Queen were in attendance, and by the special request of the King, *The Dancing Girl* was once again on the programme, with Dora attending to play the piano accompaniment. The King and Queen visited for a number of days 'partaking in a grand dinner with impromptu dance, a pheasant shoot and carriage drives around the local area – the King so enjoying himself that he would extend his visit.'[19]

The Dancing Girl and the Idol

Royal punctuality marked the entrance of their majesties, the King and Queen, into the pretty little theatre of Chatsworth House at 10.15 this evening to witness the dramatic and musical entertainment prepared for them by the Duke and Duchess of Devonshire. The theatre was already filled, indeed crowded ... the boxes at the rear of the auditorium and the gallery upstairs were crowded with the Chatsworth household ... The closing item was a pretty musical incident entitled, The Dancing Girl and the Idol, which was performed by special request. It was on the programme last year when the King was so unfortunately taken ill. The music which is oriental in character was composed by Mrs. Knatchbull (Dora Bright), who was present to play the accompaniment ... Miss Muriel Wilson danced and played with perfect grace ... it was the same in the joyous castanet dance ... Lady Maud Warrender made a noble and dignified Indian lover ... Mr. Coward was at the Mustel organ, which contributed much to the fine effect of the dancing.[20]

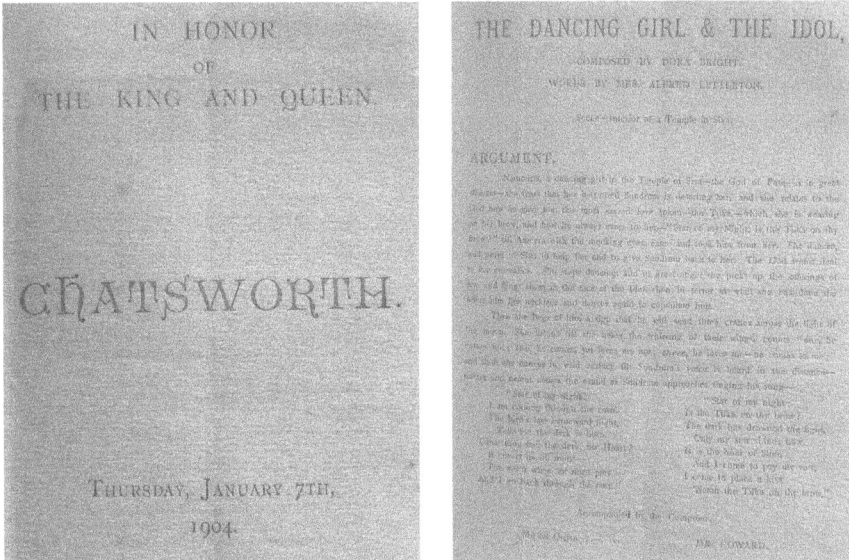

Figure 6.4. Programme from the Chatsworth Theatre 1904, *The Dancing Girl and the Idol*

Whether Dora was presented to the King is not recorded, but once again, unlike Muriel and the other performers, she was given accommodation in the Edensor Hotel (alongside the dance mistress and stage manager) rather than staying with the house party. In the household accounts for 1904, she was referred to as the 'Accompanist', and as per her trip in 1903, her board and lodgings as well as transport to and from the hotel to the house were covered in payments by the house on her behalf.

Muriel continued to take the *Dancing Girl* on tour and in September 1904, she performed in Scarborough in a 'most successful entertainment ... for the fund for restoring the old church of Routh in East Yorkshire', and once again at Chatsworth in 1906. Dora was not in attendance at either of these performances with Muriel;[21] she had already moved on to other matters, which would give her the opportunity of reaching a wider audience. However, she did not lose interest in the play and in 1909 took the work to Paris, as previously suggested:

English music on the continent is certainly looking up ... the announcement of the production in Paris, at the Théâtre Français, on the 24th, of an Oriental dance play, entitled The Dancing Girl ... music by Mme. Dora Bright. This will be produced under the direction of Mme. Mariquita, and the dancer will be Mlle. Regina Badet, of the Opéra Comique.[22]

The Dancing Doll, Chatsworth and the King

In 1905, the year after Dora Bright had played the accompaniment to her own *The Dancing Girl* in front of King Edward VII, Adeline Genée, the great Danish ballet dancer, also performed at Chatsworth in front of the King in her new performance *The Dancing Doll*. Dora had not met Genée at this point in her life, but the news of the Royal command caused a great stir and must have drawn Dora's attention.

Genée commenced rehearsals of the *Dancing Doll* at the Empire in October of 1904 and shortly before Christmas was summoned to a meeting at which she was told the King expressed a desire that she should dance before him and Queen Alexandra at Chatsworth, the following January. This was an unprecedented honour, which no other ballet dancer had received and raised further the status of ballet, already a popular Victorian entertainment.

Genée was overwhelmed by the magnificence of Chatsworth and the little theatre and during rehearsals Lord Charles Montague called Genée away and asked her to follow him. He took her to a small room where Queen Alexandra received her and spoke a few friendly words. Although extremely fearful of failure, Genée set about ensuring everything was perfect with her dress and just moments into the performance forgot the royal personages and was conscious only of her dancing.

Figure 6.5. Signed photograph of Adeline Genée as *The Dancing Doll* 1905

The performance took place on 5 January 1905, the eve of Genée's twenty-seventh birthday, and was a success. After she had changed there was a knock on her dressing-room door and a note from Queen Alexandra asking her to perform one of the dances again. She changed in double quick time and performed the piece again to applause from the King and Queen. When she left Chatsworth the next day, she carried with her a precious memento of the wonderful evening given to her by Queen Alexander – a brooch of diamonds and sapphires set in the shape of a bee.[23]

Genée had been accompanied by her uncle, Alexander Genée and her dresser, and stayed in the Peacock Hotel at Rowsley with all expenses being covered by Chatsworth House. The Chatsworth archive hold the original invoice for the hotel stay and the accounts for January 1905 record costs of £4 16s 6d (about £600 today).

Two performances in front of the King and Queen, with very different outcomes. Genée became a favourite of Queen Alexandra and would take ballet to new heights, whereas Dora had left Chatsworth with the realization that despite her much-admired music, she was not to become a member of this particular social set. However, reading of Genée's success in the papers may have set Dora's mind pondering. She went on to create a meeting with Genée, which led to a great partnership that would raise the profile of ballet further and also provide Dora a way back to her rightful place in musical history.

Concerts and festivals

The one thing Dora knew how to do well was to organize concerts. Over the past twenty years she had returned to this format as performer, composer and as a means of promoting the works of her friends and English music. With the new contacts and friendships she had made, in 1903 she proposed a National Festival of British Music. There would be six concerts, two per day, on alternate days.[24] A committee was established and included some prestigious individuals with the Prime Minister as its President. Dora was the Honorary Secretary and driving force:

Proposed National British Festival

The preliminary arrangements are now complete for the national Festival of British Music, which is proposed to be held at Queen's Hall next November. The Prime Minister is President and Sir Kenneth Muir Mackenzie is Chairman of the Executive Committee, upon which also are Mr. Herbert Gladstone and Alfred Lyttelton. The affair, however, is primarily the idea of, and is being organised by, Mrs. Knatchbull, a lady who is better known as the pianist, Miss Dora Bright … six concerts will be given … The programmes will be devoted exclusively to the works of British composers of the past and present … Such a scheme was indeed tried at the last Leeds Music Festival, but it could only end in disappointment.[25]

Despite this slightly negative view of its potential success, Dora had managed to obtain the services of the Queen's Hall Orchestra, under Mr Henry Wood, a name today revered for his creation of the Promenade season at the Royal Albert Hall in London every year. Dora had also managed to get guaranteed funds of £2000 (£250k today), but was still trying to find an additional £3000 before the festival could go ahead. This was to prove a considerable undertaking:

> In some quarters the proposed National Festival of British Music has been treated as definitely settled … the plans for the festival are still very unsettled … The committee is at present engaged in forming a guarantee fund, which, in view of the magnitude of the undertaking, will have to be a considerable one, and until this fund has been formed great advance in the scheme cannot be made. Those who care for British music have now an opportunity of supporting it in a practical way. It will certainly be a reflection on the musical taste of this country if there is any great difficulty in obtaining the requisite sum.[26]

As well as Henry Wood and his orchestra, the Sheffield Choir was to be a part of the series and Dora had been in discussion with the Sheffield Festival Committee and Sir Henry Coward, creator of the prestigious Sheffield Philharmonic Chorus.

> 1904 – January 9th – Saw Dora Bright in reference to taking my choir to British festival … This was an attempt on the part of British musicians to stem the Teutonic influence which, through skilful and shameful propogandist work of German-English and English-German agents and critics, was swamping everything in British music. Miss Bright (Mrs. Knatchbull) came to hear my choir at Sheffield, and there was a long correspondence. But the time was not then ripe for successful effort, the tentacles of the Teutonic octopus having almost strangled all British self-assertiveness and initiative.[27]

Strong sentiments indeed. But despite this view, the suggestion of amalgamating contingents of singers from choirs in Leeds, Sheffield and Huddersfield to form a Yorkshire Choir was proposed by Sir Henry, which created some disquiet in the South:

But may I humbly ask, why not a choir from the metropolis! There seems a tendency on the part of some writers to disparage London music – cheap criticism which well-informed men would avoid. But a picked 300 from London, properly rehearsed, would have nothing to fear in comparison with the best choir in Yorkshire.[28]

Dora's idea of a festival to celebrate British music was creating a storm (in a teacup no doubt), but the need to find funding, Sir Henry Coward's refusal to be party to the notion in the end, and the split between north and south became too many hurdles and the committee made a decision:

Is Patriotism in Art Extinct

One may reasonably put this question in view of the announcement that the proposed national Festival of British Music arranged for November, has been postponed until next March, mainly owing, one is left to infer, that of the required guarantee fund of £5,000 only about £3,500 has been subscribed, much of which has come from the purses of men who, without offence, can scarcely be considered absolutely English. The object of the Festival of which our music-loving Premier is the President, is to illustrate the present condition of Musical Art in this country and its historical relation to the work of past British composers, by means of selections from the works of some well-known composers, including Sterndale Bennett, Hubert Parry, Villiers Stanford, Macfarren, Cowen and Mackenzie. The scheme was laudable and worthy of support, and we trust that the postponement is not another form of interment.[29]

The National Festival did not go ahead, but ironically, in the year of Dora's death, British music was deemed to be an important part of the 1951 Festival of Britain. There was a series of eight concerts devoted to the music of Henry Purcell alongside recitals of English song. The Arts Council commissioned numerous new works such as William Alwyn's *Festival March*, the *Festival Te Deum* by Edmund Rubbra and Gordon Jacobs' *Festival Suite* for Military Band. The ceremonial opening of the Royal Festival Hall, a cornerstone of the festival's achievements, was attended by both the King and Queen and included the unveiling of a commemorative tablet by the King, a dedication by the Archbishop of Canterbury and a concert of British Music – Hubert Parry, Thomas Arne, Vaughan Williams, Edward Elgar, Henry Purcell and the honorary Englishman G. F. Handel. This was followed by a week of concerts, the first being a performance of Beethoven's Ninth Symphony. A review of the concert in *The Times* announced:

Once the new concert hall had been baptised with the music of its own land, there could be no further inauguration more immediately proper than to perform Beethoven's choral symphony in it.[30]

Sir Henry Coward comments, some fifty years earlier regarding the Teutonic octopus, still hold a note of truth. However, in much the same way as the English composers proposed at the 1903 Festival, such as Cowen, Mackenzie and Macfarren who are now largely forgotten, none of the works from the 1951 Festival made it to the concert repertoire. Even in the post-war British revival, British music was not valued, as Dora had found some decades before.

In the absence of the National Festival, Dora had to reconsider how to make her mark. She responded, in 1905, with a new series of concerts:

Miss Dora Bright (Mrs. Knatchbull) announces two concerto concerts with the London Symphony Orchestra ... [to] include works by Bach, Mozart, Beethoven, Schumann, Chopin and Hiller. Mr. Edward German will conduct his Gypsy Suite at the second of these concerts. A third concert, to be devoted to British music for piano and orchestra, will take place later in the year.[31]

Clearly Dora was reaching back to a format she knew well, with tried and tested pieces and the opportunity for her friend to display a new work. The first concert was not a resounding success:

A Concerto Concert

It is now the fashion for an instrumentalist to play three concertos at one concert, and Miss Dora Bright, once so well-known as a pianist in London, has planned two of the concerts. At the first ... she played Bach's Concerto in D minor, Beethoven's in C minor and Chopin's in E minor. Miss Dora Bright was always a sound artist, and her absence from the concert-platform has not lessened her powers. In the Bach ... she was not at her best. There were signs of nervousness. The playing in the Beethoven had much to commend it ... and the pianist's pleasant touch and vivacious style had the right material to work upon the Chopin concerto ... but there was room for further rehearsal.[32]

The *Daily Telegraph* went further in reference to the three concertos:

This capable pianist included three concertos ... in her programme, thus following a custom which has little to recommend it. The public has certainly not shown any desire to impose such exhaustive tests of strength upon pianists and violinists. Indeed, the audience is considerably thinned, as a rule, by the time the third concerto is served up.[33]

The second of the concerto concerts was well received, but once again the question of three concertos and the strain placed on the audience was raised:

> Unfortunately, programmes conceived on this generous basis are almost as great a tax on the hearer as on the performer, and Miss Bright's efforts would certainly have been none the less appreciated by her audience if she had confined them within narrower and more judicious limits.[34]

Miss Dora Bright, the clever and intelligent pianist, gave a second orchestral concert last month ... but three concertos in one programme is a fashion which we hope will soon pass away.[35]

Even more emphatic was *The Musical Times*: 'such programmes are a mistake'.[36] The third in the series of British music did not take place.

Her concert role was not completely at an end, as she would happily offer her services to charitable causes, often related to improving the lives of women. Two examples demonstrate her return to assisting the less well-off and also promoting the work of women composers. The first, a Matinée Musicale where she played, 'in aid of the Window Blind Cleaning Association, an institution formed to procure employment and to give a practical business training to unemployed women and girls'.[37] The second, a Soirée Musicale in a performance of music by Fröken Agathe Backer-Grödhal, 'the first Scandinavian women composer to obtain outside recognition. The Norse artiste was lucky in securing such a brilliant interpreter as Miss Dora Bright, who played with a verve and sympathy too rarely heard in English pianists'.[38]

Finally in 1907, she again introduced a further set of three pianoforte recitals at the Broadwood Rooms, a somewhat smaller venue than The Bechstein and Queen's Halls where she had played previously. The concerts failed to stimulate the imagination and whilst reports clearly appreciated her 'crisp, decisive touch and strong feeling for rhythm', they were more inclined to note that the music 'began to sound laboured'[39] and 'in Tausig's arrangement of the Fugue in D minor one got rather the impression that Miss Bright was trying to bully an unwilling piano into being an organ'.[40] These were her last large-scale attempts to woo the public with a series of concerts and her pianistic virtuosity. As a result she turned her attention back to the theatre and more importantly the ballet.

Throughout this period Babington remained her home and she took time running the estate, adjudicating at the Somerset Eisteddfod, and holding

parties at the house. The farms on the estate were well managed and produced high quality meats, and Christmas 1902 saw Dora giving a prime short-
horn steer to the butcher in Frome, who specifically advertised the meat as
from Mrs Knatchbull at Babington House.[41] There are also examples of flowers from the gardens winning prizes at the agricultural show in Frome, as
well as livestock: 'Mrs. Knatchbull, took the premier award for a pair of elts
[piglets] of any breed farrowed in 1904'.[42] By 1907, Dora had returned to giving
the New Year's Day party, which she had given previously with her husband:

> Mrs. Knatchbull gave theatrical, followed by a small dance, at
> Babington on New Year's Day. The first portion of the evening
> was devoted to dancing and music. Supper was served at 12, and
> dancing continued until a late hour. The programme included *The
> Dryad* (a dance play in two tableaux) set to music by Dora Bright
> (first performance).[43]

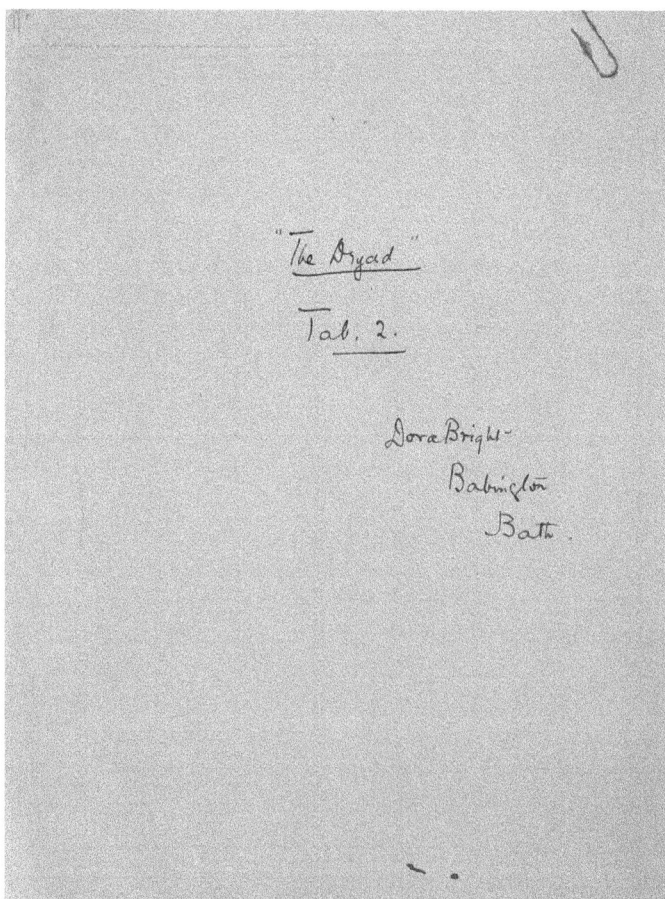

Figure 6.6. First page of Dora Bright's own working copy of the piano version of *The Dryad*

Figure 6.7. Second page of Dora Bright's own working copy of the piano version of *The Dryad*

Amongst those present were the Duchess of Somerset, her good friends the Horners and Pagets, and Ethel Boyce. Dora took the opportunity to show-case her other new work, with a recital of *The Jungle Book Songs*:

> Admirers of Rudyard Kipling should make early acquaintance of Madame Dora Bright's clever settings of these excerpts from his Jungle Book. The first is The Night Song in the Jungle, which allied to music of broad character, forms an admirable introduction. It is followed by The Seal Lullaby and the Mother Seal's Song, the music of both of which is very pleasing. The dramatic character of Tiger! Tiger! has been happily caught. The music of the Bandar-Log is pretty, but the most characteristic number of the series is The Song

Toomai's Mother Sang to the Baby, in which the idiom of Indian music is cleverly employed.[44]

Both *The Dryad* and *The Jungle Book* were a success and led Dora to return to London, more permanently, in the autumn of 1907.

BABINGTON

Harvest Thanksgiving Services were held in the Parish Church on Sunday. The ornamentation of the sacred building was very beautiful, pot plants and flowers from Babington House gardens and conservatories being kindly lent by Mrs. Knatchbull … Babington House, which has been taken by Sir Charles Hunter … Mrs. Knatchbull, who is the lord of the manor of Babington, moves in the best society, but is known best to fame, especially in the musical world, as Miss Dora Bright, both as composer and pianist. Her reputation as a composer was further enhanced at the commencement of the present year by the production of a dance-play *The Dryad*, danced by Adeline Genée, which was so popularly received in London and was given so many flattering notices in the Metropolitan press … Owing to her numerous musical engagements Mrs. Knatchbull finds she would be unable to reside at Babington during the next two years, and so she has taken a house in Cadogan Square, London, and has let her interesting country mansion to Sir Charles and Lady Hunter for this period. She has also been invited to go on tour in America, but it is doubtful if she will be able to accept the flattering offer made her to favour our American cousins with her great musical talents.[45]

It wasn't the only invitation to America, as in 1912 or 1913 she wrote to her good friend Moritz Moszkowski regarding a work of his that Sir Thomas Beecham had requested from him, and of an offer for her to tour America. In Moszkowski's reply to her letter he wrote:

My very best thanks for the happy arrangement of this affair. I send today the full score to Beecham. The parts need to be looked over so UI [you/I] send them tomorrow. I, myself, have Wednesday when I shall come in the afternoon. Thousand thanks again and Au revoir. P.S. If this tour in America is desirable depends on the fees, also on the state of one's health – and if you feel like travelling three months in a wild land![46]

If Moszkowski found America hard work, Dora would have found it impossible and so it is quite understandable why she declined such offers.

Moritz Moszkowski

Moszkowski first appeared in England at a Philharmonic concert in 1885 at the request of the Philharmonic Society. It is highly likely that such a great name drew a very large crowd including Dora Bright, who had herself played at the Philharmonic concerts in 1892. The concert was a huge success and Moszkowski returned many times to London at the request of the Philharmonic and in 1898 premiered his *Piano Concerto in E major, Op 59*, of which he remarked that, had he known he would have to play it in public, he wouldn't have made it so difficult.

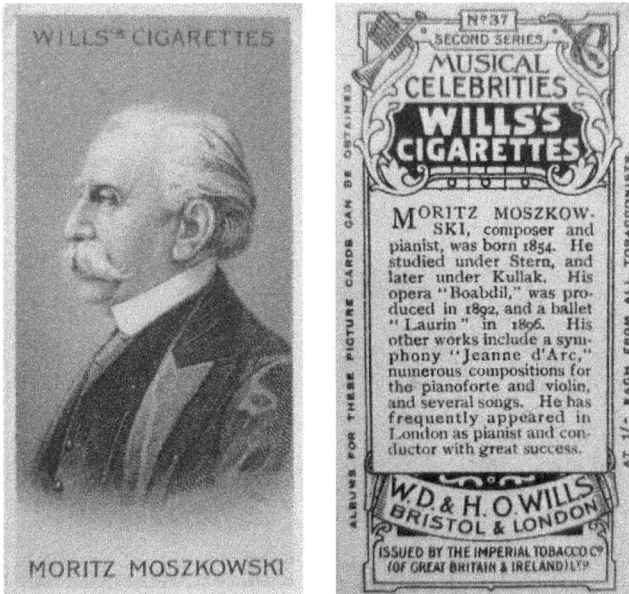

Figure 6.8. Wills's cigarettes – Moritz Moszkowski

Moszkowski was a virtuoso piano player who created many works of great beauty and elegance. His works were played frequently, and Dora had included some of his smaller works in her own concerts across the years. With the success of her association with Adeline Genée and that of *The Dryad*, in 1907, Dora travelled to Paris to meet with Moszkowski to take lessons in orchestration. Dora wrote of him:

> I thoroughly enjoyed my lessons and we became great friends. He was tolerant in all his musical ideas and most generous in his appreciation of, and behaviour to, other artists. I met brother Alexander, and was interested to note that facially the brothers resembled each other, the lines of Alexander's face went cheerfully upward, those on Moritz's went dolefully down.[47]

In 1908 he dedicated a *Pièce Romantique* to her.

Figure 6.9. First bars and dedication of the *Pièce Romantique* by Moritz Moszkowski

Perhaps as a result of this time together and Dora's long association with the Gentlemen's concerts given in Manchester, they were able to announce:

> The Directors have also much pleasure in announcing that Mr. MOWZKOWSKI, the distinguished composer, has accepted their invitation to attend the Concert on the 13th January, when he will conduct his Pianoforte Concerto, the solo part of which will be played by Madame Dora Bright.[48]

As part of his trip to England, Moszkowski took the opportunity to arrange other concerts and took the piano work and other compositions to both Liverpool on 12 February 1908 and then to London a week later. At all three of the concerts Dora played the piano concerto under Moszkowski's baton as conductor:

> Miss Dora Bright, a gifted pianist, who has not been heard much in London of late, played the solo part in the effective piano concerto which is one of the composer's best-known larger works. It is admirably laid out for the solo instrument, and contains a wealth of light and graceful melody. Miss Dora Bright played it with a charm, vivacity, and clearness of touch that brought out to the best advantage the qualities of the music.[49]

Moszkowski gave a copy of the piano concerto score to Dora, inscribed by himself, 'to Dora'. This now resides in the library of the Royal Academy of Music as one of three pieces donated by Dora to the institution during her lifetime; the others being her scores of the *Piano Concerto in A minor* and the *Variations for Piano and Orchestra*.

Dora visited Paris for a number of years to study with him, completing the *Variations for Piano and Orchestra* in Paris in 1910, and was reported visiting in 1912:

> The English Colony is fast settling into its winter quarters in Paris … Miss Alice Williams gave her first reception this week and among her guests were Mrs. Knatchbull (Dora Bright), who is staying with her … also visiting the house M. Moskowski.[50]

Moritz became a frequent visitor to Babington and was, as with so many of her good friends, party to some of Dora's more exuberant charitable works.

Patronage

Dora Bright, unlike many other musicians of her period, had not been fortunate enough to have a wealthy and generous benefactor. Consequently she worked as an accompanist and pianist across London and at private parties. However, after the death of her husband she had become a woman of some wealth, status and a seemingly unending energy for organizing both her own life and that of others.

Now a lady of means she turned to patronage to assist other musicians to attain their potential. Her new circle of friends had grown to include a number of young musicians from Cambridge University, one of them being a promising pianist, O'Neil Phillips. She had taken him under her wing and supported him financially and suggested he spend time in Berlin, learning with Busoni the Italian composer and pianist. During Phillips's time in Berlin he became acquainted with Edward J. Dent, a scholar at King's College, Cambridge and later to become Professor of Music at Cambridge University. Dent wrote frequently of his endeavours and difficulties with Phillips to his friend Clive Carey, a baritone, who was also a good friend of Dora Bright and a frequent visitor to Babington House.

Phillips was by all accounts a party animal and after a series of wild parties ran out of money and could no longer afford to pay his rent and refused to accept help from his friends. Dent wrote to Clive asking if he could raise some money for Phillips from Mrs Knatchbull, as payment for imaginary work done. Dora sent some funds but Phillip's behaviour did not improve, leading Dent to write angrily about Phillips:

> …who stays there (on other people's money) long after Busoni has gone, mooning about, doing nothing except writing cynical and suggestive things to me, and doing his utmost, by saying rude and unpleasant things, to break off his friendship with Mrs Knatchbull,

who really was entirely the cause of his going out, and has done her best to help him.[51]

Clearly Dora's well-intended patronage was not always well rewarded, but she remained undeterred by such behaviours and continued to support Phillips, who failed to become the brilliant pianist she had hoped and committed suicide in Montreal, where he had taken a job teaching.

Clive continued his friendship with Dora, visiting her frequently at Babington, and after moving to Cambridge, dining with her before a concert at which she was performing. He wrote to Dent: 'Mrs Knatchbull is to play in Cambridge, and I believe I dine with her. Odder programme than ever. She telephoned me the other day and made more din, bawling, than a Holbrooke symphonic poem'. Once again her friendship and patronage are met with unpleasantness. Even Clive's mother failed to appreciate Dora's support, resenting her possessiveness and calling her Mrs Snatch'em.

Figure 6.10. Dora Bright with friends on the beach. One of the very few photographs of her remaining. From left to right, Francis Jekyll, Francis Toye, A. M. (unidentified), Dora Knatchbull, O'Neill Phillips

Dora took Clive firmly under her wing and introduced him to Moszkowski. Clive moved to Paris to take up composition and spent the summer holidays with Moszkowski and Dora in France. He remained friends with Dora for many years, working with her on a production of *The Dryad* some years later, and spent time in 1911 at Babington House as a guest alongside Moszkowski and Adeline Genée.[52]

It is not recorded how many young musicians Dora Bright supported through patronage or friendship, but it is clear that she was committed to helping others to reach their potential, whatever that was and wherever it would lead.

***

In many ways the story of *The Dancing Girl and the Idol* epitomises this short period of Dora's life, who having been promised love, fears she has lost it and dances her heart out to get it back. Finally, her efforts are rewarded and her life continues. Perhaps in the case of Dora Bright the three cranes were the National Concerts, *The Dancing Girl* itself, and finally the success of *The Dryad*.

7 London Calling, 1908–1920

The first years of the twentieth century found Dora Bright discovering a new direction for her musical, and increasingly theatrical, calling. She had started the century a widow and, over the course of a few years, tried to become part of a socially elite amateur dramatic company with Muriel Wilson to no avail, attempted a concert series which did not grab the imagination of the public, and finally found success in her association with Adeline Genée and her first ballet work, *The Dryad*. The years ahead would be the most productive of her life, with over twenty-five works written for the ballet and the theatre forming the backbone of Dora's return. She was to be the stage star she had once been and would now become again.

The Dryad

With the premiere of *The Dryad* at Babington, in front of a captive New Year's audience a success, Dora needed to find a larger outlet that would present the work in front of the public. Such an opportunity arose through her good friend, the Duchess of Somerset, who organized a charity matinée at the Playhouse early in 1907. Mr Cyril Maude, actor and manager of the Playhouse Theatre in London, was persuaded to lend the theatre for a charity performance:[1]

> In aid of the Alexandra Hospital for Children and The Southwark Invalid Kitchen … an attractive feature of the programme was The Dryad, a new dance play, in two tableau, with music by Dora Bright. This proved a charming little idyll, with a tragic ending … It is a quaint and fanciful little piece, which, with Mlle. Adeline Genée as the exponent of the wood nymph, naturally enjoyed the benefit of the most artistic presentation, and as such found general favour … An essential ingredient of the little piece is, of course, its music, and this is full of grace and charm – of no great depth, it may be, but delicate, imaginative, and in keeping with its subject.[2]

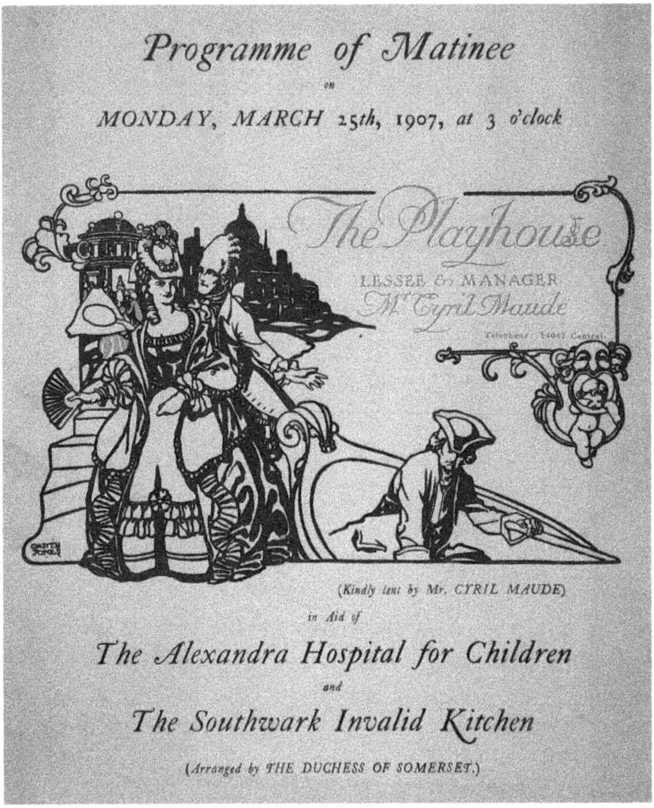

Figure 7.1. Front cover of the programme from the 1907 performance of *The Dryad*

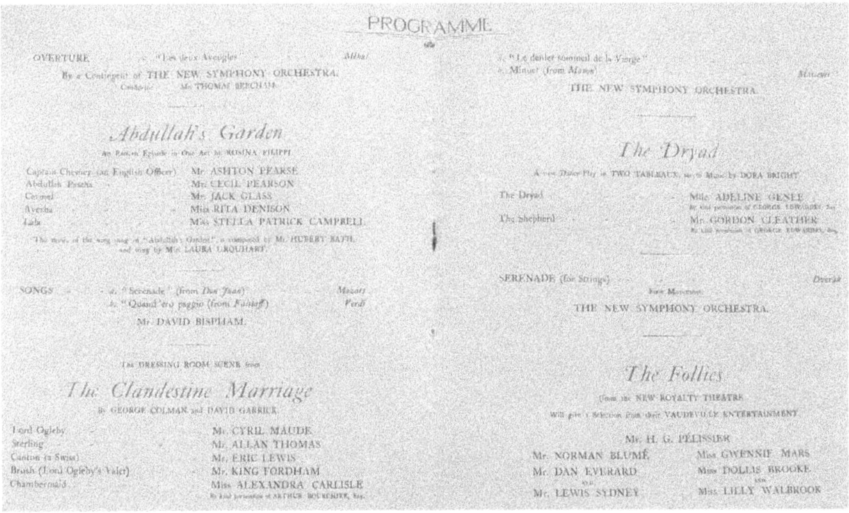

PROGRAMME

OVERTURE - "Les deux Aveugles" - *Méhul*

By a Contingent of THE NEW SYMPHONY ORCHESTRA.

Abdullah's Garden

Captain Chesney (an English Officer)	Mr. ASHTON PEARSE
Abdullah Pasha	Mr. CECIL PEARSON
Cevmel	Mr. JACK GLASS
Ayesha	Miss RITA DENISON
Lala	Miss STELLA PATRICK CAMPBELL

SONGS - a. "Serenade" (from *Don Juan*) - *Mozart*
b. "Quand' ero paggio (from *Falstaff*) - *Verdi*

Mr. DAVID BISPHAM.

The DRESSING ROOM SCENE from

The Clandestine Marriage

By GEORGE COLMAN and DAVID GARRICK.

Lord Ogleby	Mr. CYRIL MAUDE
Sterling	Mr. ALLAN THOMAS
Canton (a Swiss)	Mr. ERIC LEWIS
Brush (Lord Ogleby's Valet)	Mr. KING FORDHAM
Chambermaid	Miss ALEXANDRA CARLISLE

a. "Le dernier sommeil de la Vierge"
b. Minuet (from *Manon*) - *Massenet*

THE NEW SYMPHONY ORCHESTRA.

The Dryad

The Dryad	Mlle. ADELINE GENÉE
The Shepherd	Mr. GORDON CLEATHER

SERENADE (for Strings) - *Dvořák*

THE NEW SYMPHONY ORCHESTRA.

The Follies

(from the NEW ROYALTY THEATRE

Mr. H. G. PÉLISSIER

Mr. NORMAN BLUMÉ	Miss GWENNIE MARS
Mr. DAN EVERARD	Miss DOLLIS BROOKE
and	and
Mr. LEWIS SYDNEY	Miss LILLY WALBROOK

Figure 7.2. Inside the programme from the 1907 performance of *The Dryad*

Dora had plucked up the courage to ask if Genée would play the part of the little nymph, and had in part written the work in the hope of getting her to take on the role, the *East Anglian Daily Times* reporting, 'the fantasy was apparently created by Miss Dora Bright for the specific purpose of Mdlle. Genée demonstrating her bewitching art'.[3]

Normally, Genée made it a strict rule to accept no other engagements while she was dancing daily at the Empire, but she was instinctively attracted by the poetic theme of the ballet and consented to give her services … *The Dryad*, in which Genée first danced on this isolated occasion with Thomas Beecham conducting his newly-formed Orchestra, was not only to figure largely in her career, but to mark the beginning of a friendship which continued until Dora Bright's death at the end of 1951. This first association with Genée revealed exciting possibilities to Dora Bright, who went to Paris to take lessons from Moszkowski in preparation for the work she sensed lay before her … Like Genée she was a traditionalist. Her music was composed with a consistent competence marked with no unusual originality of style, but its happy melodies and deft and delicate orchestral colouring were as Genée saw at once, admirably suited to accompany the dance. Thus the bond between them was reinforced by a mutual understanding of each other's art.[4]

The die was cast and Dora would write many more ballet works for Genée over the coming years. They would become firm friends and Genée, as with so many of her other friends, would be more than willing to assist Dora in her charitable endeavours.

MISS DORA BRIGHT

Figure 7.3. Dora Bright as pictured in the 1907 *Dryad* programme (Reproduced with permission from the Royal Academy of Dance, London)

At the end of the season in 1908, Genée decided to take her new favourite work, *The Dryad*, with her on tour in America. She persuaded the management of the Empire Theatre in London to alter the bill for the final two weeks to include the work, and the little dance was a huge success, resulting in a very favourable review in *The Times*:

> Miss Dora Bright's Pastoral Fantasy is an interesting thing, partly because in itself it is affecting and charming, partly because it brings together in an unusual way the three arts of music, acting and dancing … This is Mlle. Genée's last week at the Empire. Three nights of it might be worse spent than in seeing *The Dryad* three times.[5]

In the USA there was eager anticipation of the impending tour:

> Mlle. Genée made her first appearance Monday night at the Empire Music Hall (London) in the ballet *The Dryad*, which was written especially for her by Dora Bright, a non-de-plume of Mrs. Knatchbull, a close friend of the Duchess of Somerset. Her success was instantaneous and pronounced. Mlle Genée sails for America September 23.[6]

Figure 7.4. Postcard of Adeline Genée, postmarked 1908

Figure 7.5. Postcard of the Empire Theatre in the early 1900s

So firm had the friendship between Dora and Genée become, that she stayed at Babington House prior to sailing to America. The US tour was a huge success, but in the end *The Dryad* did not form part of the tour, which was a great disappointment to Genée. Her American management had suggested the possibility of special matinées in Philadelphia and Chicago, but these did not materialize. Apparently, American audiences were not prepared to forgo vaudeville for ballet and consequently the work was not performed.[7]

Returning to England Genée agreed with the management at His Majesty's Theatre to allow her to perform the work:

> I want to have the chance of illustrating the deeper feelings in human nature, she said on her return to London. To fulfil the desire she chose Dora Bright's delicate pastoral fantasy, *The Dryad.* She was seen performing *The Dryad* at four special matinée performances presented by the Afternoon Theatre at His Majesty's Theatre, London, on June 4th, 8th, 10th and 11th. After these performance she returned to The Empire for her next season on July 5th, where ballet was firmly back on the bill.[8]

Whilst *The Dryad* remained a success with London audiences, it never achieved a similar standing outside of England. Genée, thwarted at introducing the work to American audiences in 1908, took the opportunity in 1911 to fulfil this long-standing ambition, and with a week to spare before her return to England she organized a special Matinée. The concert, played at Carnegie Hall on 4 May 1911, proved an unsatisfactory affair, being hurriedly prepared.

The stage management was poor and with gaps in the scenery the stagehands could be seen moving items around as the dancers performed. In a mixed programme together with Morris dancers and child dancers, the performance was reported as 'pleasant but rather weird'.[9] Presented a few days later in Boston the work fared no better, the ballet was criticized as weak and dull with too much singing in the first scene and too much mime in the second.[10]

Genée was twice invited to perform the work in Paris for the Comtesse de Béarn, but *The Dryad* continued to bring her bad luck. The first time, flooding of the Seine prevented the performance and on the second occasion the electricity failed only hours before the show: 'for a time Moszkowski and Widor kept everyone amused by engaging in a contest to see who could produce the most impressive sounds from the organ … but finally the performance, to which all fashionable Paris were invited, had to be cancelled. As a result Genée never danced in Paris'.[11]

Returning again to a London audience, *The Dryad* became the success it had been when first revealed in 1908 for both Genée and Dora Bright. When it was revived some years later in 1914 it was also well received:

> If we were asked to name the production in which Genée gives the most exquisite facets of her art, we should name, *The Dryad*, from the pen of Dora Bright, who is responsible for both story and music … no Genée season would be complete without it.[12]

Adeline Genée

Genée was born Anina Margarete Kirstina Petra Jensen in Denmark, January 1878. Her father was a talented musician and according to Genée herself, his playing is what made her want to dance. Her parents sensed her love of dance and encouraged the passion so much that when she was five years old they asked Alexander Genée, the great ballet dancer and uncle to Anina, to visit the family in Aarhus to decide if she had the right qualities to be a ballet dancer. Alexander and his wife Antonia Zimmerman, herself a ballet dancer, were happy to help:

> My earliest recollections of dancing was partnering my sister in a waltz … That waltz was to decide my future. I was only five at the time, and we danced in honour of my uncle and aunt, who were paying a family visit. At the end of our waltz I was seated on a throne-like chair while Uncle Alexander examined my foot. He was impressed by my high in-step, said I had a dancer's foot and was born to become a dancer. It was agreed that I should go to them for training as soon as I was old enough, and as I approached my ninth birthday I joined them to study in Copenhagen.[13]

Anina was given the name Adeline Genée, after Adelina Patti, the opera singer whom Alexander adored and for whom he had choreographed the dances in *Carmen*. Her uncle and aunt taught her the basics of the five positions and were relentless in the daily studies which Adeline was made to follow. Her technique took 'the French style of the early nineteenth century, which had been adopted by the Russian School, described as the French School, only the French have forgotten it'.[14]

The summer of 1888 saw Adeline's first public performance in Oslo, after which she moved with her aunt and uncle to Stettin, now in Poland, where she very soon became part of the Corps de Ballet and a principal dancer under her uncle's management. Some years later the family moved to Berlin where Adeline débuted at the Opera in 1896. The people of Berlin took her to their hearts and she had a very successful summer season before moving on to Munich. Her fame spread quickly and in 1897 she received a proposal to dance at the Empire Theatre in London as part of the celebrations for Queen Victoria's Diamond Jubilee.

The management of the Hoftheater in Munich would only allow Adeline leave of absence to undertake the performance in London if she agreed to sign a five-year contract, which Alexander refused as it would restrict Adeline's future. The Alhambra Theatre in London was also interested in acquiring Adeline as their principal dancer and contracts were nearly agreed until a misunderstanding led to the contract being withdrawn. Alexander, unhappy with the Munich theatre and now desperate to find a position for Adeline, took her on the first train to Vienna only to find that there were no vacancies. As they returned to their hotel they found a telegram waiting for them, which read:

> Have arranged for Adeline guest appearance six-weeks Empire Theatre £20 a week and travelling expenses for two starting 16th. Telegram is contract. Reply prepaid.[15]

There was only one answer and the six-week engagement at the Empire lasted ten years:

> England became my home and I was happy to dance for audiences who had a real appreciation of ballet. Then came my American tours. These lasted five years and were followed by my visiting Australia and New Zealand. After leaving the Empire I staged my own ballets at the Coliseum, the most notable being ... *La Camargo*, *La Danse* and *The Dryad* ... Music in most of my ballets was by Dora Bright.[16]

Her association and friendship with Dora Bright lasted for the rest of Dora's life and Adeline was a regular guest at Babington. At Adeline's marriage to Mr

Frank Isset in 1910, Dora was a guest and gave the couple a wedding present of a sapphire and diamond ring, which had been given to her on her own wedding day by her husband Captain Knatchbull. Over the next decade they would, between them, take ballet to new heights both in England and around the world.

Dame Adeline Genée was one of the greatest ballet dancers of the twentieth century and through her vigorous hard work she established the Royal Academy of Dance, becoming President, where she presided for thirty-four years. There have been only three other Presidents to date, Dame Margot Fonteyn, Dame Antoinette Sibley and, since 2012, Dame Darcey Bussell.

Coleford Workmen's Institute

As early as 1879, the residents of Coleford met to discuss the desirability of establishing a reading room and Workman's Institute in the village. Over the years the location of the Institute varied from building to building and village to village, until in May 1911:

> the following munificent offer has been made by Mrs. D. Knatchbull of Babington. Recognising that the young men of the district are without an institute, or a reading room, in which to spend the long winter evenings, Mrs. Knatchbull has not only generously offered to give a suitable site for the erection of a commodious and comfortable institute in a convenient position, but has also intimated her intention of interesting her friends in the work of raising the necessary funds for the erection of the room, so that the young men of the village will have eventually, the building they have so long been wishing for. Mrs. Knatchbull proposes that the club room and Institute shall be erected in the memory of her late husband, Capt. Knatchbull of Babington.[17]

Dora was as good as her word and rallied her friends and family in support of the Institute and hosted a matinée of music in the Market Hall in Frome. The small town had never seen such famous individuals, as Dora brought Adeline Genée, Moritz Moszkowski, the talented violinist M. Emile Sauret and the famous tenor Mr Gordon Cleather to the Market Hall stage.

MUSICAL PERFORMANCE AT FROME. MATINEE OF MUSIC AND DANCE IN THE MARKET HALL. RHYTHM IN SOUND AND GRACEFUL MOVEMENT. DANCING BY MDLLE. ADELINE GENÉE. MUSIC BY CELEBRATED COMPOSERS AND TALENTED ARTISTES

To Mrs. Knatchbull, of Babington House, who as Dora Bright is known throughout the musical world as a talented artiste, a distinguished musician, and a clever composer, Frome and district owe many musical treats such as only could be heard and seen in London, but never was the locality under deeper obligation to this popular lady than it was yesterday, when some of the best London talent gave a matinee of music and dance in the Frome Market Hall, before, if not crowded, a select and appreciative audience. The object of the performance was to raise funds for the erection of a men's club at Coleford ... To this end she arranged to give two performances in the Market Hall, and added to her kindness by securing the service of some of the best talent in London, who as her friends kindly gave their services. Among these were Mademoiselle Adeline Genée, the great Danish dancer, and of whom the Times said 'she could pirouette on a daisy and it would not bend,' and who refused an engagement this week for £500 (£60,000 today) in order to help Mrs. Knatchbull ... Then the musicians included M. Mauritz Moszkowski, the celebrated composer and pianist, who was associated with Mrs. Knatchbull in an impressive and expressive duet by Schumann ... An orchestra of 30 performers and composed of professional players from Bath and Bristol was under the conductorship of Mr. Clive Carey, and the audience was delighted with the tasteful selections rendered ... The concluding item and to which all the others had led was the pastoral fantasy *The Dryad*, which is the clever composition of Mrs. Knatchbull, and which has held many audiences entranced, both for the beauty of the music and the performance of the artistes, especially the descriptive, realistic and passionate dances of Mdlle Genée.[18]

The performance was repeated the following evening and no doubt many of Dora's closest friends stayed at Babington House to enjoy her extensive and generous hospitality. Although a considerable success and a great show for the people of Somerset, the matinée failed to raise even the amount Adeline Genée had turned down in order to be part of the event. Making less than £100, the good people of Coleford would be forced to wait several more years before their Institute became a reality.

Ballet, Bright and Genée

Adeline Genée returned from her first American tour in May 1909 and immediately reported, 'I should like to mention that Miss Dora Bright is writing and composing another little piece for my use in which she seeks to show the varying phases and moods of a young girl's character'.[19] Because of her next tour of

America, Genée missed the opportunity to play the part in this ballet and the role was played instead by Mlle. Kyasht at the Empire the following October.

The Faun is a one-scene fantasy in which a bored young girl tempts a stone Faun down from his fountain and dances madly with him until the Faun's time runs out and he must return to stone. Once again, the short ballet work was a success: 'fanciful in idea and very charming in execution is the little piece by Miss Dora Bright which was last night presented to an appreciative audience',[20] although not quite as well thought of as *The Dryad*:

> To Miss Dora Bright London owes the two best ballets it has seen of recent years – *The Dryad* ... and here *The Faun*, which was produced last night. Both are really lyrical; both imaginative and (as one might say) poetical; both tell their stories by means of the music and the movement, and need no elaborate printed argument to explain them, and both have the unity of a thing that grows and is not pieced like patchwork. In this respect *The Dryad* was perhaps better than *The Faun*; but since Miss Bright makes the music of her ballets as well as the story, and has imagination and skill in both, she can achieve little works of art that have qualities of form and spirit lacking in most ballets.[21]

A Charming Ballet

> There is no denial of the fact that ballet stories are apt to be conventional; and a writer who can break through this circumscription of fantasy will do much. Miss Dora Bright has the disposition, and to an extent has succeeded – first with *The Dryad*, in which Genée was charming; now in *The Faun*.[22]

Genée returned to the London stage in June 1911, performing in a number of ballets at the Coliseum, and then at the end of the season went to stay with Dora Bright at Babington. During her stay she and Dora discussed the possibility of further ballets. Genée had a special interest in the lives and careers of the great ballet dancers and suggested a ballet based on the life of the eighteenth-century dancer Camargo. Dora was happy to oblige and worked on the score through the winter of 1912.

Genée arranged the choreography and, as she explained, the first thing is to learn the music. 'That done, we fit the sentences to the rhythm of the movement, and remember that a ballet is written like a play ... coming to yet closer detail the steps must be arranged.'[23] In creating these steps, Genée took a daring decision to change shoes, in front of the audience, mid-scene from high heels to ballet shoes. This was an anxious moment and Dora Bright arranged the music so that a long chord could be held if the conductor felt it necessary. In a vivid dream Genée failed to change her shoes and the orchestra fell silent.

As a result of the dream she changed her new ballet pumps for an old pair which would slip more easily on to her feet.

LA CAMARGO. MLLE. GENÉE'S DANCING AT THE COLISEUM

Whatever Mlle. Adeline Genée chooses to do, it is always delightful to see her ... when she gets so good a little ballet as *La Camargo*, twice a day for a week seems the least number of visits one could be content to pay ... While it is delightful to see Mlle. Genée do entre-chats and pirouettes, there is a new interest in seeing her do them in *La Camargo*. We see the dawn of that new dancing which our wider knowledge of its later achievements in Russia, in France, and in England only enables us to enjoy the more ... Miss Dora Bright has caught the note admirably, both for the purposes of the ballet and for the period. Her music is either founded on or imitated from the music of the time. There are some very engaging airs in the little gavotte, the gigue that Mlle. Genée dances to, the music for the King's entrance and that for both the dances with which La Camargo wins her request from him. And in the merely descriptive music Miss Dora Bright contrives to keep the right spirit, so that there is no shock of contrast between the dance-tunes and the music of the action, the whole being light, tuneful and rhythmical.[24]

Figure 7.6. Adeline Genée as Camargo

Such was the success of *La Camargo* that Dora Bright went on to publish four dances for the piano in August 1912, and then the gavotte on its own later in the year.[25] Genée took the ballet on tour with her to America in 1912 and then to Australia in 1913 and in 1914 it was shown in London at the Coliseum to more success.[26]

ADELINE GENÉE AND SOME OTHERS

Whatever else there is beautiful on the London music-hall stage just now, I am sure there is nothing quite so charming as the ballet *La Camargo*, with Adeline Genée in it … Judging from the enthusiasm with which it was received, it had largely been the cause of the crowded state of the auditorium. Look where one would, there was not an empty seat, or a person who was not clapping when the curtain fell. And surely it was rather a pleasure to think that a piece so delicate and music so delightful, so Mozartean, without being a mere imitation, had been designed by and composed by an Englishwoman, Miss Dora Bright. All honour to her! And why will so many of our managers be forever going abroad for their musical scores? Miss Bright can write as well as the best of the foreigners.[27]

Following the success of *La Camargo*, Genée asked Dora to collaborate on another historical ballet, *La Danse*. This was to be an evocation of ballet from 1710 to 1845 represented through six tableaux. Dora visited the British Museum, toiling away to find suitable music. The ballet was first presented in America at the Metropolitan Opera House in New York on 17 December 1912. The American dancer Ted Shawn described *La Danse* as one of the most beautiful and finished dance performances that had been the privilege of his generation to see.[28]

Figure 7.7. London Coliseum Theatre programme – Adeline Genée farewell season

ANOTHER GREAT ACHIEVEMENT BY MLLE. GENÉE

It would be exceedingly difficult to imagine anything more entranc-
ing, more completely artistic, or more truly eloquent of the high
perfection which Mlle. Genée has achieved in her great art than the
record of dancing and dancers between the years 1710 and 1845
… And the music, arranged and partly composed by Miss Dora
Bright, is exquisite. The charms of Lully and Rameau are revived;
there is the music of Gretry, Mozart, Boccherini, Gluck, Strauss,
Mendelssohn and Chopin – a joyous procession of stately and
light-hearted airs.[29]

Genée announced her decision to retire after the performance of *La Danse*:

but for all the joyousness the dances carry a shadow of regret that
so soon Mlle. Genée will say good-bye.[30]

Mlle. Genée's appearance in *La Danse* at the Coliseum is the finishing touch to her career of fascination, and the finishing touch to
the public's loss in her impending retirement. Of all the delicious
things that she has done, this new work, which she and Miss Dora
Bright have put together, is the most delicious.[31]

Within months of her farewell performance, war broke out and Genée felt
honour-bound to return to the boards in support of the troops and to do her
bit to keep up morale in England. As well as supporting the war effort she also
gave her time to alleviating distress amongst the poor. *The Princess and the
Pea* was the work she chose to dance to, and on 2 July 1915, she performed at
a matinée for the Invalids Kitchens of London. The work, based on the Hans
Christian Andersen story, had been set to music by her good friend Dora
Bright. It was a whimsical work and meant only to raise money and a smile.
The outing was its only performance.[32]

Genée became resigned to a full return to her career and took up prepara-
tions for another season at the Coliseum with the assistance of Dora Bright in
a new ballet, *The Dancer's Adventure*, based on the life of the ballerina Marie
Taglioni. The ballet met with a mixed reception:

Mlle. Adeline Genée returned to the programme of the Coliseum
yesterday with a new ballet written and composed by Miss Dora
Bright … music for this ballet is not quite up to the level of her
others, perhaps, and it suffered from some little uncertainty in the
playing.[33]

Despite positive reports of Genée's dancing, the action was unconvincing and the music, though tuneful enough, was unremarkable. It did not give Genée the opportunity to dance as much as she wished and the ballet was withdrawn at Genée's request before the end of the season.

In 1915 Dora Bright composed a *Ballet Suite* which was performed at St George's Hall in Bradford. The work was described as a novelty:

> in the shape of a clever and attractive suite by Miss Dora Bright, illustrating a fairy story, The Shoes that were danced to pieces … It is a concert version of a practicable Ballet Suite, and one can fancy that its graceful measures would prove highly effective when translated into dance movements. As a concert piece it is brilliant, most happily orchestrated, and full of life.[34]

Figure 7.8. Cigarette card featuring Adeline Genée

The work may have been an orchestration of the *Dancer's Adventure*, but it no longer exists.

Ballet at the Coliseum went from strength to strength and through the rest of 1915 to 1917 Genée continued to dance, performing numerous works but always coming back to some of her favourites, *The Dryad*, *La Camargo* and *La Danse*:

> In the Summer of 1917 America joined the war and Genée took part in a Heroes Invitation Concert at the Albert Hall to celebrate the event. Ten thousand soldiers packed the hall and when Genée finished her dance they roared with approval and would not stop until she agreed an encore. After many encores she threw her hat and whip into the cheering throng. One might read into this spontaneous casting of the hat and whip into the audience not only of her gratitude for an unforgettable ovation, but a symbolic gesture indicating her withdrawal from the stage. Having given her official farewell in 1914, she did not announce her retirement again, but discreetly and graciously withdrew into private life.[35]

This, too, was the end of Dora Bright's time in the spotlight as a composer of ballets and theatrical works. The music that accompanied so many of these works and performances created by Genée, and composed by Dora Bright, have now been forgotten despite their importance to the history of dance.

Historically, the work of Adeline Genée and Dora Bright represents one of the three main facets of early twentieth-century dance. Their greatest triumphs, *The Dryad* (1908), *La Camargo* (1912), *La Danse* (1914), *The Dancer's Adventure* (1915) and *The Love Song* (1932), showed Genée at her very best to admiring audiences around the globe:

> The revelation of the Russian ballet which swept across Western Europe obscured the manifestations of ballet which preceded it and to a large extent the writers of the last century dismissed what went before as of no real interest. It is important to consider that ballet audiences now and then are very different, with the primacy of classical ballet at the great Opera houses. The Empire ballet was designed for a far wider audience than today, and for a public which came to be diverted and entertained at a popular theatre or the music hall. The ballet of the early twentieth century was a minor art, played side-by-side with jugglers, popular singers and other vaudeville acts, but it remains an important link in the tradition of British ballet. Consequently, the great figures at the Empire, who put on the very costly ballet performances are now forgotten, although the techniques they developed in mime, as taught in the Royal Ballet School, and of performance management are now central to the way ballets are created.[36]

Whilst the Russian ballet, under Sergei Diaghilev, brought exotic passion and mystery, and in the US, Isadora Duncan enhanced the humanity and expressive content of the dance, Genée perpetuated and preserved the classical tradition, which would become English ballet's life blood under her tenure at the Royal Academy of Dance.

Genée returned to the stage several times in her official retirement for charitable reasons, some associated with Dora Bright, but her main focus in retirement was to raise the standard of dance teaching. With that in mind she began to meet with like-minded individuals:

> With additional leisure on my hands, I found more time to attend those Dancers' Circle Dinners, where ballet enthusiasts used to meet to discuss the best way of developing their favourite art in England. The Association of Operatic Dancing of Great Britain emerged from these dinner-table talks, and in 1920 I was elected first president. Eight years later the Association was honoured by Her Majesty Queen Mary, who graciously consented to become its patroness. In 1935 the title was by the King's Command, altered to The Royal Academy of Dancing, and King George V approved the grant of a Royal Charter.[37]

Music hall

Spurred on by the success of *The Dryad*, Dora turned her attention to the theatre as well as ballet works with Genée. Her first steps saw her return to incidental music, with *The Hampton Club*, a three-act play based on Robert Louis Stevenson's *Suicide Club*, being performed at the Coliseum Theatre in 1909.[38] This work had previously been performed at the Grande Gaignol Theatre in Paris, most likely during Dora's autumn 1908 trip to visit Moszkowski.

Then, in 1910, with 'her pleasing gift of imagination and her considerable skill as a musician, miss Dora Bright has fashioned in *The Portrait* ... a little play of undoubted charm. In the trifle, which was cordially received, the author-composer makes effective use of the pianoforte and the orchestra.'[39] There are shades here of her mother as an author and playwright.

The Portrait was a success and became one of two dance works Dora's good friend, the Duchess of Somerset, chose as part of a special dance matinée in aid of the Invalid Kitchens of London. The other work by Dora, returning to mimodrama, was a new work *The Abbé's Garden*.[40] 'There's an attractive afternoon for you', one paper reported.[41] The matinée was a success, but Dora Bright's new work was not well reported:

> I will not say that *The Abbé's Garden* was the special thing ... but it was the longest; and but for the extremely pretty music Miss Dora Bright has composed ... I should say that the mimodrama was more than a trifle over-long. As writer and composer, however,

> Miss Bright may shake hands with herself and compliment her-
> self alike as dramatist and composer upon the taste and skill with
> which the composer of the music has interpreted the fancy of the
> writer, and upon the inspiration the writer of the play has given to
> the composer of the music.[42]

Amongst the dancers was Miss Phyllis Bedells, who together with Adeline
Genée, were founding members of the Royal Academy of Dance.

Charity continued to be important to Dora and in 1912 she wrote a new
work, *In Haarlem There Dwelt*, performed at a matinée in aid of the Three
Arts Club, a place where young lady actresses, artists and musicians may
board, lodge, work and study.[43] Dora must have been very aware from her
own experiences, and those of her family, of the difficulties actors faced in
finding decent accommodation whilst on tour. This club led the way in providing a safe harbour, in the big provincial centres, where artists could 'find
congenial company and lodging – often a rather difficult matter'.[44] *In Haarlem
There Dwelt* went on to be played commercially at The Playhouse in 1913 and
was met by a slightly puzzled report from the *Sheffield Daily Telegraph*:

> Perhaps combining pantomime with music to take the place of dia-
> logue at the critical moments gives one the impression of selection
> – the essence of art being carried to the extreme – of the big things
> not being said because the writer could not say them. But at any
> rate, it is better to say too little than too much, and one must now
> forget that the music and the scenery and the pantomime did have
> an effect. Perhaps this is the dramatic art of the future.[45]

A somewhat dour Yorkshire response.

A further one-act wordless play, *The Magic Pipe*, was a feature of the 1917
season at the Royalty Theatre. The play, by Jules Delacre, was set to Dora
Bright's music, and represents the carnival of 1838 in the Latin Quarter of
Paris. The author played the lovelorn Pierrot, who found his opium dream a
reality,[46] and also featured Li-si-fou (a Chinese medical student) and Claudine,
a little milliner.[47] Perhaps not to modern tastes.

The year 1917 saw the end of Dora's involvement with the theatre and ballet, and other than publishing the score to *The Dryad* in 1919,[48] the next two
years were very quiet by comparison to the heady and busy war years.

Society of Women Musicians (1911)

The Royal Society of Musicians was founded in 1738, with the express aim of
providing relief to its distressed male members. Its refusal to allow women to
join led to the establishment of the Royal Society of Female Musicians in 1839,

with a similar aim. Twenty-seven years later the two societies joined forces with the word Female being dropped from the society's title. Whilst the society flourished, it failed to meet the needs of its women members, as it did nothing to support women trying to establish or develop their careers.

The new musical academies were producing many gifted and talented female musicians who remained unable to work in large orchestras, or to overcome the prejudices that women do not compose large-scale works. As a consequence in 1911, 150 women composers, singers, instrumentalists, teachers, critics and musicologists gathered in London to form the Society of Women Musicians. Their key objectives were to allow a forum for women musicians to discuss musical matters, advice on the business side of their professional work and to bring together composers and players with a mind to playing each other's music.

The Society was founded by three women with a music college background. They were strong-minded women involved in the Women's Institute and the suffragette movement and very vocal on the position of women. None of them were ever considered a serious composer, their strengths being their work as activists and writers on behalf of the Society. By 1920, the Society had grown to 423 female members and 49 male associates and included amateurs as well as professionals.

Women composers were given a special focus and in later years there was a considerable emphasis on chamber music as a result of the philanthropist Walter Willson Cobbett, an early male associate, donating the Cobbett Free Library of Chamber Music he had amassed, and providing sponsorship of competitions which notably produced more male winners than female. In trying to build a body of chamber works for the members of the society to utilize, two of the founders, Katharine Eggar and Marion Scott, encountered considerable difficulties due to the reluctance of publishers to publish chamber music by women or chamber music at all. One publisher's response made the position clear, although the name of the composer was not revealed: 'The only thing we handle in the way of chamber music is … X's pianoforte quintet. That, we take it, will not interest you, as the composer has the misfortune to belong to the sterner sex.'[49]

Eggar and Scott did go on to trace a quantity of music, printed or in manuscript, which included three works by Dora Bright. The society continued until 1972 and throughout its time continued to campaign for the rights of women musicians as well as organising concerts and meetings.[50]

Despite being a professional musician and composer of some note at this time, Dora Bright was never a member of the Society. She was an avid supporter of women's charities, such as the Window Blind Cleaning Association of Unemployed Women and Girls[51] and even promoted the lives of young women overseas, performing at a concert to raise funds for a high school in Iceland,[52] but she clearly felt that the Society had nothing to offer her and its image as an amateur society may have been another factor. At this point in time, Dora Bright was a rising star, therefore the Society for Women Musicians had nothing to provide and it seemed that Dora had little time for them. Certainly, there is no evidence of Dora Bright being persuaded by any political cause and it is most likely that the strong individuals at the centre of the Society and some of its members, Ethel Smyth being one example, with their suffragette allegiance, did not meet with the values of a country lady.

Compositions away from the theatre

Dora's attention was not entirely focused on the theatre and ballet during this period and she remained committed to extending her musical offerings into new and sometimes eccentric arenas.

Her interest in producing music to stimulate the young remained, and in 1908 she wrote a song-cycle, *A Child's Garden*, first heard at the Broadwood Rooms in London. The work was well received, but its outing seems to have been a one-off and is now lost, other than this short news report:

> The humour of these little poems by Stevenson is so delicate, and the childish point of view so happily caught, that a corresponding degree of fancy and perception is required of a composer if the settings are not to sound sophisticated and self-conscious. On the whole Miss Bright has accomplished her task very skilfully, and her music strikes the right note of simplicity without ever becoming obvious. Some of the verses do not really call for musical treatment, but they are well contrasted, and one, *Every night my prayers I say*, is very charming.[53]

Dora's interest in songs remained in the background with only one other single work in the period, *I Know a Lady Sweet and Kind*, published in 1913 and mentioned specifically as one of her key works in her obituary.[54] She did write some further children's songs in collaboration with Ethel Boyce who published *The Orchard Rhymes* in 1917 and included four pieces by Dora.

Charitable works remained a cornerstone of her work and Dora dedicated much time to the war effort. In 1916 she took part in Women's Tribute Week at the Royal Opera House, Covent Garden, organizing a whole day of entertainment in support of the Sailors and Soldiers of the Empire.[55] Then, at a concert in aid of the funds for British Prisoners of War and Interned Civilians in Germany, she provided a new work:

> The first performance of a set of four Russian dances by Dora Bright. They are part of the incidental music to a dramatized version, which has not yet been produced, of the well-known novel,

My Official Wife. They are melodious and well scored, and their rhythms are vigorous and piquant.[56]

There is no further reference to the play but the Russian dances were heard once more, played by the BBC Theatre Orchestra on the radio in 1939.[57] A further work may have been the result of the conflict in France with Dora writing to stir the spirits of the nation. In 1915, a curious *Concertstück for Six Drums and Orchestra* was presented as part of the Harrogate Symphony Concert season.[58] Her association with military bands from her youth may have provided some influence on the production of this one-off work; it is certainly not a format that many other composers have ever adopted, before or since.

Dora presented her Piano Concerto at a Promenade Concert back in 1888, but had never returned to the promenade concerts either as a composer or performer. The BBC Proms, as they are now, were established some years later in 1895, with Sir Henry Wood as the established conductor. Although Dora and Henry were at the Royal Academy of Music together, it was not until 1917 that one of her works was finally conducted by him:

> The Promenade concert season has been extended to the close of October and never have the concerts been so well patronised. Saturday evenings which are devoted to popular music always draw a full house and last Saturday's performance was made particularly notable by the first appearance of a composition by Dora Bright. Miss Bright's *Suite Bretonne* for the flute and orchestra was based upon a genuine Breton folk tune, divided into an aubade, chanson, angelus and dance. It was exquisitely scored, and the last movement entranced the audience, which accorded the composer an ovation at the close.[59]

Looking forward

The year 1918 was a largely restful one, with no reports of Dora in the newspapers and the only key document which gives any insight into her life at this time is her first will, signed on 10 February 1918.

A letter from Ethel Boyce reports, 'Dora is staying at the Orchard [Ethel's home in Chertsey where she lived with her parents] and her bronchitis was influenza!'[60] Dora recovered from her bout of the 'flu, unlike so many others across the globe, but it may have made her consider that the time had come to ensure that in the event of her death her hard-won wealth would go to her nearest and dearest. The will includes gifts to members of the Knatchbull family as would be expected, but also offers a little insight into her other friendships and those close to her.

Her long-standing friend Miss Paget was appointed one of her executors and was to receive 'my ruby and diamond brooch ... as a memento'.

To her dear friend Dorothy Beazley of Birkenhead, she bequeathed:

> my diamond plaque, my diamond brooch with single drop, my five-row pearl necklace with topaz and diamond clasp and my topaz diamond brooch to match and my marquise diamond ring, also my gold chain with cigarette case (D in diamonds), gold case with diamond snake and ruby eyes, gold chain sovereign purse, pencil and matchbox, and all my lace and furs belonging to me at my death.[61]

Sister Georgie was to be the main recipient of her wealth and along with the 'gold locket containing my father's portrait and hair', she left to Georgina de Lara Kennedy Allen, 'the income of my trust fund' during Georgina's life. In the event of Georgie's death the trust fund and income would revert to members of the Knatchbull family.

The final feature of the will was Dora's desire for:

> the portrait by Sargent of myself to remain hanging at Babington House for twenty-one years after the death of the children of my nephew who will inherit the house, only then, or after the sale of Babington House, to present the said portrait to such public collection of pictures in London worthy of the artist.[62]

Dora appears to have realized that she would not live forever, but through these few, not inconsequential gifts and requests, her legacy might live on a little longer.

***

The retirement of Adeline Genée heralded the end of an era for Dora Bright. She had been at Genée's side to provide the music to her new ballet ideas, but had also made use of her knowledge and understanding of the theatre with other dance works, incidental music and more orchestral works making Dora a well-known cornerstone of popular music. Approaching the age of sixty and with a very successful decade behind her, it was time for Dora Bright to take stock and slow down.

8 Return to the Country, 1920–1939

In July 1920, Dora announced that she was to return to Somerset and one of her many local responsibilities would now include the presidency of the Mid-Somerset Musical Competition, to be held in Bath.[1] The return to the country heralded yet another era in Dora's life, in which she would settle into local charitable works, continue to compose, but more importantly find yet another way of presenting her music to the public. Radio and TV were in their infancy, but in a changing world embracing these new developments would open up a new audience for Dora's works.

A Somerset lady

With the retirement of Adeline Genée, Dora's work in London had started to slow down with fewer stage productions. Dora chose this as her time to return to Babington and resume her social life in the country. Babington remains a beautiful location and the house is designed for socializing, parties and balls. On her return, numerous friends and acquaintances were invited to dinner and to stay for extended periods.

One such distinguished guest was Helen, Countess Dowager of Radnor, closely connected to the Royal Family and the first woman to conduct her own women's orchestra in 1881. Whether she was a regular visitor is not documented, but in her book, *From a Great-Grand-mother's Armchair*, she recalls a day when she was invited to lunch at Babington with Mrs Knatchbull:

> One Sunday in September 1920, I started off in the car to go and lunch with Mrs. Knatchbull. When we had gone a few miles, however, the car broke down ... we telephoned for a taxi which took me back to Bath ... later in the afternoon Mrs. Knatchbull sent a car for me to go over to tea, and I flew over hill and dale and reached her place in Babington in half an hour.[2]

Dora's chauffeur earned his wages that day, driving the narrow lanes of Somerset for hours so his mistress could have tea with an important and well-connected musical figure.

Dora was also good friends with William Inge, Professor of Divinity at Cambridge and Dean of St Paul's Cathedral in London. He visited her frequently at Babington and recorded the visits in his diary: 'September 11 1929 – A very pleasant visit to Mrs. Knatchbull … She is extremely hospitable. Among others we met and liked very much, Mr Vachell the novelist, who lives at Bath'. In May 1930, he stayed for a number of days: 'May 19–22 – At Babington; Mrs. Knatchbull is a perfect hostess, and knows everything about cookery and wines. We met the Hannays, Lady Horner, and Lady Hylton; also Mr Vachell the novelist, whom we met last year'. The following year after visiting friends around England, he returned to visit Lady Horner at Mells and Mrs Knatchbull at Babington and quite prophetically wrote, 'so we saw something of the doomed country house life, which will soon be a thing of the past'. His final report, in 1933, is of lunch with Mrs Knatchbull, the Danish Minister and his Russian wife.[3] No doubt the Danish Minister had been introduced by Adeline Genée on one of her many visits to Babington.

Of course there were still parties and balls to be held, and a letter from Ethel Boyce provides an interesting insight into some of the guests Dora invited to Babington. The letter indicates that not all the guests got on with one another all of the time, but that Dora knew how to smooth things over and keep the guests from bickering. Who the guests were is not made obvious, but they seem to have been well fed and watered and provided with plenty of entertainment. The letterhead is also worthy of note.

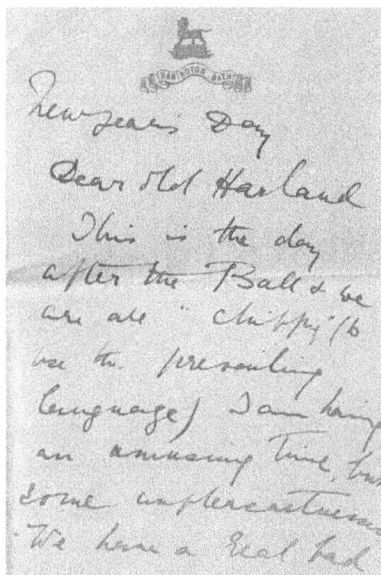

Figure 8.1. Letter from Ethel Boyce to Harland Chaldecott

New year's Day. Dear old Harland. The day after the ball and we are all chippy (to use the prevailing language). I am having an amusing time, but some unpleasantness. We have a real bad woman staying in the house, a type I have never seen before, American, brilliant, charming in some ways but the trail of the leopard is over it all. Dora has been splendid in the way of managing a quite undesirable conversation breaking cliques and so on. I've now had 2 Balls and have 2 more to come and shall then be quite a corpse unless I am critically kept up by champagne and such. What a different life! There's been an awful man here, a swell brute. A sort of Lord Weller. He has spent his time between me and the hard woman, talking properly to me in a series of grumphies [grunt-like utterances] and being bored (only he likes my face) and paying her violent attention under the eye of her poor and observant husband. Feline amenities have prevailed. Altogether I have had considerable amusement … Pantomime rehearsal went well.[4]

One further example gives an insight into Dora, less as a socialite, but more as a quieter and personable friend. George A. Birmingham, the pen name of James Owen Hannay, was a prolific novelist with over sixty titles to his name. He was also an Anglican minister and became the vicar of Mells in 1924 and a good friend of Lady Horner. He met Mrs Knatchbull at Mells Manor as one of Lady Horner's guests and speaks very kindly towards her:

I must count myself singularly happy and Mells a fortunate parish, for it was not only at the Manor House and in Lady Horner's company that we met well-known and delightful people. Babington is another house to which I often go. We met Mrs. Knatchbull on the first evening we spent in Mells, for she was a guest at the Manor House. She does not live in Mells, but she soon became a valued friend. They say that true friendship must be based on some community of interests. This sounds plausible, but in fact is not true. Mrs. Knatchbull and I have scarcely any common interests. She does not belong to Mells and the 'rustic murmur of our borough' means nothing to her. She is very musical, a brilliant pianist and composer whose works are well known. I have all my life disliked music and my feeling hardened into actual hatred during my years in Budapest … Nor does Mrs. Knatchbull care greatly for the things which chiefly interest me. Yet, almost at once, we became friends and the friendship ripened. An evening at Babington is always something to look forward to, even if I know that all the other guests are eminent musicians. The evenings she spends with me at the rectory are pleasant to me – I hope perhaps to her – even if there are no other guests at all. It is indeed fortunate for me that friendships can be formed and persist in spite of sharp divergences of tastes and interests.[5]

It is an interesting reflection on a side of Dora Bright, which rarely surfaces in the hurly-burly of her musical and theatrical world, and one that shows a woman at peace with herself, happy in the simple friendship of others.

The people of Somerset were also proud to have Mrs Knatchbull back in their county and took great pleasure in making her welcome at every opportunity, inviting her to charitable events where she was the starring attraction. She attended many of these events with presence and dignity and some interesting news reports arose as a result:

> A delightful little building was the description given by Mrs. Knatchbull, of Babington, when on Saturday afternoon she opened the newly built Methodist Sunday School ... Mrs. Knatchbull expressed her pleasure for the privilege, observing that Sunday Schools in these days had a tendency to go down instead of up, but if they went up instead of down it would be better for England. Mrs. Knatchbull after expressing a hope that children who would be taught there would grow up as good as their forebears, turned the key and led the way into the room.[6]

TAKE SHELTER – FÊTE

> Window frames were removed from the conservatory and all the available outhouses were utilised ... in order to prevent buyers and sellers getting wet. People came to the conservatory ... and made their purchases, which were handed to them through the windows. The Rev. K. C. Jackson (vicar) said that a vicarage fête demanded two things – a fine day and the right person to open it. (It was raining a steady drizzle with intermittent gusts of wind when the opening ceremony took place). But even if they had not the fine weather, they certainly had the right opener in Mrs. Knatchbull of Babington, who was also 'Dora Bright', a celebrated pianist and composer ... the Vicar of Frome expressing thanks to Mrs. Knatchbull, said that owing to her friendliness and cheerfulness, people are always happy wherever Mrs. Knatchbull was ... She wished to congratulate them on their picturesque village, their beautiful inn, their marvellous church tower, and last but not least their Vicar and his wife.[7]

As well as presiding over fête openings Dora was active with the Vobster Bright Hour, a church group meeting at the Vobster village Hall in Somerset, and was happy to entertain them at Babington:

The party were taken to Babington House, where they were very heartily welcomed by Mrs. Knatchbull. The hostess conducted them over the house, and Mrs. Knatchbull spared them no effort in showing them the many interesting and historic features for which Babington House is noted.[8]

This included the

King James bedroom, which contained an oak four-poster, dateable to about 1595 with Swan marquetry inset in the richly carved head. A note in the Rev. J. Skinner's diary, 1822, states that the bed belonged to the Hungerfords of Fairleigh Castle. According to tradition James II visited Babington, and beside the bed is a magnificent saddlecloth embroidered in silver thread, said to have been left in the house by him. A watch is also preserved with the King's miniature on its face surmounted by a crown of diamonds.[9]

Remaining in demand as a pianist, in January 1922 Dora played for the Avonmouth and Shirehampton Choral Society, who had been able to persuade none other than the great Dr Ralph Vaughan-Williams to conduct them in some of his own songs. Dora was acquainted with the great composer and most likely attended as a favour.[10] A letter from Ralph to Dora in 1939 apologizing for not being able to visit her, goes on to ask, 'I am being worried by a Russian refugee who wants to give piano lessons – do you happen to know if there is any Society for befriending foreign evacuees which could help him?'[11] There is no evidence of a response from Dora, but given her charitable nature, numerous contacts and the chance to add an interesting Russian to her network, it was most likely impossible for her to ignore such a request.

Coleford Welfare Hall

Back in May 1911, Dora had been made aware of the requirement for a new building to house the Workman's Institute in Coleford. At the time she generously offered to provide both the site and a matinée performance to raise funds for the institute. Despite her efforts, the money raised did not lead to the immediate construction of the building. At a village meeting on 5 November 1919, the subject of constructing the hall was again raised and once again Dora, in attendance, agreed to be party to the work. She described how she had always been in favour of the scheme, but that 'due to living away from the neighbourhood, and also through the war, it had not been possible to complete it'.[12] Offering them the proceeds of the previous fundraising, amounting to £83, she offered to make this a round £100 (£5,300 today) as a start to the new scheme.

Figure 8.2. Coleford Hall as it stands today

Not until 1927 did Coleford finally got the Welfare Hall, as it was now titled, only a mere sixteen years since Dora's first assistance, and some thirty-eight years after it was first considered:

> The hall was very fine with a spacious hall, which contains a roomy cloak-room for ladies and lavatories for the men. The billiard room … accommodates two full size tables. One is already present and another will shortly be presented by Mrs. Knatchbull … On the second floor is a large concert hall … and the room will comfortably accommodate 300. A Broadwood grand piano has been secured for a nominal sum through the kind offices of Mrs. Knatchbull … Mrs. Knatchbull who was received with prolonged applause, expressed her gratification that the movement she had set on foot some years ago had at last attained its object.[13]

St Margaret's Church, Babington

The little church of St Margaret's is set very close to the main house at Babington and was the local parish church for local residents and Dora, who would have attended when she was at home, the church having a private family box pew at the front next to the altar. According to the *Somerset Standard* of 1937[14] the church was reputed to be one of the smaller masterpieces of the master-architect, Sir Christopher Wren. This is unlikely as the church was built a generation after the death of Wren and it is more likely that the church was designed by a Bristol architect, either John Strahan or William Halfpenny. The previous Norman church was razed to the ground to make way for the new church completed in 1748 and then remained unchanged since that date.

First alerted to the dilapidated state of the church in 1902, Dora staged a concert to raise funds for its restoration, raising £30 (£4,000) for the fund. It seems there had been little maintenance of the church in the intervening years as a result of Dora's move to London, the war and the general economic depression. As a consequence the interior, the roof and the organ were in a sad state of disrepair.

On the eve of the Second World War, Dora focused her attention on the little church and organized a series of three concerts to raise monies for its repair, and with her inimitable style organized some big-name artistes to visit and perform. Isolde Menges, the world-famous violinist, was to attend the first concert with other celebrities such as Herbert Heyner, the well-known baritone, alongside promising young singers and cellists taking part in the other events. Plans were drawn up with The Marquess of Bath attending the first concert, the second by Lady Horner of Mells Manor and the third by the film star, Cyril Maude.

Figure 8.3. St Margaret's Church, Babington

Figure 8.4. Interior of St Margaret's Church, Babington, with Georgian box pews

Somewhat inevitably, the local papers reported the event as a huge success and covered it in some depth:

> Introducing the first of a series of concerts in the charming music room at Babington House on Saturday, Lord Bath congratulated Mrs. Knatchbull, of Babington House, on her energy in working for the restoration of the tiny Wren church which stands on the lawn near the house. It is to this end that Mrs. Knatchbull has arranged the concerts of chamber music, at which the composer-pianist of Babington House is supported by well-known artistes. The first concert provided rare entertainment for the company, which packed the room.[15]

> The second of the Babington concerts took place last Saturday ... Lady Horner opened the proceedings with an unusually witty and interesting speech. She referred to the time when Mrs. Knatchbull first came into the neighbourhood, when there were no motors, no wireless and no cinemas! – she said that Mrs. Knatchbull had provided all three in herself, and lit the houses free of charge. In speaking of the church she said she highly approved of the way the interior was to be restored.[16]

> There must have been some regret that Saturday's concert ... was the last of the series ... Though it was the last it was the most outstanding for its length and its variety.[17]

Dora kept the best to the last of the concerts using the occasion to play her own music including her *Jungle Book Songs*, *Two Pieces for Cello*, the *Variations on an original theme of Sir G. A. Macfarren* and her newest work

Neu Wien. The news report of the final concert ends with an interesting hint of more to come: 'In Babington church the music is less sweet, but we are glad, for its sourness promises that there will be fairies dancing upon the lawn at Babington in the month of June.'[18]

Despite the success of the concerts, the need for a new organ remained. Dora spoke to her good friend, Adeline Genée, and organized a children's dance fundraiser with Genée in attendance, alongside a troupe of young dancers from the newly formed Royal Academy of Dance:

Ballet Dancers and Bishops at Babington House

Pupils of England's most famous academy of dancing took part in the sunshine of Tuesday evening on the lawn adjoining Babington House ... Madame Adeline Genée, president of the Royal Academy of Dancing, had brought from London eleven of her pupils. The entertainment lasted for about 80 minutes but seemed much shorter. With a tall yew hedge as a back-sheet and the lawn as a stage, solo ballets were performed depicting a mother's lullaby, a butterfly and a torch bearer, these being followed by a spring fantasy, in which the whole company took part ... The entertainment concluded with a ballet on the old rhyme, *Monday's child is fair of face*. The music for this is the composition of Dora Bright (Mrs. Knatchbull) who was at one of the two pianos ... At the close the Vicar said that he had been requested by Mrs. Knatchbull not to say anything, but he felt they would like him to disobey and just say 'Thank you' to her for arranging the dances ... Hearty applause endorsed his remarks, and Mrs. Knatchbull replied, 'We are very grateful' ... Mrs. Knatchbull's Lady Secretary was present and was as helpful and obliging to the Press as usual.[19]

Yet again there was more bad news and in 1939 the deathwatch beetle was found to be causing havoc amongst the rafters in the little church. Dora organized another concert:

The sum of £200 [£13,500 today] is needed in order that the little church at Babington may be completely restored. Recently an appeal was made in order that the interior of the church might be redecorated. An examination of the roof, however, revealed that the rafters were almost eaten through by that sinister insect the Death Watch Beetle ... Recently Mrs. Dora E. Knatchbull of Babington wrote pointing out that Her Majesty Queen Mary had sent her, through Lady Cynthia Colville, the following message, 'The Queen hopes you will succeed in raising the sum you require for so excellent an object.'[20]

Once again, Dora turned to her good friend Adeline Genée:

> Dancers from the Royal Academy of Dancing performed on the lawns at the home of Mrs. Knatchbull on Tuesday afternoon and evening ... There was a large audience which included the Bishop of Bath and Wells ... Before the commencement Madame Adeline Genée asked the audience to remember as they watched the dancers that the girls were not professionals, just scholarship girls who were pleased to come a second time for what they would term an outing ... The applause recalled the girls the second time to take a bow. A shower during the popular *My Lady's Minuet* [specially written for the concert by Dora Bright], for which Mrs. Knatchbull played, caused a little disturbance as some of the people found it necessary to take shelter. By special request the item was repeated minus the dancers ... Lady Horner, at the conclusion, expressed thanks to Madame Adeline Genée for her generosity in giving such a lovely show ... Her ladyship remarked in humorous vein that an apology was due to Madame Adeline Genée for the weather. 'We in Somerset', she added, 'feel very sorry and ashamed'.[21]

Aside from the weather, the restoration was a success and the church remains in use to this day as a wedding venue and for other occasional ceremonies such as baptisms and funerals.

A voice on the radio

The advent of radio was yet another way in which Dora promoted herself and her music and she had a number of works premiered on the BBC, as well as accompanying some concerts on the piano. The first appearance of one of her works was the *Jungle Book* songs, sung by Kenneth Ellis on 13 November 1924,[22] then in 1926 a specially written work for the Hallé in Manchester, *Un Soirée de Vienne*, featured on 7 January. The year 1928 saw a production of her incidental music, *Scrooge*, on Christmas Eve, and then in 1937, she starred in a concert with the BBC Orchestra playing her *Variations for Piano and Orchestra*, heralded by the *Radio Times* as '(First performance in England) The variations to be heard this evening were composed in Paris in 1912'.[23]

Some months before the advent of the Second World War, Dora was invited by the BBC to host a concert and evening of entertainment from her home at Babington.

' Myself '

Figure 8.5. Portrait of Mrs Knatchbull as drawn by J. S. Sargent and featured in the *Radio Times*, 28 April 1939

The programme went out live on the radio to the nation and she regaled listeners with stories of her time with Moszkowski in Paris, and played settings of her *Six Songs from the Jungle Book*.[24] The programme aired on 28 April 1939 from 7.31pm until 8.02pm. What a story it would provide if it was still available. The play list is still stored in the BBC archives and amongst the items played were her *Siciliano and Gigue on a theme by Arne* and a *Prelude and Fugue* by Moszkowski. For the pleasure of her company, the BBC paid her £10 10s (£740 today). The Babington concert of 1939 was her last radio performance.

Reminiscences

In 1932, Dora attended a small reunion dinner for members of the old Empire ballet team. Other attendees included her good friend Adeline Genée and may have led to the idea for a final farewell by Genée, to the music of Dora Bright. The news report reads: 'what memories the names recall, and what audiences! Genée stayed at the Empire for ten years … Well that was yesterday. To-day, at the Empire there is the unrivalled Greta Garbo.'[25]

After this meeting Genée was approached to appear in aid of the Hertford Hospital in Paris at a charity matinée to be held at the Drury Lane Theatre in the summer of 1932. She agreed but could not decide what to dance and after viewing an eighteenth-century painting, she turned to Dora, telephoning her to ask whether she had anything that would be suitable. The next day they met and Dora produced a cycle of period dances – pavane, minuet, passepied, galliard and rigadoun – for which the old painting seemed to provide the perfect setting. The work proved a success and was added to a programme at the Coliseum in 1933 and then in what was to be Genée's final performance together with Anton Dolin, 'in a series of dances founded on a picture, *The Love Song*, music by Dora Bright'.[26] The performance was recorded using the Baird process and televised nationally at 11pm on 15 March 1933, the only work of Dora's to have appeared on television:

> **LONDON NATIONAL PROGRAMME** (1147Kc/S.) (261.6 M.) 11.0–11.30 Television Transmission by the Baird Process; Adeline Genée, the Famous Dancer, in her World Farewell by Television, dancing with Anton Dolin; Traditional Dances 'from a Picture, "The Love Song"; Music by Dora Bright; Eric Bertner (the Danish Musical Comedy Star), Maisie Seneshall (Period Song Cameos in French.) (Vision, 261.6m.; Sound, 398.9 m.)[27]

Further reminiscences did not have quite such a dramatic outcome, but they give some indication of just how much Dora was admired locally:

> At the meeting of the Vobster Bright Hour Association ... the members were favoured with the company of Mrs. Knatchbull. Mrs. Knatchbull can claim to be a stage star of days when the term screen star was not coined. The members were given delightful entertainment as she related her reminiscences of her associations with distinguished people and her home life among the very quaint servants on the Knatchbull estate.[28]

Dora went on to judge the knitted hot water bottle cover competition, and competitive games concluded the meeting. A further report included a telling story of Dora and her time with the Babington Strollers some years earlier:

> Seated in a favourable position at one of the performances in Wells of the Babington Strollers, the writer was particularly struck with the marvellous musical memory of Mrs. Knatchbull. She accompanied throughout and gave the various incidental music with extraordinary ability, but without any copy of the music before her. There was never the slightest hesitation on her part.[29]

There is no pathos in this looking back, simply the joy of a life well lived, and one full of such interesting and varied encounters that it should be revisited.

Further works

These latter Babington years were also a period of composition with eleven works written in two bursts between 1922–27 and 1933–39. Her *Romanza and Scherzetto for piano*, originally written and published in 1889, was reprinted in 1922 and the Romanza dedicated to her good friend Ethel Boyce.

During this period Dora also had a flirtation with the music of Strauss, starting with the short work *Neu Wien*, her only work to be recorded on a 78rpm record at the time. This was followed by *Un Soirée de Vienne*, for the Hallé, which was transformed into an operetta. The work was reported in *The Times*: 'Miss Dora Bright has written music for a new opera, called *The Waltz King*, the book of which is the work of Mr Frank Stayton. The opera deals with the life of Johann Strauss, and many of his melodies are incorporated into the score.'[30] The libretto, without music, is located in the Library of Congress in Washington DC, USA, the only copy to remain in existence.

Finally, the *Radio Times* offered a tantalizing glimpse of 'a third opera to be written', but there is no other record of the work.[31]

***

Dora had settled back at home in Babington and become part of the fabric of Somerset. She had a reputation as a hostess, but things weren't always as they seemed:

> Meanwhile, the house became increasingly fossilised. Sir Orme Sargeant (famous as Moley in the Foreign Office) told me of the shock he had on retiring for a siesta as a guest of Mrs. Knatchbull. He pulled down the blind of his bedroom window and a bombshell of flies, undisturbed for years, broke over his head.[32]

Consummate host requires cleaner would perhaps be apposite. The impending war would bring privations for many and would finally lead to Dora taking a step back from the limelight, but not quite retiring from her more expensive lifestyle.

9 Swansong, 1940–1951

Throughout the latter part of her life Dora continued to work and split her time between London and Babington. War brought changes to lifestyles, society and musical tastes with the old pre-war world being brushed aside as people struggled to live under rationing, bombing and the threat of invasion. Despite this, Dora's lifestyle did not alter to any great extent. In 1942 she advertised for staff at Babington:

> **WANTED**
>
> MAID or suitable EVACUEE, over 40 to help Parlourmaid and Housemaid; country. – Apply, Mrs. Knatchbull, Babington nr. Frome.[1]

It seemed there weren't many candidates left in the area so later in the year Dora was forced to amend the advert to:

> **WANTED**
>
> AN ELDERLY PERSON to help Parlourmaid and Housemaid. Country near station and bus – Mrs. Knatchbull, Babington, nr. Frome.[2]

Whether the position was filled is not recorded, but certainly living the country lifestyle was still high on her agenda, despite the privations of so many others.

A new job

Approaching the age of seventy, Dora became the radio critic for the magazine *Musical Opinion*. Her time with them has become part of the journal's folklore and she remains admired by the editor and staff despite a gap of eighty years. Her reviews 'were not always positive and her style was considered to be "bitingly scornful" at times, particularly of modern music'.[3] In a 1941 article titled 'What has happened to music', she deplores the music of Debussy, Strauss [Richard], Schoenberg and Stravinsky[4] and, in 1942, reviewing Benjamin Britten and others, she talks of their

> perverted sense of key, melody, harmony and form comparable to an aural distortion or disorder ... I often wonder that the old stagers in the good orchestras do not rise in revolt at the things they are made to play.[5]

Dora's own music and musical tastes were conservative. Her musical style changed little over the years. Her training stemmed from the nineteenth century and even her efforts to improve her orchestration and composition with Moszkowski was based on his own training from the mid-1800s. Both he and Dora were Romantic in style and for Dora the new sounds arising from modernism had no place in her musical world.

However, not all her reviews were scathing and after a positive review of a Schumann recital given by Adelina De Lara, she contacted Dora and recollects:

> I happened to write to the critic of *Musical Opinion* to thank him for a good notice. To my surprise Dora Bright replied, as she was the critic! She invited me to a house party. Unfortunately I was unable to go, but in June 1947 a friend drove me to Dora Bright's lovely home, Babington. As we drove into the great park, with its lake and church built by Wren, my heart quickened. The sight of the house made me gasp. Some parts of it date from the 13th century and it contains twenty-five bedrooms, one of which is called James II's room. King James' saddle, a dull rose in colour, and his watch are kept in a glass case in the room. My own bedroom was enormous with a four poster, but the peaceful view from the tall windows was comforting and uplifting. I found Dora delightful. So youthful too for her years. I think there were quite six grand pianos in the house and her music-room might have belonged to Buckingham Palace. I played Schumann to Dora each evening after dinner, and to talk to her was joy. Best of all were the duets we played together on two pianos, and Dora's playing of her own compositions.[6]

This meeting of minds and music provides a delightful insight into Dora's last years and continuing lifestyle.

Dora's music slipped off the radar and by the end of the 1940s, now in her eighties, she spent much of her time socializing, entertaining and as ever on charitable works. During this period there are two final works recorded from her pen; one of the pieces, the work, *Melody*,[7] was written for a London wedding in 1944 and has not survived, and the other is a transcription of a work by Arne, the *Siciliano and Gigue from the Suite in D minor*, which she published in 1948.

In May 1950 her suite from *Four Ballets* was played by the West of England Light Orchestra on the radio. This was the last time her work was played to the public, until Catherine Wilmers, the eminent cellist, introduced *Two Pieces* dating from 1934, into her concert repertoire in the 1990s.

A final journey

After a short illness in London, Dora returned to Babington for the final time, where she died on 16 November 1951. There was very little response to Dora's death in the press. *The Times* issued an obituary written by a friend, the Sheffield newspapers did not respond at all, and it was largely left to the local *Somerset Standard* to fill the gap:

> Death of Mrs. Dora Knatchbull. Former Concert Pianist. The death has occurred, at her home at Babington, near Radstock, of Mrs. Dora Estella Knatchbull (89) widow of the late Capt. Wyndham Knatchbull, 3rd Dragoon Guards. Before her marriage Mrs. Knatchbull was well known on the concert stage as Dora Bright, the pianist. Many of the leading figures of music and literature have visited her country home.[8]

The Musical Times was short and to the point:

> **MRS. WYNDHAM KNATCHBULL**
>
> formerly well known as a composer and a pianist under the name of Dora Bright. On one occasion she played a piano concerto of her own at the Promenades under Sir Henry Wood. Recently she was for some years critic of radio music to *Musical Opinion*.[9]

Ignoring her importance to the concert audience, *The Stage* newspaper wrote only of her ballet works and, from its tone, had Dora not worked so closely with Adeline Genée it seems possible they may not even have recorded her demise:

> We regret to announce the death, at the age of 89, of Dora Bright, who wrote the music for a number of ballets in which Adeline

Genée danced at the old Empire. Perhaps the most famous was *The Dryad*, in which Genée appeared as a lovely wood nymph. Miss Bright also arranged the music for *The Love Song*, a suite of dances, for Genée and Anton Dolin, when the great ballerina danced for the last time in 1933.[10]

Despite the lack of interest from the newspapers, her good friends Adeline Genée and Sir Kenneth Barnes provided a suitably touching epitaph:

MRS WYNDHAM KNATCHBULL

Dame Adeline Genée and Sir Kenneth Barnes write:

The death of Mrs. Wyndham Knatchbull will be deeply felt as a loss to her many friends. She was a lifelong friend of both of us, from the days when, as Dora Bright, she made her mark in the professional world of music as a composer and pianist, the first woman to be awarded the Lucas Gold Medal for Composition at the Royal Academy of Music. She was a brilliant executant on the piano, chosen to play her own concerto by Sir Henry Wood at the promenade concerts at the Queen's Hall; and in the first years of this century she composed a series of ballets which were produced with remarkable success in London at the Empire and Coliseum and afterwards in New York.

She loved music and was blessed with an intellectual power which enabled her to appreciate all the great masterpieces. Her musical memory was phenomenal; and she made this a great joy to her friends, as she was able to give them anything they asked for on the piano. She studied harmony under Maurice Moszkowski, and he, as well as many other famous musicians, regarded her friendship and criticism as a spiritual influence of high value. She was frankly critical of our contemporary music, and puzzled by it. As a hostess at Babington she entertained her guests with a warmth of welcome and hospitality which permeated every gathering. Whatever she did she made worth doing, and appreciated her friends, whom she never lost through a long life.[11]

She was buried at Babington:

Death of Mrs. Knatchbull

Internment at Babington Church. The death occurred on Friday, 16th November of Mrs. Knatchbull, at the age of 89 years. Her maiden – and professional – name was Dora Bright, a musician whose compositions and renderings were noted above all for grace and charm. Although a composer of many songs, she will perhaps be remembered most for her unique little ballads, such as *The Dryad*, *The Princess and the Pea* and others, founded upon fairy tales well known to children, and in which Adeline Genée, the premiere of her day, co-operated. As a pianist, Dora Bright had a wonderful gift of touch and expression. On one occasion at a rehearsal before a Mozart concert at which she was the pianist, the conductor, the late Landon Ronald, said to the orchestra, 'let's run through that bit again and put a little more Dora Bright in it' – with admirable result. During the first world war she held many drawing-room concerts for deserving causes and, by her personal efforts, raised an appreciable amount of money for the restoration of the little church which stands in the grounds of her home.[12]

It is good to see that despite the limited coverage in the press, Dora's funeral was very well attended, by the family (nephew, niece and other senior members), Dame Adeline Genée, Sir Kenneth Barnes, the Director of RADA, as well as members of the great and good of Somerset and locals from the vicinity. This gives a final perspective of how much she was admired and respected across many aspects of music, drama and society.

After the service, Dora was laid to rest next to her husband Wyndham in the family vault, which sits in the corner of the small graveyard to the rear of St Margaret's Church. A plaque commemorating Captain Knatchbull and Dora sits above the Knatchbull family pew at the front right of the little church. Her date of birth is mis-recorded as 15 August 1862.

Figure 9.1. Church memorial to Captain Knatchbull and Dora in St Margaret's; note the date of her birth is incorrect

A few months later Dora returned to the newspapers when her will was published:

> Mistress of Music. Mrs. Dora Estella Knatchbull, whose will was published recently, was well known as a musician, pianist and composer of a very high order … She was described in the *Musical Standard* as a charming mistress of English music, and *The Observer* once said of her, Miss Dora Bright becomes more and more valuable.[13]

In her final will, written in 1948, she left a pansy ruby and diamond ring and her war savings, certificates amounting to £100 (£3,200 today) to her sister Georgiana, evidence that they had remained in contact throughout their lives. Her net assets amounted to £1,545 (about £50,000 today) and after a number of other bequests the estate was left in the hands of a friend from Frome to dispose of 'as previously instructed'.

The house was sold by the Knatchbull family in 1952 to the Jennings family, who in the summer of 1953 set about selling off some of the house's possessions at an auction at the house. A portrait of Dora, which had hung in the house, drawn by the portraitist John Singer Sargent, was bequeathed to the Royal Academy of Music, but was stolen from the house during the auction of the remaining contents. Its present location is unknown.

Dora's partying spirit meant she neglected the house, leaving it in a very poor state of disrepair. It also appears that, as the new owners outline, she had been

> an enthusiastic bidder at auctions. Cases would arrive from Sotheby's or Christie's, the contents sometimes retaining their labels, with lot numbers, as they stood on window-sills or chests. It was far from unknown for the cases to remain intact as they had arrived. The final sale at Babington had thus an element of a lucky Dip.

The writer continues:

> Under a brilliant August sun, crowds, local and beyond, rallied at Babington. The Church stands only a hundred yards from the house … Outside, tombs of previous owners lie scattered in the turf. It was a perfect setting for what holiday brochures call 'an outing for the family'. Picnics were eaten, drinks poured and babies in push-chairs received, as if it were a baptism of fire.[14]

A very fitting end, and how similar to many a garden party thrown by the great lady herself on the same lawns. Perhaps her spirit was in attendance, smiling on the gathering as she once again provided pleasure to the public.

***

Unfortunately, after her death most of the manuscripts in the house were destroyed and only a few songs and Dora's memoir were retained by the family. The post-war years were hard and the whole estate was reportedly run down when Dora died, making it almost inevitable that anything seen as of no value would be thrown away and destroyed.

Dora and her music had been out of public view for over ten years and her music had been largely forgotten. It would remain that way for the next fifty years until one of her cello pieces, *Polka à la Strauss* (1934) was included on a CD in 2000 and finally in 2019 with the recording of her two major piano and orchestral works.

Despite being out of the public eye, a series of stories written by author Susan Albert in 2009 following on from the *Cottage Tales of Beatrix Potter*, included a reference to Dora Bright:

> 'So it seems', Beatrix said thoughtfully, 'Caroline wrote me that she wants to study composition, she wants to become a composer'. 'A composer!' Margaret said blankly. 'But there are no women composers!' 'There's Ethel Smyth', Beatrix reminded her. 'And Dora Bright. Both of them had their music performed – although I'm sad to say that I've never had the opportunity to hear it myself'.[15]

Sad indeed. It seems that for far too many of us and for too many of her works, this remains the case.

10 Women in Music Today

Seventy years since the beginnings of the feminist movement, the world of music remains anchored in the 1880s, and the issues faced by Dora Bright and her compatriots have altered little. In recent years there have been legal requirements placed on institutions to address gender inequality and diversity issues. This has led corporates, opera houses, theatres and the like to develop policies on equality in employment, recruitment, visitor access and a host of other areas. But they have not addressed the central question of hiring performers and musicians to ensure gender equality.[1]

The BBC has pledged to ensure that the 2022 Proms are fully gender neutral, but in many other areas the world of music does not live up to these standards. Back in 1903 the New York Metropolitan Opera House seemed to lead the way by playing Ethel Smyth's opera *Der Wald*, but it took over a hundred years before another opera by a woman composer appeared at the same venue in 2017.[2]

Examination of the classical repertoire shows it remains biased against women composers to the extent that the 2015 season playlist in the USA contained only 1.8 per cent of music written by women. More recent analysis of 2020 worldwide performances by 100 orchestras (14,747 works) showed that women composers accounted for 5 per cent of works with over 88 per cent of concerts featuring only works by men. This does suggest some movement in attitudes, but indicates that for many women composers their works are unlikely to receive an audience and may end up, as with Dora Bright and others, being consigned to history. Unsurprisingly the top three composers were Beethoven, Mozart and Tchaikovsky.[3]

Clearly, audiences pay to hear what they know, but unless they are offered new works or composers, the old classics will remain at the core of performances and the repertoire cannot expand. Marcia Citron, musicologist, suggests one reason for this imbalance:

In the 1800s, women composers typically wrote art songs for performance in small recitals rather than symphonies intended for the performance with an orchestra in a large hall, with the latter being seen as the most important genre for composers; since women composers did not write many symphonies, they were deemed to be not notable as composers.[4]

Whilst this is a valid argument, it cannot excuse the many large-scale works written by women failing to make it into concert performances or, even, why so few small-scale works, including chamber pieces and song cycles, remain unplayed.

Employment for women players also lags behind, with a survey of London orchestras in 2019 identifying that there were more percussionists called Dave than there were female percussionists,[5] and analysis of the two largest orchestras in the United Kingdom indicated that women account for only around 35 per cent of players. Henry Wood, founder of the Promenade Concerts, allowed six women violinists into his orchestra, the Queen's Hall Orchestra in 1913: 'I do not like ladies playing the trombone or double bass, but they can play the violin, and they do'.[6] Some hundred years later women are represented in most of the sections of the orchestra, but still have some way to go before they are equal in number to men.

Life in popular music fares no better, although at first glance there appear to be many women in prominent positions and winning awards. But, in reality, female acts have seen a decline in the top ten spots on the Billboard Hot 100 since the 1990s and analysis of the Billboard Hot 100 artists for w/e 6 August 2021 showed only sixteen of them to be women. With the advent of streaming and access to web-based platforms, it seems surprising that women still lag behind their male counterparts. Lara Baker, a music industry diversity consultant, finds the gap worrying:

> I'd like to see streaming platforms, festivals and radio stations giving more attention to equal representation than they currently do. If you look at any of the major streaming playlists, or radio station playlist, – chances are in many cases you'll find male artists taking up more slots than female artists. They might argue they are reflecting the market and what the consumer or listener wants, but are they? Or are they part of the problem. There is no lack of appetite and lack of talent when it comes to women writing and making music, so clearly what we do have is an old-fashioned and biased industry which needs to work together to achieve better gender balance.[7]

Modern media echoes the publishers of the nineteenth and early twentieth century, who failed to consider the wider audience and put profit before art.

Sexuality and music provide a further example that spans the hundred and fifty years from the 1870s to the present.

> The popular cartoons in *Punch* from the turn of the twentieth century show women musicians as objects to be leered at or ridiculed. The cartoon *The Fair Sex-tett (Accomplishments of the Rising Female Generation)*, drawn in 1875 only three years after the first woman violinist was admitted to the Royal Academy of Music, shows a band of women playing exclusively for a group of men; the cellist adopting the male position considered shocking at the time (with the instrument between her legs), and another playing a strange serpent instrument suggestive of Eve the temptress.[8]

Today women pop stars remain under this cloud in which sexualization is a recurring theme. Lily Allen's controversial video for *Hard Out Here* (2014) illustrates how, despite trying to challenge the view of women musicians as objects, it merely reinforces the case:

> The song's lyrics criticize many of the double standards about sexuality, ambition, and physical appearances faced by women not just in the music industry, but in everyday life. The video is meant as a parody, but Allen's backup dancers – all of them skinny, conventionally beautiful, scantily clad black women – twerk and grind pretty much the same way you'd see in any modern MTV video. Few visual ethics are challenged, and the treatment isn't absurd enough to be satirical. Meanwhile, Allen sings, 'Don't need to shake my ass for you 'cause I've got a brain.' No doubt she meant to empower women and young girls, to put out the message that a female is more than the sum of her parts and in doing so, she denigrates the very women around her whose sexuality is a celebrated part of their livelihood.[9]

Plus ça change, plus c'est la même chose, might seem the inevitable conclusion, but a more positive end to Dora Bright's story would be the words of the singer-songwriter Taylor Swift: 'My hope for the future, not just in the music industry, but in every young girl I meet, is that they all realize their worth and ask for it.'[10]

11 Overview of Major Works

This chapter provides the reader with details of the major works of Dora Bright that are available in print and in Library archives, and also those works where only newspaper reports provide an outline of a lost work. Newspaper reports of the time gave considerable detail and ably demonstrate the breadth, complexity, grace and musicality expressed in Dora Bright's music. So many of her works did not survive her death, very few were ever published and so it is only through third-party handwritten review that much of her opus can be enjoyed. The chapter is not exhaustive, but outlines numerous works, across a number of genres, to demonstrate the quality of the music and also how well they were regarded during Dora Bright's lifetime. Where available, a few bars of the main themes have been included. The works included are:

- *Whither?* (1882)
- *Variations on an Original Theme of Sir G. A. Macfarren for Piano and Orchestra* (1888)
- *Concerto for Piano and Orchestra in A minor* (1888)
- *Romanza and Seguidilla* (1891)
- *Suite of Five Pieces for Piano and Violin* (1891)
- *Quartet for Pianoforte and Strings in D major* (1894)
- *Three Pieces – Berceuse, Liebesleid, Tarantelle* (1895)
- *The Dancing Girl* (1899)
- *The Ballad of the Red Deer* (1904)
- *The Dryad* (1907)
- *The Faun* (1910)
- *Variations for Piano and Orchestra in F major* (1910)
- *The Portrait* (1910)
- *The Abbé's Garden* (1911)
- *In Haarlem There Dwelt* (1912)

- *Poor Pretty Columbine* (1912)
- *Monday's Child* (1912)
- *La Camargo* (1912) – Piano Solo and Orchestral
- *Garrick* (1913)
- *The Colour of Life* (1914)
- *La Danse* (1914)
- *The Waltz King* (1926)
- *Two Pieces* (1934)

Whither? (1882)

Although printed in 1882, the work could have been written some time earlier, and may have been part of a number of works provided to the Royal Academy of Music as part of Dora's application to join the College. The piece is published by a little-known publisher and was possibly paid out of Dora's own pocket. Her next known work, another song, *The Task of the Flower*, did not make it to publication and either she felt it not good enough to publish or, more likely, was financially unable to publish more works at the time.

The song is based on the poem by Henry Wadsworth Longfellow.

I heard a brooklet gushing

I heard a brooklet gushing,
From its rocky fountains near.
Down into the valley rushing,
So fresh and wondrous clear.

I know not what came o'er me,
Nor who the counsel gave,
But I must hasten downward,
All with my pilgrim stave.

Downward and ever farther,
And ever the brook beside.
And ever fresher murmured,
And ever clearer the tide.

Is this the way I was going?
Whither, O brooklet, say!
Thou hast with thy soft murmur,
Murmured my senses away.

What say I of a murmur,
That can no murmur be.
'Tis the water nymphs that are singing,
Their roundelays under me.

Let them sing, my friend,
Let them murmur,
And wander merrily near.
The wheels of a mill are turning
In ev'ry brooklet clear.

Based on Wilhelm Müller's 'Wohin?', translated by Henry Wadsworth Longfellow (1807–1882).

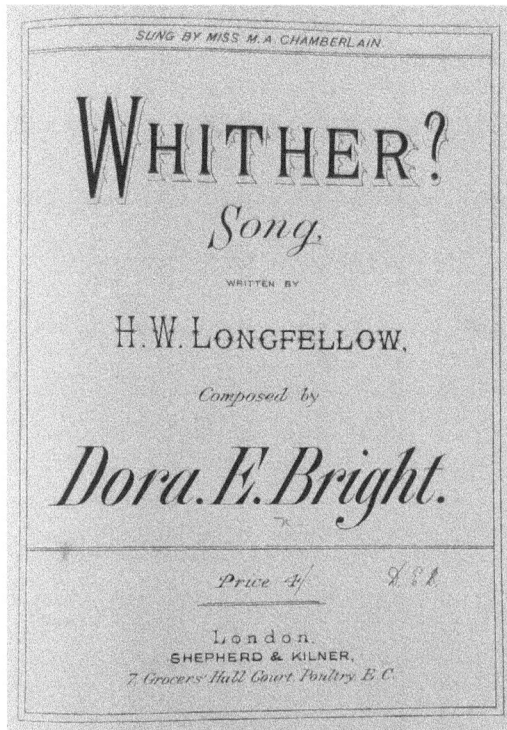

Figure 11.1. Cover of Dora Bright's first published work, *Whither?*

The song consists of five pages and is in three sections. Opening in E major the first two verses are played allegretto and then at bar twenty-two, after a rising arpeggio, moves to C major, marked Plus lentement for the middle two verses. Seven bars of moody incidentals take the work back to E major and at bar thirty-nine the piece returns to the original tempo for the final two verses, ending with a further arpeggio flourish to the final chords marked pianissimo.

Figure 11.2. The first five bars of *Whither?*

Variations on an Original Theme of Sir G. A. Macfarren for Piano and Orchestra (1888/1894)

Said to be the last theme written by Sir G. A. Macfarren, the variations were originally written for piano and orchestra in 1888, whilst Dora Bright was still at the Royal Academy of Music. The piece was first performed at an Academy concert on 17 April 1888:

> The work presented by the pupils at this Concert may be divided into creative and executive. In the former department the most important was a set of Variations for two pianofortes on a theme by the late Sir G. A Macfarren, composed by Miss Dora Bright. In this effort a high degree of musicianship and considerable knowledge of effect are to be found in combination, and as the rendering by the composer and Miss Ethel Boyce was in every respect satisfactory it was exceedingly well received.[1]

It would become a staple work which she would play frequently and it was published in 1894:

> It is undoubtedly a serious composition, the Theme itself being very earnest if not pathetic; but the variations are conceived in a very broad spirit, and are treated in a thoroughly artistic and musician-like manner. In a word, the Duet is not only interesting, but very effective in in performance. Edwin Ashdown Ltd.[2]

The sombre theme is not very remarkable, but Miss Bright has evolved some highly interesting and effective music from it, in which abstract beauty and ingenuity of device are well matched.[3]

Figure 11.3. Opening bars of the first piano part from the four-hand version of *Variations on an Original Theme of Sir G. A. Macfarren*

Concerto for Piano and Orchestra in A minor (1888)

The *Piano Concerto in A minor* was first played at a Royal Academy concert on 25 July 1888 and was very well received by the press. It was Dora Bright's second large-scale orchestral piece and a work of which she was sufficiently proud to ensure it was saved for posterity, by her donation of the full score to the Royal Academy of Music archive. She played it on a number of occasions, and after its success on her German tours she brought it to London and the Crystal Palace Afternoon Concerts, for which she had revised the third movement.[4] It is likely that the work was also played in two-piano format[5] although a copy of this version has not survived, although it has been recreated by Valerie Langfield as part of the publication of the orchestral version on CD.[6]

The full score of the work is held in the Royal Academy of Music archive and is labelled in blue pencil as First Concerto.

The work is in three movements and only 24 minutes in length. The first movement, marked Allegro, is in classical sonata form having two themes, both of which are very appealing with simple attractive melodies.[7]

Figure 11.4. First theme of first movement of *Piano Concerto in A minor* (piano part)

Figure 11.5. Second theme of first movement (piano part)

The second movement is a charming Intermezzo in E major, using a simple rocking theme, which after first being played by the piano is taken up by the orchestra and then developed between piano and orchestra in combination to a fortissimo climax and rapid return to the peaceful, lilting conclusion.

The final movement starts with a brief dialogue between timpani and piano and moves rapidly into a Rondo Tarantella which is brisk and spirited.[8] Bar 150 sees a brief reintroduction of the first theme from the first movement and leads to the return of the Rondo and a virtuosic ending marked 'con amore'.

Figure 11.6. Initial intermezzo six-bar theme – four-hand version of the score

Figure 11.7. Initial three bars with piano theme – four-hand version of the score

After Dora's marriage the work received few outings and the *Fantasia No.2 in G* replaced it in the concerts given in the early 1890s. Had it not been for Dora's foresight in preserving it, no doubt it would have been lost with so many of her other works.

Some comments from the papers at the time give a view of its reception:

> Her concerto is highly meritorious, and is distinctly original while free from the eccentricities and crudities which followers of the modern German school have vainly sought to popularise in England. The opening movement has a touch of Scottish character. It is furnished with effective themes, which are well worked, and Miss Bright proved herself a mistress of the pianoforte by playing with finished execution the difficult passages she has written for the solo instrument. A very pretty intermezzo – too short to be called a movement – was followed by a final movement which did great credit to the composer.[9]

> Miss Dora Bright ... played a pianoforte concerto of her own composition, and won well merited applause both as pianist and composer ... there is a Scottish flavour about the opening movement; its leading theme slightly resembling the air, Charlie is my darling ... it is none the worse for that ... The first movement is followed by a too brief intermezzo, which we should have been glad to hear repeated. The final movement is full of spirit and animation, and brought the work to a triumphant close.[10]

Special mention must be made of Miss Dora Bright's pianoforte Concerto in A minor (M. S.). It displays a creative faculty altogether out of the common, and is full of bright original fancy, and melodious inspiration of a high order. The second subject of the first movement and the succeeding Intermezzo are worthy of almost any living composer. The sparkling Finale is unfortunately rather too short – a fault on the right side, however – and would probably be improved by the interpolation of a sostenuto subject. The orchestral colouring is exquisite throughout. The work was capitally rendered by the gifted composer, who, together with some other lady composers, is destined apparently to negate the generally accepted belief the female mind is destitute of creative power in music.[11]

Romanza and Seguidilla (1891)

One of the few published works includes this item which most likely originates from a *Spanish Suite* written in 1891 for a performance in Cologne that autumn. The Philharmonic Society requested that this work should be included in their 1892 season. Dora Bright refused on the grounds the work was too light for such a prestigious event, and instead wrote her *Fantasia No.2 in G*, which she played with great success on 11 May 1892.

The original work was a five-movement orchestral suite: Prelude, Liebesleid, Seguidillia, Romance and Finale. Whether the work was played in Cologne is not recorded, but in the same autumn Dora published this *Romanza and Seguidilla for Flute and Piano*.

The work was published in the Flute Players' Journal in 1891 and was dedicated to the Welsh flute player, Frederic Griffiths, a student of the Royal Academy and Principal flute of the Royal Italian Opera Orchestra in London. Mr H. A. Chapman played the piece as a flute solo at a concert in Hampstead in May 1891, and was recorded as very successful in the papers.[12]

The piece did not become a standard concert work, but remains in print and under copyright.

Suite of Five Pieces for Piano and Violin (1891)

Written in 1889 the work was first performed in 1890 in London:

The accomplished English pianist, Miss Dora Bright, gave a Chamber Concert at the Prince's Hall, Piccadilly, last week; an interesting feature of the programme being a new Suite for violin and pianoforte from the concert giver's own pen. The suite comprises five movements in all, namely, a Prelude, a Scherzino, a Scotch Air with variations, a Romance, and a Moto Perpetuo. The themes employed in each division of the work are fresh and melodious, and the several movements are marked by considerable constructive skill. Altogether the Suite proved a very genial and interesting production and it was received with manifest favour by the audience.[13]

After a few more outings around London, Dora took the work to her home town of Sheffield in February 1891, hosted by the Sharrow Literacy Society at the Schoolrooms on Psalter Lane. The work was a success with the local audience, and an encore requested.

> ... the piece of the evening – as far as local interest is concerned ... was Miss Bright's suite for violin and piano, and from the commencement of the plaintive prelude through the scherzino, Scotch air with variations and romance, the interest was kept alive not only by the splendid performance of Miss Bright ... but by the music itself, which is written on rather advanced lines. The effort was crowned with success, a vigorous, but fruitless, encore being asked for.[14]

Figure 11.8. Front page of the *Suite*

Figure 11.9. First page of the *Finale*

Quartet for Pianoforte and Strings in D major (1894)

Most likely this work was composed in 1892 and first performed in Germany at a concert in Cologne. Similarly, the work appeared as new in the third of the 1893 Prince's Hall concerts. Then once again this is reported as newly written for the second of Madame Serruys' matinees in Norwich, 1894.

Probably the work went through a number of iterations and refinements over the course of the two years and so at each concert the work was new. Since the quartet(s) has not survived it is impossible to know for sure.

Thanks to the reporting of the *Norfolk News*, there is a very detailed description of the work:

> Undoubtedly the greatest interest of the afternoon centred in the new work specially written for the occasion by Miss Dora Bright. Among English pianists of the day, this talented lady occupies a foremost place, and she has moreover again and again proved her claim to be considered as a composer of remarkable ability. The work presented to the public for the first time on Saturday is a quartet for pianoforte and strings (violin, viola and violincello) ... Miss Bright here displays not only high purposes, but some very notable achievements. As a rule, her utterances are clear and well-defined, her themes, in themselves refined and melodious, are dealt with in a most felicitous manner; of striking harmonic effects there are not a few, and the entire work may be pronounced entirely free from any tinge of intimacy. In truth, the robust nature of much of the music is very extraordinary. The quartet consists of the usual number of movements. The first, an *Allegro Maestoso* in the key of D major, opens with a bold subject, march-like in character, and the whole of this section is full of life and vigour. The second movement takes the form of an air with eight variations. Here the writer reveals considerable power, the air, consisting of eight bars in the key of D minor, being treated with rare musicianly skill. The first variation is in 2–4 rhythm; the second in 6–4 time, with the melody flowing on gracefully; in the third a return is made to 2–4 rhythm, with the theme divided into responsive phrases for the various instruments; variation four is marked *scherzando*, and 6–8 time is employed; the fifth (*vivace*, 2–4 time) finds plenty of employment for the first violin; in number six the air receives simple treatment in the key of tonic major, 2–4 time; in number seven (4–4 time) the pianoforte has an important part; the last variation is in triple time (3–4) *leggerissimo*. Miss Bright has labelled this portion of her work onward. The third movement is entitled a Scherzo, and is in the key of B flat. The Rondo (key of D major), which ends the quartet, contains some very clever writing. It may be guessed that the pianoforte is lovingly provided for, but it cannot be said to the detriment of the other instruments, for the composer has provided each of them with some exceptionally graceful parts ... Great care had evidently been spent upon its preparation, and the result was a thoroughly successful and highly gratifying performance. The appreciation of the audience was shown by an outburst of enthusiastic applause that compelled Miss Bright to come forward to bow her thanks.[15]

Three Pieces – Berceuse, Liebesleid, Tarantelle (1895)

The Liebesleid was orchestrated and first performed on its own at a Henry Wood Promenade Concert on 6 March 1897, and described as 'exceedingly graceful'.[16] 'A very pleasing Liebesleid for orchestra by Miss Dora Bright, a graceful and melodious piece scored in a picturesque and refined manner'.[17]

> Distinctly artistic as these pieces are, they have yet a charm beyond what could have been given them by means of the learning of all the schools: in other words, they are spontaneous, rhythmical, and replete with choicest harmonic combinations. The Berceuese is in the key of G minor, and very pleasant pianoforte music: it reminds us curiously of Chopin's *Andante Spianato*, and having the same tonic and dominant as that piece furthers the illusion. The Liebesleid is in the key of B flat and full of the unique charm which distinguishes the Lady's music. The Tarantella takes us back to G minor, and is distinguished by the restless life and motion which are characteristic of the dance.[18]

> Three pieces for the pianoforte, by Dora Bright, may well be added to the repertory of an average good player. Berceuse looks more difficult than it is, it should be committed to memory; Liebesleid is a tuneful melody; Tarantella is a showy and brilliant example of its popular type.[19]

> These three pieces well sustain the reputation of one of the foremost lady composers. Considerable elaboration has been bestowed on the Berceuse, which, however, the interest of the themes fully justifies. In the Liebesleid, in which the path of love apparently runs through pleasant places, the two-voice parts are effectively treated, and the Tarantella is a brilliant example of its class.[20]

The Dancing Girl (1899)

The play was first performed by the dancer Violet Vanbrugh.[21]

The work was taken up by the drama group, sometime known as Lord Roslyn's Men and was performed at Chatsworth House in 1903 and 1904. Specially requested by King Edward VII in 1904, Dora accompanied the work. Later in 1909, the work was performed in Paris.

The words to the play were written by The Honourable Edith Lyttelton and the play is described here:

The scene is the interior of a temple of Siva, the God of Fate. Namouna, a dancing girl in the temple, is in great distress. She fears that her betrothed Sundrum is deserting her, and she relates to the god how he gave her the most sacred love token – the Tilka – which she is wearing on her brow, and how he also sang to her Star of my Night, is the Tilka on thy brow?, until Ameera with the mocking eyes, came and took him from her. She dances and prays to Siva, to help her and to give Sundrum back to her. The god seems deaf to her entreaties. She stops dancing, and in great anger she picks up the offerings of rice and flings them in the face of the idol, then in terror of what she has done she offers him her necklace, and dances again to conciliate him. Then she begs of him a sign that he will send three cranes across the light of the moon. She listens until she hears the whirring of their wings, counts one, he comes not, two, he comes, yet loves me not; three he loves me – he comes to me; and then she dances in wild ecstasy until Sundrum's voice is heard in the distance. Nearer and nearer comes the sound as Sundrum approaches singing his song –

> Star of my night:
> I am coming through the corn,
> The bird's last homeward flight
> Tells' me the dark is bore.
> Canst thou feel the dark, my heart?
> It covers us till morn –
> The morn when we must part,
> And I go back through the corn.

> Star of my night;
> Is the Tilka on the brow?
> The dark has drowned the light,
> Only my star shines now.
> It is the hour of bliss,
> And I come to pay my vow;
> I come to place my kiss
> 'Neath the Tilka on thy brow.[22]

Namouna the beautiful, dancing to please the idol Siva. Jewels glitter about her arms, her neck, and breast and glint from the folds of her gossamer robes. Will the god not send her lover back to her – the lover who gave her the token she wears on her brow? The dumb god makes no sign. Namouna tears her jewels from her own fair neck, and places them about the neck of Siva, but he hears her not. False god! She will pray to him no more; she will make sacrifice. Her lithe body moves in graceful undulations; her diaphanous draperies seem to fill the air; the diamonds at her breast are flashing everywhere as she whirls. He gives a sign – three cranes shall fly before the moon; Sundrum, the lover, is true and he comes to Namouna, singing.[23]

The work still exists in full and is housed in the Library of the Royal Academy of Dance in London.

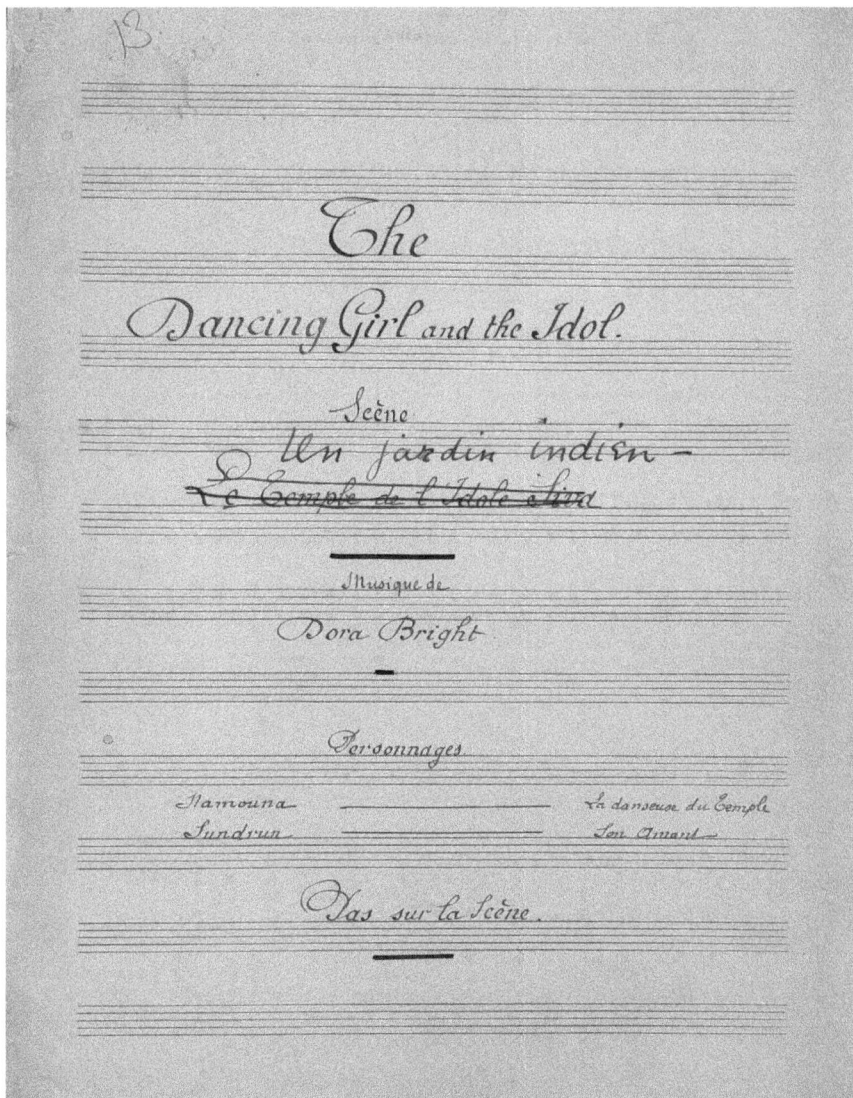

Figure 11.10. Cover page of Dora Bright's working copy of the score of *The Dancing Girl*

Figure 11.11. Page 1 of Dora Bright's working copy of the score of *The Dancing Girl*

Figure 11.12. Page 3 of Dora Bright's working copy of the score of *The Dancing Girl*

The Ballad of the Red Deer (1904)

Dora set this work as two pieces, No. 1 in E flat for low voice and No. 2 in F for high voice.

The text of 'The Ballad of the Red Deer' is simply announced as being written by F. H. Apparently the verses are an allegory, and the moral would seem to be that when you go a-hunting you should not give heed to any stray Earl's daughter who gazes forth from a lattice window, for it is told that of the three knights who rode by he who mounted the castle stair, ne'er more the world shall roam. The song is cast in true ballad form with a refrain which leaves room for the play of the imagination of the listener, and the accompaniment is appropriately simple.[24]

Princes went riding to hunt one day
Into the forest green
As they rode the wall of a castle grey
The Earl's daughter forth did lean

O green is the Oak
And brown is the beech
And red is the red deer, red deer

The Eldest Looked up
Your tresses are fair
But they do not shine as bright
As glistens the coat of the red
Red deer that I shall bring home tonight
The second turned round
O bright are your eyes
But they do not pierce so keen
As the glance of my goshawk that flies to day in the forest green

O green is the Oak
And Brown is the beech
And red is the red deer, red deer

The third he drew rein
O your lips are red
And sweet as the brier rose
Let him hunt who will
But I fain would wed
Up the castle stair he goes

O green is the Oak
And Brown is the beech
And red is the red deer, red deer

The first galloped back with his red deer
The goshawk was borne home
But he who mounted the castle stair
Ne'er more the world shall roam

O green is the Oak
And Brown is the beech
And red is the red deer, red deer

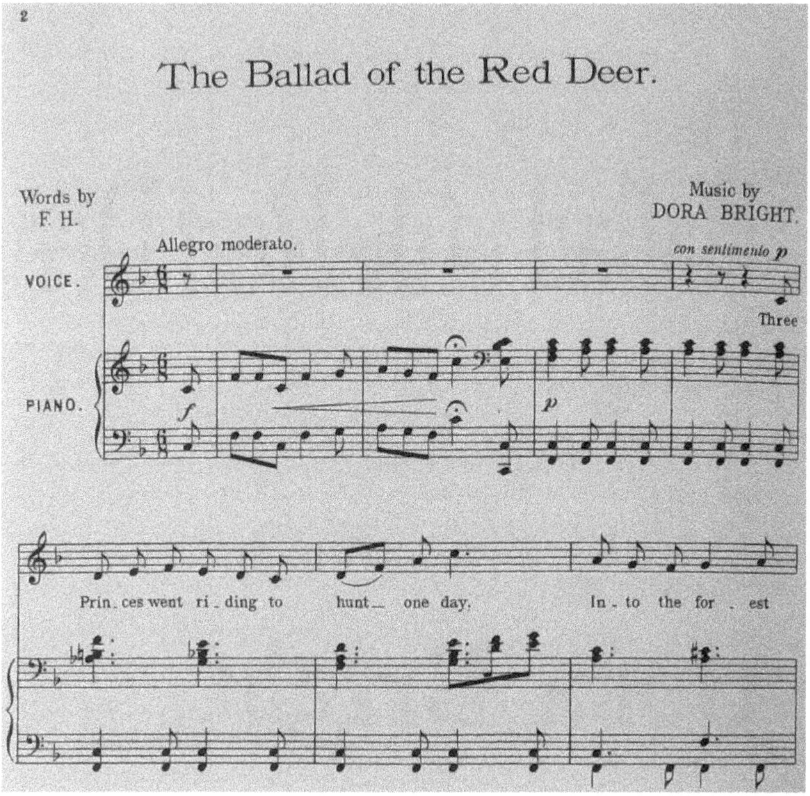

Figure 11.13. Opening bars of the Ballad in F

The Dryad (1907)

Premiered at the Babington New Year's party in 1907, the work went on to be played many times by Adeline Genée and toured America and Australia with her.

> It is only short – there are only two brief scenes, and the whole is over in a half an hour ... In the first scene she comes out of the tree trunk in which she has been imprisoned by jealous Aphrodite. Once a year only is she allowed to see the earth again, and she is on fire with joy at the flowers and the leaves and the sunlight. A still greater joy is in store for her. She meets a shepherd, and he falls in love with her. She tells him, in a language far plainer than his own, though she speaks not a word, her story. He must go away ten years – the tale of years is counted out heavily on flowers that she gathers : and if he will return, still true to her, ten years hence, she will be released and his for ever. A passionate parting and she returns

to her tree-trunk, to wait. The ten years pass, and on an autumn evening she comes out again. Will he come? She is sure of it, and dances with joy. Will he come? She searches for him eagerly, yet still gaily, through the glades. Will he come? Of course he will. She is rippling and blazing with joy. There is his voice. He is singing the old love song. He comes in : and on his arm is a human shepherd-ess, to whom he is singing the song that once was the dryad's. They pace out of sight down the glades, and the dryad, alone with her despair, returns to her tree-trunk, to find that even that is closed against her. She kneels before it, pleading for admittance : she beats on it with her hands, and at last it slowly opens to admit her to its desolate shelter from a world that is yet more desolate. Miss Dora Bright's pastoral fantasy is an interesting thing, partly because in itself it is affecting and charming, partly because it brings together in an unusual way the three arts of music, acting and dancing.[25]

Figure 11.14. Opening bars of Tableau I of the Dryad Pastoral Fantasy

Figure 11.15. Opening bars of Tableau II of the Dryad Pastoral Fantasy

The Faun (1910)

First produced at the Empire Theatre in October 1910, *The Faun* is a fantasy written in one scene, written and composed by Dora Bright.

> The scene is a Tuscan hill village. In the open space outside the west end of the church stands a fine old fountain, and over its wide basin rises the statue of a Faun. Russet and weather-mellowed, he is the very colour of the wall and the houses; and you hardly notice him as you watch the few inhabitants moving lazily about in the sun and Ginestra, the only busy person there, trying in vain to sell them flowers. She has brought a basket from her home somewhere away

there beyond the line of cypresses that runs towards the campo santo, and she is very tired and very sad because no one will buy them. And while she is bathing her face and dipping her flowers in the fountain she sees the Faun, and you see him too. He is leaning against his tree-stump with his pipes to his mouth, taking no notice. Lonely Ginestra finds someone who, if he will not take any notice, at least cannot order her away, and she begins to talk to him, to flirt with him, to dance to him. She dances her very best to him – to music very artfully embroidered on some old simple tune, full of sunlight and girlhood, but with just a touch in it of loneliness and sadness. And the Faun takes no notice. Then she chooses him a rose from her basket, dips it in the fountain and throws it at his feet, reaches up, and pats his red-brown arm. And when she has done that a strange sleepiness comes over her. She lies down by the broad basin of the fountain, falls asleep – and wakes to find the Faun peering into her face, gloating timidly but hotly over its beauty. For the drops of water which sprinkled him from her rose have brought him to life; and half afraid, half glad, half stiff from ages of standing still, and half-drunk with the new joy of motion, he has crept down from his tree-stump to see who this lovely mortal might be. Fauns as we know, are wicked pagans and have only one notion of the proper use of lovely mortal maidens. It is the old battle, the spell of his pipes against her training in virtue; and his pipes with their quaint, dropping little air, prevail over her so far that she dances with him, a mad dance that gets madder and madder, until, just when the danger is nighest the Faun's time of freedom expires. His last effort snaps her belt, and still bearing it in his hand he climbs back to his tree-stump and turns again to stone. But Ginestra, of course, must recover her belt – and her scattered senses; and she must tell the returning villagers all about it and prove the truth of her story by the broken fragments of the Faun's pipe which fell when he snatched her belt away … *The Faun* is a delightful thing; its music always appropriate in colour and rhythm, and its performance enchanting.[26]

Variations for Piano and Orchestra in F major (1910)

Completed in Paris in 1909 and revised in 1910, the work was one produced under the guiding hand of Moszkowski and is one of Dora Bright's later orchestral pieces. The orchestration differs from her *Piano Concerto in A minor*, showing more complexity and depth with much greater use of the orchestra throughout.

The piece starts with a five-note theme on the piano which is repeated to a five-bar phrase, which then provides the basic content around which all the other variations revolve.

Figure 11.16. Initial five-bar theme of *Variations for Piano and Orchestra in F major*

The work contains the following movements and is only 16 minutes long:

Thema – Semplice – Moderato
Variation 1 – Grazioso
Variation 2 – Con Brio
Variation 3 – Andantino
Variation 4 – Tempo di Valse
Variation 5 – Allegretto Tranquillo
Variation 6 – Lento
Variation 7 – Scherzo

The piece is very elegant and makes expressive use of the theme across the variations. After an explosive scherzo finale it ends very quietly and simply with a final motif, reminiscent of the theme in the woodwind and a single piano chord.

Oddly, the theme gives an impression of the Dambuster's theme written by Eric Coates many years later.

There is only one report of the work being performed and this is on BBC radio on 8 April 1934 played by Dora Bright and the BBC Orchestra. However, the Royal Academy of Music holds a number of scores of the Variations and one set is written with French instructions suggesting it may have been performed initially in Paris.

The Portrait (1910)

The Portrait is based on *Pygmalion*, the one-act fantasy play first performed at the Prince of Wales's Theatre in November 1910.

> The theme is sufficiently familiar. A young artist is painting the picture of his life and falls in love with his own creation. While he sleeps, a Spanish dancer, more beautiful on the stage than on the canvas, steps out of the frame and proceeds to make love to the sleeping artist. Before he awakes she is startled by the sound of voices, and returns to the frame, while the painter, persuaded that the whole thing has been a dream, goes off disconsolate to supper.[27]

The Abbé's Garden (1911)

Written for a benefit concert for the Invalid Kitchens of London and first played at the Globe Theatre in London on 31 March 1911, the piece is a wordless play based on an incident in Guy de Moupassant's *Clair de Lune* with the music written by Dora Bright.

> As in *L'Enfant Prodigue*, the story is of a flight from home and of the pathos of return. In this case the runaway is a girl, the niece of an Abbé whose asceticism blinds him to the fact that the girls are susceptible beings, especially when soldiers and artists hover outside his garden gate. The awakening of the Abbé and his reconciliation with the girl is the finale of the work.[28]

In Haarlem There Dwelt (1912)

First performed at a charity matinée given in aid of the Foundation Fund of the Three Arts Club at His Majesty's Theatre, London, on 21 May 1912. The music has not survived.

> An altogether charming little Dutch idyll which Dora Bright has taken from a short story by Pieter Van De Meer. The scene takes place in a delightful Dutch interior, with the quaint tilings and suggestions of characteristic freshness and cleanliness, and the story is concerned with a love episode, which comes across the grey life of Minna, the wife of Gerritt. Gerritt neglects Minna, scarcely ever speaks to her in fact, and had not even wept when their only child died. Polman on the other hand, appreciates what Gerritt values but lightly; and Minna and he fall in love with each other, and

eventually resolve to go away together. It is here that Gerritt's very indifference proves to be a sort of binding chain between himself and his wife. 'Before you leave me for ever', he says, 'will you kindly sew on a couple of buttons to my waistcoat? You will find them in the left-hand pocket.' Minna in short, finds the bonds of wedded life too strong, and the memory of her dead child too sacred, to yield to her passion for Polman, and the final Picture shows her quietly reconciled to her weary life by the side of her indifferent husband … The music by Dora Bright is melodious and illuminative … and its reappearance, one hopes, is only a matter of time.[29]

Poor Pretty Columbine (1912)

First produced at the Kilburn Empire on 3 June 1912, the work is a one-act wordless dance-play with a cast of four, each representing a flower. The music has not survived.

Poor Pretty Columbine has gone to Flowerland; and in a pretty stage-set depicting a regular galaxy of floral beauty she tells how Columbine is unsuccessfully wooed by Monkshood to the undoing of her own happiness with Sweet William. It happens that Monkshood, being deeply jealous of her preference for Sweet William, by some means or another induces that capricious young gentleman to transfer his affections to Marigold, who is supposed to be a richer match, and the end finds poor, pretty Columbine, after some pathetic assumed gaiety, entirely overcome by misery. It is a pretty story, allowing for some clever and dainty dances, and its pantomimic representation upon the stage is eloquent enough to allow one to dispense with the synopsis which is given away with the programme … Miss Dora Bright is melodious and attractive throughout, notwithstanding a suggestion of reminiscence in Columbine's final dance; and, with the added advantage of particularly pretty costumes, there should be no apparent reason why Poor Pretty Columbine should not delight audiences for some considerable time to come.[30]

Monday's Child (1912)

Monday's Child was first performed at a matinée at the Royal Court Theatre in London at 2.30pm on 28 December 1912. The original manuscript for the work is retained by the Royal Academy of Dance. The manuscript is complete and penned by Dora Bright for two pianos.

To arrange the old nursery proverb of Monday's Child as a ballet introducing seven characteristic solo dances for children was a capital idea; and it has been cleverly carried out by Miss Morris, who has invented the movements and dances, and by Miss Dora Bright, who is responsible for some pretty and tuneful music. In this quaint little dancing scene, Miss Morris appears as an early Victorian lady, surrounded by a group of children representing the seven different temperaments associated in nursery proverbs with the seven days of the week. Monday's child is fair of face; so the little maid who represents her pirouettes with childish vanity before a tiny mirror. Tuesday's child is full of grace; and so the ballet goes on through the other days of the week to Saturday's child who having far to go, appropriately appears in the national dances of far-off lands, while the child who is born on the Sabbath morn is represented with white lilies. Following the pretty fancy, we have a series of selected dances … a bagatelle (Beethoven), in which all the children move with swift rhythmic grace about their instructress, their pretty dresses being of just the right design for showing off the symmetry of slim childish limbs.[31]

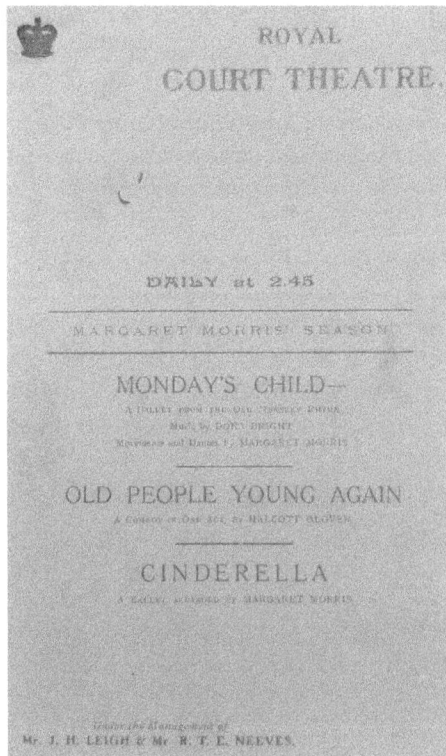

Figure 11.17. Front cover of programme for *Monday's Child*

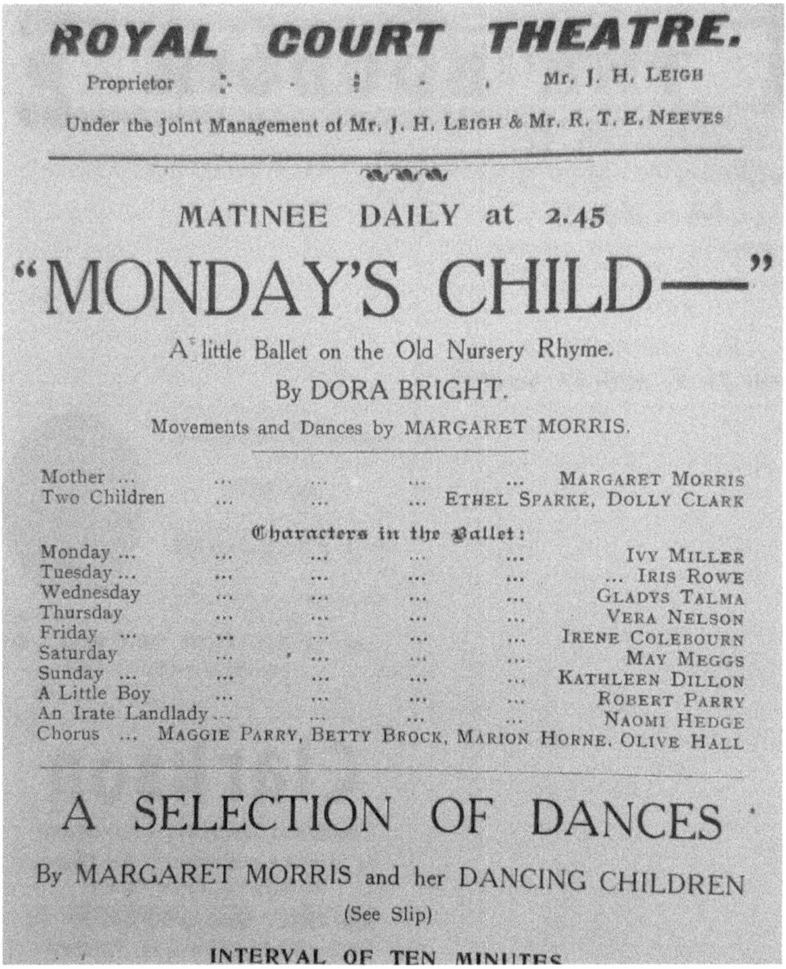

ROYAL COURT THEATRE.

Proprietor ... ... Mr. J. H. Leigh

Under the Joint Management of Mr. J. H. Leigh & Mr. R. T. E. Neeves

MATINEE DAILY at 2.45

"MONDAY'S CHILD—"

A little Ballet on the Old Nursery Rhyme.

By DORA BRIGHT.

Movements and Dances by MARGARET MORRIS.

| Mother ... | ... | ... | ... | ... | MARGARET MORRIS |
| Two Children | ... | ... | ... | ETHEL SPARKE, DOLLY CLARK |

Characters in the Ballet:

Monday ...	...	...	...	...	IVY MILLER
Tuesday ...	...	...	...	...	... IRIS ROWE
Wednesday	...	...	...	...	GLADYS TALMA
Thursday	...	...	...	...	VERA NELSON
Friday ...	...	...	...	...	IRENE COLEBOURN
Saturday	...	...	.	...	...	MAY MEGGS
Sunday ...	...	...	...	...	KATHLEEN DILLON
A Little Boy	...	...	...	...	ROBERT PARRY
An Irate Landlady ...	...	...	...	NAOMI HEDGE
Chorus ...	MAGGIE PARRY, BETTY BROCK, MARION HORNE. OLIVE HALL

A SELECTION OF DANCES

By MARGARET MORRIS and her DANCING CHILDREN

(See Slip)

INTERVAL OF TEN MINUTES

Figure 11.18. Programme outline for *Monday's Child*

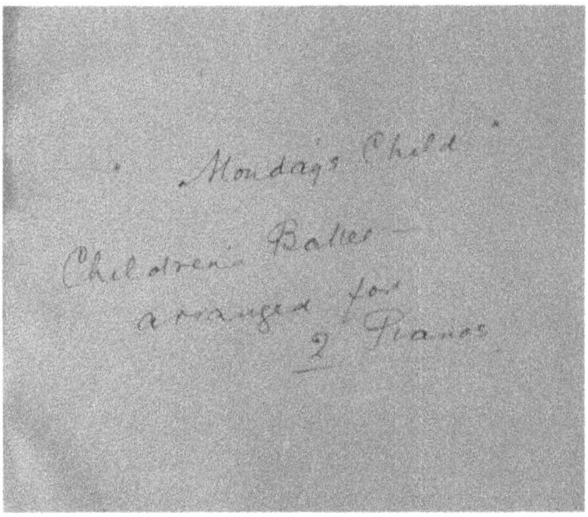

Figure 11.19. Front cover of the manuscript to *Monday's Child*

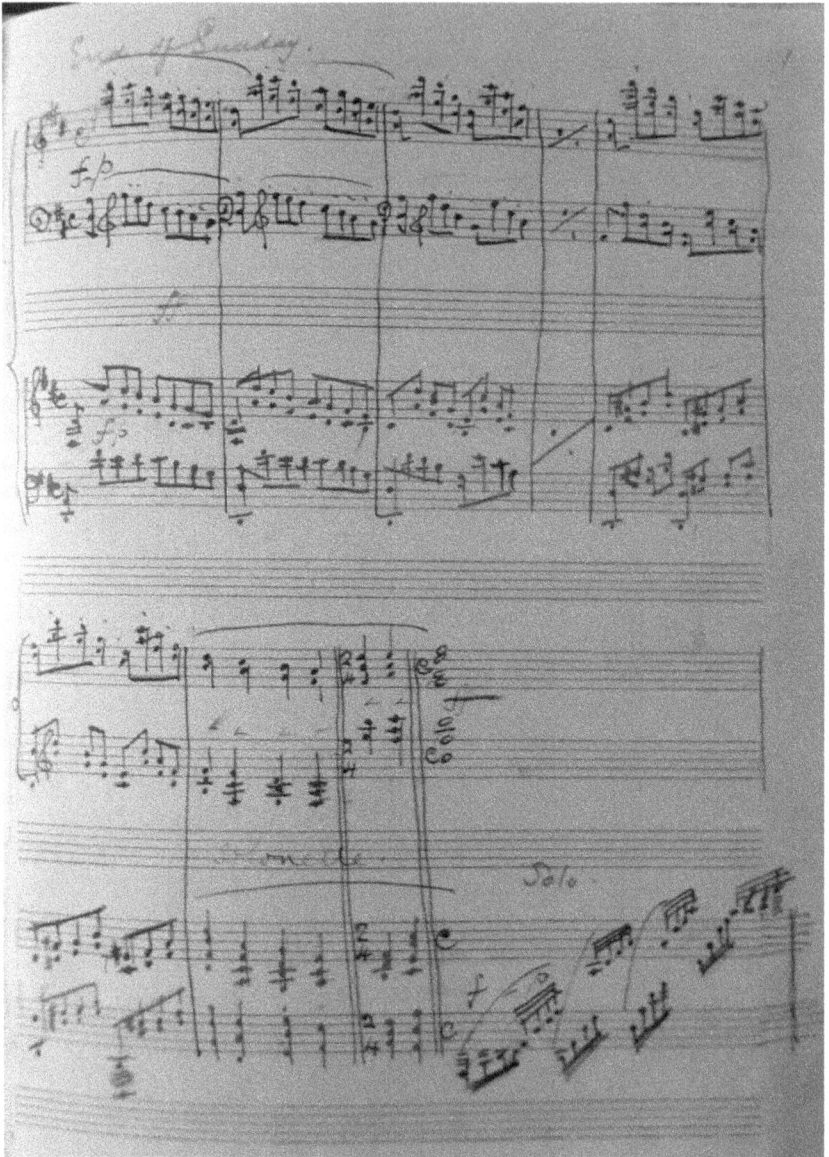

Figure 11.20. Excerpt for the end of Sunday from the manuscript to *Monday's Child*

La Camargo (1912)

Marie Camargo was a celebrated eighteenth-century ballet dancer. With her interest in the history of ballet and the careers of her great predecessors, Adeline Genée approached the celebrated scenery designer, C. Wilhelm, to help her produce a ballet on the life of the great Camargo. Genée asked her good friend Dora Bright to write the music and in May 1912, the work was first performed at the Coliseum. The work was a huge success and Genée took it with her on tour to America and to Australia.

The original music, written by Dora Bright, was orchestrated by the composer A. W. Kettleby for a substantial sized orchestra consisting of piano, Mustel organ (improved harmonium), first and second violins, viola, cello, bass, B flat clarinets, B flat cornets, trombone, bassoon, flute, oboe, horns in F and timpani. Following the success of the music Dora Bright published a piano reduction of the work.

The ballet illustrates an incident in the career of La Camargo, the favourite court dancer of Louis XV, the action taking place in her boudoir. She is trying on a new costume, and, while her maid, Felicie, and Toinette, the costumiere, are expressing their admiration, a note is brought in, the contents of which causes La Camargo great annoyance. She feels that the writer has insulted her, and determines to show the note to the king. Just then a message is brought to La Camargo that an old woman wishes to see her. This is Madame Laroche, who had been a great friend of La Camargo in the days before she became famous. The old woman is in deep distress, and successfully enlists the great dancer's sympathy on behalf of her son Gaston, who had struck an officer. This officer happened to be the Comte D'Aurillac, the writer of the insulting note to La Camargo, who had, in the hearing of Gaston, now a private in the King's Guards, made some insulting remarks about La Camargo, which so enraged Gaston that he struck the officer, and was thereupon arrested. La Camargo calls for the sergeant of the guard, who chances to be her maid's sweetheart, and asks him to bring in the prisoner. He demurs at this, it being irregular. Accustomed to instant obedience, La Camargo alters the request to a command, and reluctantly the sergeant does as he is told. While Gaston and his mother are talking with La Camargo, the king is announced. They are hurried into an adjoining room and Louis enters. La Camargo proceeds to show him a new dance. The king, delighted, asks her what gift he can offer her. She asks him to sign a pardon for Gaston, but the king shakes his head. This is no affair with which she should concern herself. Hiding her disappointment she again begins to dance, this time with the king as partner. So delighted is he that she again ventures to ask for his signature, at the same time showing him the insulting note she has received. The king is incensed at the officer's conduct, seizes a pen, and signs the pardon. He takes leave of La Camargo, who triumphantly hands over the pardon to Gaston and his mother. Overcome with gratitude, they would pour blessings on her, but she dismisses them.

Left alone, she recalls the old happy days with Gaston, the playmate of her youth, and would call him back to her, but feels how futile that would be, and, with a deep sense of depression, realizes she is a lonely woman amid the glittering splendour of a Court.[32]

Figures 11.21 to 11.25 show the opening of the piano reduction produced and published by Dora Bright and the comparative opening bars for a selection of the instrumental parts.

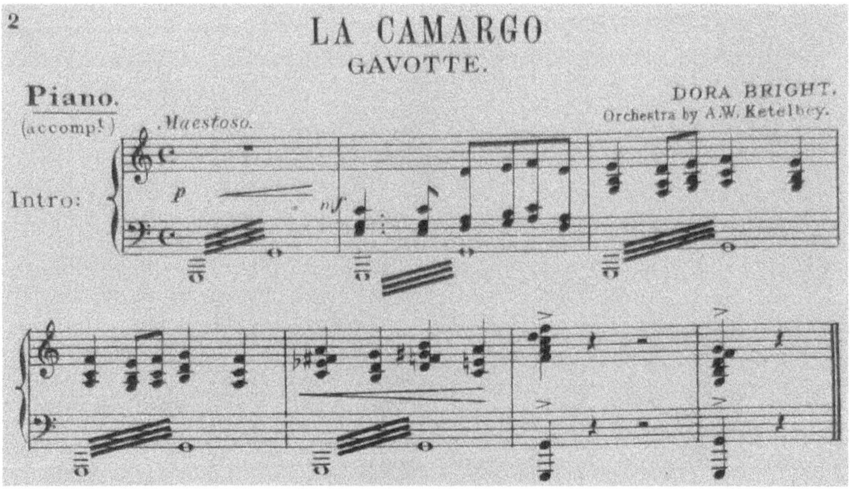

Figure 11.21. Opening bars of the Gavotte for the piano from the orchestral version

Figure 11.22. Opening bars of the Gavotte for the violin from the orchestral version

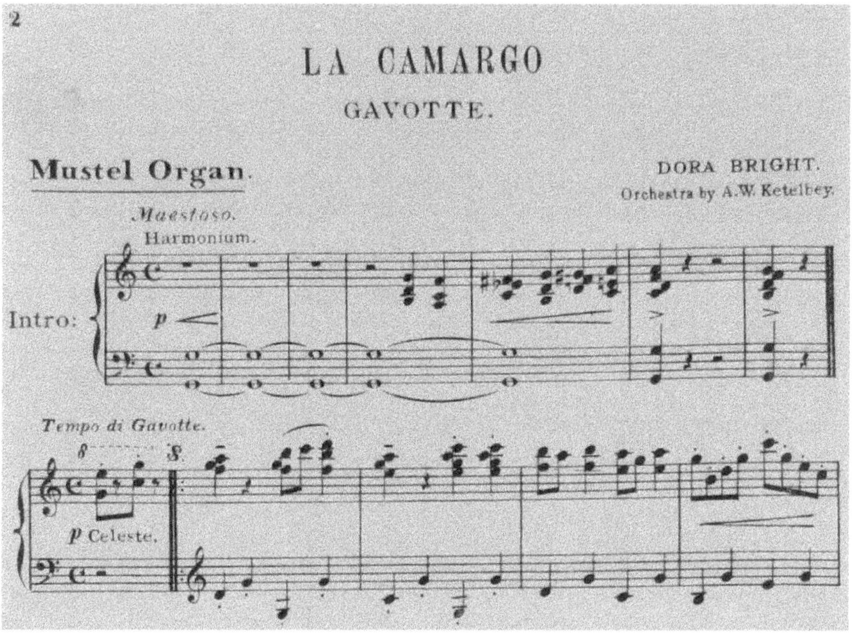

Figure 11.23. Opening bars of the Gavotte for the organ from the orchestral version

Figure 11.24. Opening bars of the Gavotte for the clarinet from the orchestral version

Figure 11.25. Opening bars of the Gavotte for the horns from the orchestral version

Garrick (1913)

This is a play written by Max Pemberton on the subject of the great actor Garrick, in eight scenes. The music, specially written by Dora Bright, no longer survives.

The curtain rises on the Battle Scene in Richard III on the stage at Drury Lane, with Garrick in the character of Richard. Other scenes take place in one of the boxes at Drury Lane Theatre, in a corridor at Drury Lane Theatre, in Garrick's dressing-room, and in Marylebone Fields, which is the scene of a duel between Garrick and Lord Fareleigh.[33]

The Colour of Life (1914)

The score, titled *Danses des Couleurs*, is retained in the Library at the Royal Academy of Dance.

The Colour of Life, a dainty dance poem by Captain Janesen, with music by Dora Bright, specially written for Madame Karina ... The accomplished dancer appears as Blanche, called the Fairy Flower, to whose charms while dancing a passer-by quickly capitulates. The dances typify various emotions. Innocence is garbed in white; modesty in pink; passion in orange; jealousy in yellow; sorrow in black. In the lighter of these Madame Karina dances like a joyous nymph on a May morning, and in the more serious her miming is always expressive and graceful. Her associates, as a passer-by and friend of whom she is jealous, are both good.[34]

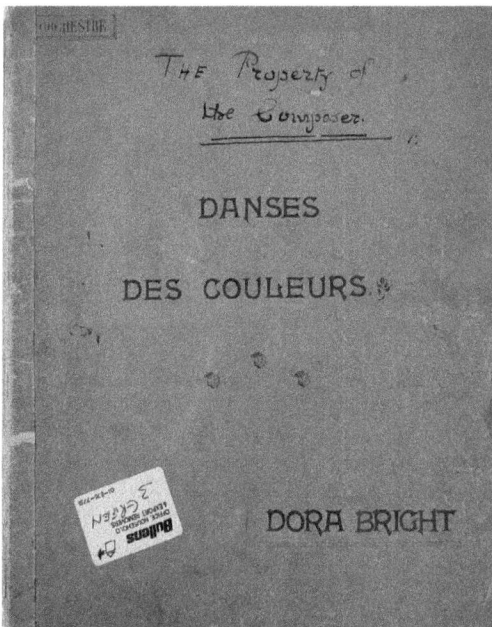

Figure 11.26. Outer cover of the composer's copy of the *Colour of Life* orchestral score

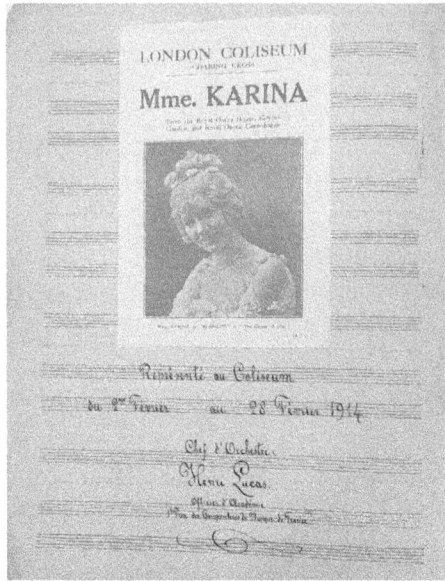

Figure 11.27. Presentation page of the *Colour of Life* orchestral score

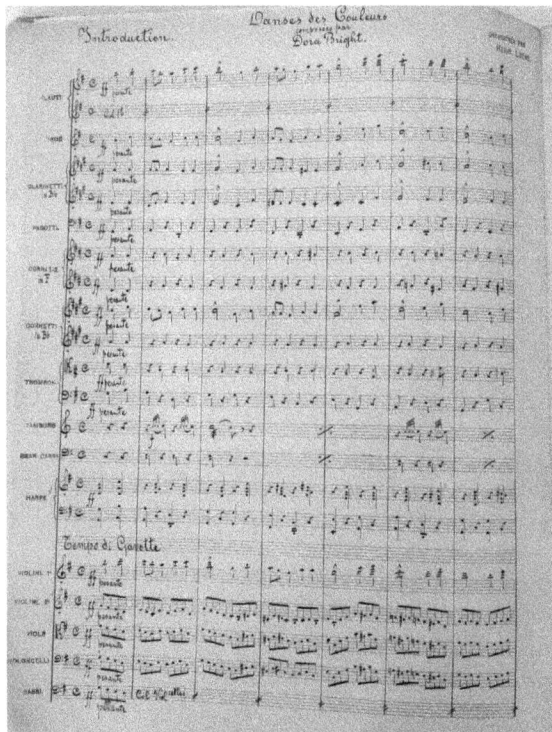

Figure 11.28. First page of the Introduction from the *Colour of Life* orchestral score

La Danse (1914)

First performed at the Metropolitan Opera House in New York as part of Adeline Genée's 1912 tour of America. Subsequently premiered in London as part of the farewell tour of 1914. Finally danced at the Coliseum theatre, London as part of her final season.

> *La Danse* tells the story of dancing from 1710 to 1845. It begins with the Prévost; then come Camargo, Sallé, Guimard, Taglioni; and it is Genée who impersonates all these dear dead women. From *passepieds* and *chaconnes*, we come to gavottes and minuets; we see the introduction of the Valse, *Hons d'Arlequin*; and it is Genée who is dancing them all. From the stateliness of the Court of Louis XIV, we see the dance growing freer and gayer; and it is Genée who illustrates all the changes, starting with the haughty Prévost (and who were more-haughty than this resuscitated Prévost?) and ending with the absolute Genée in the mischief and thistledown lightness of the Columbine, who teases Pierrot. We listen to the music of Lull and Rameau, Guetry and Mozart, Gluck, Chopin, and Johann Strauss; and it is Genée who turns it all to movements, making it music for the eye. The ballet has its historical value; in its pretty Watteau landscape it revives long-dead graces and amenities. But, best of all, it shows more of the range of the great artist who dances it, and allows for the exercise of more, perhaps, of her personal charm – the charm that makes her beloved as admired – than any other ballet in which Mlle. Genée has appeared.[35]

ADELINE GENEE

World-Famed Danseuse

Assisted by M. VOLININ and CORPS DE BALLET

Mr. C. J. M. Glaser, Conductor   Management of R. E. Johnston

PROGRAM "LA DANSE" An Authentic Record by MLLE. GENEE

of Dancing and Dancers Between the Years 1710 and 1841.   Music of Each Period Compiled and Arranged by Dora Bright.

PRELUDE, "OLD PAVANE AND PASSACAILLE".................(Died 1750) J. F. Rebel

TABLEAU I—MADEMOISELLE PREVOST

DANCES

PASSEPIED, From the Ballet "Triomphe de l'Amour".................................(1663) J. B. Lully
CHACONNE, From "Le Menage de Molière".................................(1663) J. B. Lully

Danced by MLLE. GENEE

PARAPHRASE on Rameau's "Rigaudon"...Dora Bright

Corps de Ballet

FRANÇOISE PREVOST was almost the earliest of the great dancers and the teacher of the brilliant "CAMARGO." Noverre said, "Composers write Passepieds because Mlle. Prevost dances them with such fluent elegance." She became intensely jealous of "La Camargo," and even joined an intrigue to harm her. Finally, when Mlle. de Camargo and Mlle. Salle became the idols of the Parisian public, Prevost could not bear a diminished popularity and retired.

TABLEAU II—MLLE. DE CAMARGO

DANCES

(a) Gavotte in F...Padre Martini
(b) "Rigaudon"...(1683) J. P. Rameau

(First Performance in 1760)
Danced by MLLE. GENEE and Mons. Volinin

CORELLIS CHACONNE, with Variations....................................(1653) Dora Bright

Corps de Ballet

MLLE. de CAMARGO, daughter of a dancing master, was born in Brussels. At the age of ten the Princess de Ligne offered to pay all expenses for her education as a dancer, and she became a pupil of Françoise Prevost. At sixteen, she gained an incredible success in "Les Caracters de la Danse." This so enraged her teacher that she relegated her to the first row of the ballet. One evening Dumoulin, the famous male dancer, failed to appear, when the orchestra struck up his music for the "Danse du Diable." Before anyone could intervene Mlle. de Camargo sprang to the front of the stage and executed a brilliant, improvised version of the dance, to the amazement and enthusiasm of the audience.

After this crowds fought at the doors of the Opera House for a sight of her. She was the first dancer to introduce the "entrechat" (the crossing of the feet while springing in the air) in 1730. She was a great court favorite, where her brilliance of achievement and spontaneous gaiety were alike admired, but in her private life there was a touch of melancholy about her. She retired definitely in 1741, greatly honored and respected.

TABLEAU III—MADEMOISELLE SALLE

DANCES

TAMBOURIN AND MUSETTE...(1683) Jean Philipe Rameau
COLINETTE...(1782) Gretry

Danced by MLLE. GENEE

OLD BRETON AIR (for strings).
SERENADE—"Don GIOVANNI"...Mozart

Orchestra

MARIE DE SALLE, a contemporary of La Camargo, inspired an enthusiasm verging on idolatry. Crowds of impassioned admirers of her art having paid dearly for their places, had usually to fight for standing room when she appeared. When dancing for a charity at His Majesty's Theatre, London, as she made her final curtsy, purses of gold and jewels were thrown at her feet. On this memorable evening the receipts were £8,000 ($40,000.00).

Salle was the first dancer to discard the rigid ballet costume, and to appear in simple Greek draperies, and with no head ornaments. She was also one of the first to combine dancing with expressive gesture (pantomime) which, strangely enough, was—at the time—more appreciated in England than in France.

JEAN BAPTISTE LULLY was the Court "Master of Music" to Louis XIV. He began life as a kitchen scullion to Mlle. de Montpensier, then was later in the Princess' private band. He became a great favorite of the King, who loaded him with favors—principally on account of his entertaining powers, but he was a great scholar in his art, nevertheless.

TABLEAU IV—MLLES. GUIMARD, ALLARD and MONS. DUPREZ

PAS DE TROIS-PANTOMIME and ALLEGRO, from "Les Petits Riens"..............................Mozart
MLLE. GENÉE, Mons. Volinin and Mlle. Schmolz

MENUETTO IN "A"..Luigi Boccherini
Danced by Corps de Ballet

GAVOTTE IN "G" from "Paris and Helen"..C. von Gluck
Orchestra

Gluck was Singing Master to Marie Antoinette in Vienna, before her marriage to Louis XVI, and followed his patroness to Paris, where all his most famous works were produced.

MADELEINE GUIMARD, the most illustrious dancer since Salle and Camargo, was a very interesting personality. She had enormous influence at Court (Louis XVI and Marie Antoinette). Her sumptuous hotel was close to the Palace, and her fetes were attended by princes of the blood, noblemen of the court and presidents of the Parliament. She took a mischievous delight in fixing her receptions on days when there were royal functions, that the latter (which was invariably the case) might be altered to suit her. Notwithstanding all this, she was intensely charitable, and always exchanged the Prince of Soubise's annual gift of jewels into money that she might give to the poor. The Revolution, which ruined so many, ruined "La Guimard." After experiencing all the joys and splendors she died at 73, almost in want.
Mozart was barely mentioned for his Ballet, but he managed to gain a few guineas to pay his journey to seek a place as organist.

TABLEAU V—DEBUT DE LA VALSE

FANTASIE on Waltz Themes..Strauss
Orchestra

WALTZ. Promotionen...Johann Strauss
Illustrated by MLLE. GENÉE and Mons. Volinin

The Valse was danced for the first time during the Revolution, brought from Germany in a Tyrolean form, but it was actually developed through the agency of the Walz-Meister, Johann Strauss, to its present shape in the years 1826-28, up to 1860.

ORCHESTRA—Who is Sylvia...Schubert
Das Fischermädchen...Meyerbeer
Du Bist Wie Eine Blume...Schumann
LIEDER OHNE WORTE...(18..) Mendelssohn
Danced by Mlle. Peters, Mortimer, Pruzina
Illustrating Lucile Graham andFanny Cerrito and Carlotta Grisi

TABLEAU VI—MADEMOISELLE MARIE TAGLIONI

PRELUDE—(a) Mazurka...(18..) Frederic Chopin
(b) Valse...(18..) Frederic Chopin
Danced by MLLE. GENÉE

Marie Taglioni, born at Stockholm, of an Italian father and Swedish mother, made her first appearance in Vienna. Her success in all ballets arranged by her father was immediate, but in the Sylphide she was unrivalled. The Queen of Wurtemberg was her devoted friend, and notwithstanding her overpowering success, she remained sweet, simple and reserved.
NOTE—There were two Marie Taglionis, aunt and niece; I represent the niece, daughter of Paul Taglioni, Balletmaster of the Opera House in Berlin, who wrote "La Sylphide" for his daughter. She married a Furst, Windisch-Gratz, and died in Vienna in 1891. Another of the famous Pas de quatre was Lucile Grahn, like myself a Dane by birth, and whose acquaintance I made when I danced at the Opera in Munich, where she died only a few years ago. Carlotta Grisi died in Italy seven years ago; Fanny Cerrito being the only surviving one living at Passy, near Paris.

ADELINE GENÉE.

TABLEAU VII—THE FAMOUS PAS DE QUATRE (1846)

BALLADE, from the Ballet "Coppelia"..Leo Delibes

INTERMISSION

PART II.

OVERTURE—"Merry Wives of Windsor"....................................Nicolai
Orchestra

Meyerbeer's
"ROBERT LE DIABLE"
(Divertissement)

Bertram, an Evil Spirit..Henry Miller
Robert, Duke of Normandy...M. Volinin
Helena (Superior Nun)..MLLE. GENÉE
And Corps de Ballet
The Interpolated Numbers Composed by C. J. M. Glaser

STORY OF "ROBERT LE DIABLE"

Bertram, an evil spirit, doomed to wander the earth, leads Robert, Duke of Normandy, his illegitimate son, who is an exile into Sicily, where he is affianced to Isabella, the King's daughter. But the marriage is prevented, and Robert, persuaded by Bertram, wishes to try black magic to restore his bride to him.
Bertram leads him to a ruined cloister, where he resuscitates the nuns. They try to seduce him by wine, by play and by love. In the last Helena, the most beautiful of them, succeeds, and gives him the cypress-branch, a talisman by which he may enter his bride's chamber unchallenged.
This eventually happens, but overcome by Isabella's tears and appeal to his honor, he breaks the talisman and is seized by the now awakened soldiers.

"SOUTHERN ROSES"...Strauss
Orchestra

"PAS DE DEUX"
I. Adagio...M. Hauser
II. Mazurka..F. Chopin
III. Butterflies..A. Steinke
Mons. Volinin and Mlle. Schmolz
POLKA COMIQUE, from "Les Millions d'Arlequin"....R. Drigo
MLLE. GENÉE and Mons. Volinin

Figure 11.29. Pages from the souvenir 'program' to *La Danse* from Genée's 1914 tour of America (Author's collection)

The Waltz King (1926)

When Lilac Time brought Schubert and his music on the stage, it was prophesised that other composers' lives would be encompassed in semi-operatic form … and Mr Frank Stayton, the well-known dramatist, has just put the finishing touch to Johann Strauss, under the title Waltz King. Miss Dora Bright, next to Dame Ethel Smyth our most distinguished woman-composer, has woven the score from Strauss's wealth of waltzes, through which a transcription of The Blue Danube will run as a leit-motif.[36]

Miss Dora Bright has written for a new opera called The Waltz King … The opera deals with the life of Johann Strauss, and many of his melodies are encompassed in the score.[37]

The Webber-Douglas Theatre production of the Waltz King was well worth its transference to the Ambassadors … I am relieved to find a Viennese-flavoured musical entertainment on tasteful and utterly unpretentious lines … The Waltz King has been devised by Miss Dora Bright, who not only is as adept at arranging Strauss waltzes for Virtuoso pianists but composes excellent music on her own account.[38]

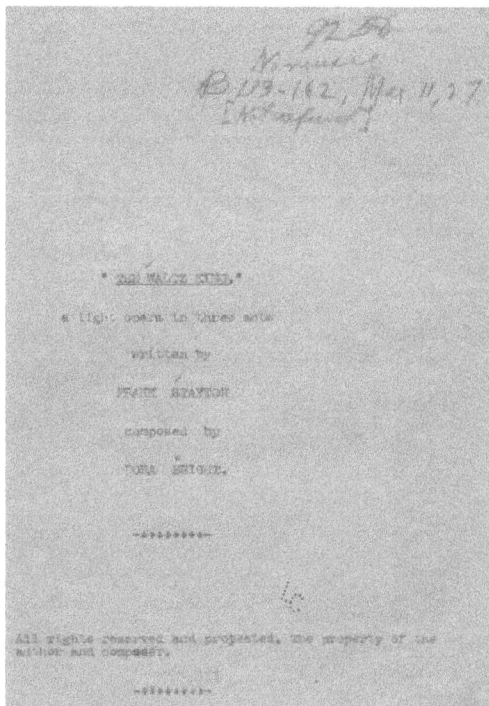

" THE WALTZ KING."

(The story is purely fiction, and disregards all facts.)

Johann Strauss, Senior.
Mme Strauss.
Johann, their son.
Johannes Brahms.
Baron Josef von Auerbach.
Hiram van Soutter.
Herr Tannhauser.
Herr Kinzler, a banker.
Louise.
Hetty.
Freda.
Lily.

Act I.   Garden of the Strauss' villa at Sommandorf, near Vienna.
Act 2.   Johann's studio in Vienna.
Act 3.   .... on the steps of the opera House, Vienna.

Time: the eighteen-fifties.

A few months elapse between each act.

The author apologizes for taking liberties with the lives of famous people.

ACT I.

A charming scene. Backcloth shows glimpse of river, with lovely garden in foreground. Formal hedge, broken R. & L., runs from R. to L. L., a wing of the villa, with steps descending from first floor. R., another wing of house, with open french-windows leading into a living room. Paved floor-cloth. Some seats, a table. Atmosphere of summer. Time: late afternoon.

No.1. Overture.

No. 2. Some students enter, one at a time, look round as though searching for someone - during introduction, and finally break into song.

No.2.

STUDENTS   Are you there, Mister Strauss?
We have come to your house
      To beg you to join us in fit celebration!
Master great, it is late,
Pray do not desitate,
      Come down and accept our polite invitation!
A surprise we devise,-
Come with us, Master wise,-
      The tavern is open, and, if you are willing,
'Tis our right to invite
You as guest for to-night,
      To pay for the wine that your glass will be filling.

(Enter Freda, from stairs: a pretty serving-maid. Quite young.)

FREDA   What do you want? Mister Strauss is asleep,
          He has dined, he has wined, he is full!
STUDENTS Will you tell him he has an appointment to keep?
          And we promise he shall not be dull!
FREDA   Mister Strauss is too old to go drinking with you -
STUDENTS   Mister Strauss is too great, too grow old.
FREDA   But I may not disturb him...oh, what shall I do?
STUDENTS   Do nothing but do as you're told!

(ff)   Are you there, Mister Strauss? etc.

(Madame Strauss enters from stairs. A charming, sympathetic woman of 47.)

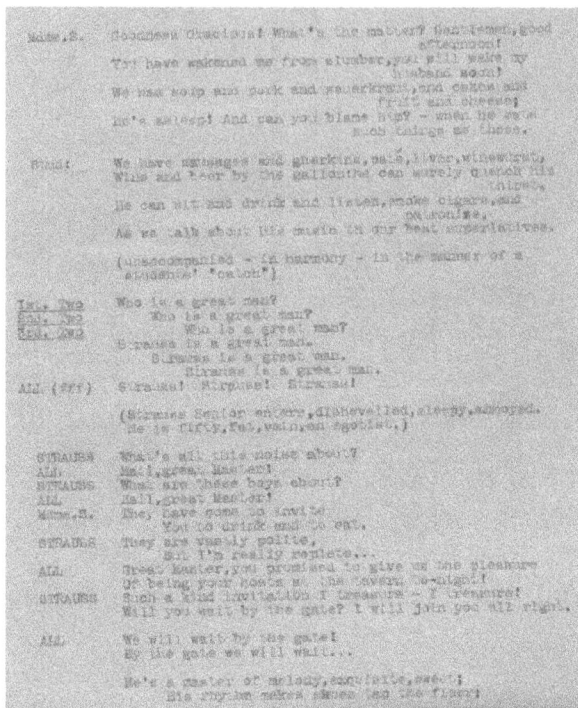

Figures 11.30–11.33. First four pages of the libretto for *The Waltz King* (only surviving copy)

Two Pieces (1934)

These works were published in 1934 as a set for cello or violin and piano. They are included here as two of the few works which remained in the repertoire after Dora Bright's death in 1951. The eminent cellist, Catherine Wilmers, included these items in a number of her concerts and provides her own perspective on the two short pieces.

Das Fischermädchen

Das Fischermädchen is a delightful short gem for cello and piano lasting 2 minutes. There is a two-bar pizzicato introduction and then the theme is introduced. It returns thrice more thus making the piece easy to listen to with an easily discernible theme to pick out! The third appearance is in the piano with a pizzicato interlude for the cello. It makes a perfect encore piece! (Catherine Wilmers – Cellist)

Das Fischermädchen

A Melody by MEYERBEER

Arranged by
DORA BRIGHT

Figure 11.34. *Das Fischermädchen* pizzicato opening and theme in the cello part

Polka à la Strauss

Polka à la Strauss for Cello and Piano was one of only four works by Dora Bright ever to have been recorded.

> Audiences love to hear the Polka à la Strauss. It is light music, beautifully composed with an important and equal piano part taking over the theme in the middle section, with large chords sometimes spread arpeggiando style and sometimes played simultaneously. There is soft delicate writing for both instruments. The piece allows room for the cellist to be free and take their time at several points in this charming miniature lasting three minutes. (Catherine Wilmers – Cellist, personal communication)

Figure 11.35. *Polka à la Strauss* opening with theme in the cello part

Figure 11.36. Middle section with theme taken over by the piano

Appendix 1: Catalogue Raisonné 2021

Catalogue Raisonné: Dora Bright (1862–1951)

The preliminary catalogue of works by Dora Bright was prepared by 'Maj-Britt Peters'(?) on the basis of the Pazdérek 1904 catalogue. This was updated by Silke Wenzel in a paper under the 'Musik und Gender im Internet' project undertaken by the Hochschule für Musik und Theater Hamburg, and also by Sophie Fuller in her PhD thesis on women composers.

Further work reviewing library catalogues from across the globe, lists of works in articles and news sites, as well as contemporary websites and research, are incorporated into this listing. Items not in the previous catalogue(s), i.e. new works, and new information regarding each work is highlighted in italic. Existing copies of works have been identified and are underlined.

Revised and updated by Anthony Bilton, November 2022.

Opera

Tuong Lung's Shadow
Opera based on the novel by Charles William Doyle.
Three-act opera based on the story of life in the Chinese quarter of San Francisco. Opera written fully (libretto & music) by Dora Bright. Mentioned first in the Shepton Mallet Journal 31/10/1902 and also Dresden Neuste Nachrichten 18/10/1902.
Reported first in RAM Club News No. 10 10/1903, p. 9. Taken by Dora Bright to Germany and submitted to the Director of the Dresden Opera House by Dora Bright reported in the London Daily News 23/10/1902. The Sketch 29/10/1902 reports from the German paper Neuste Nachrichten the music of the opera 'is

*so captivating, and, above all, holds on so strongly, that one exclaims in aston-
ishment, 'can this be the work of a woman".*

The Waltz King
Light Opera (Libretto: Frank Stayton), 1926 (The Times 25/11/1925, p. 12).
*First reported in the Westminster Gazette 25/11/1926 as to be performed in
the New Year. Performed 20/5/1935 at Webber Douglas Theatre London as
reported in The Stage 16/5/1935. Libretto and lyrics reported in The Stage
16/5/1935 as by Arthur Davenport and Rodney Bennett. The Illustrated
London News 1/1/1927 reports the score is woven from Strauss's wealth of
waltzes through which a transcription of 'The Blue Danube' runs as a leit-motif.*
© D79847 26/2/1927.
<u>Copy of libretto in the Library of Congress, Washington DC, USA, ML50 B8526
W2</u>

Suggested third opera *Referenced without name in the Radio Times 8/4/1937,
p. 58.*

Ballets and Theatrical Works

The Dancing Girl and the Idol
Ballet, 1903. The Times 6/2/1903, p. 7. *Oriental Fantasy. Performed at
Chatsworth 1903 and then 1904 as requested by King Edward VII, Sheffield
Daily Telegraph 6/3/1903. Performed in Alloa Scotland 29/1/1903 reported
in The Dundee Telegraph 30/1/1903 and London Evening Standard 6/1/1904.
Played at the Theatre Francais Paris 1/5/1909 reported in the Sheffield
Independent 26/4/1909. First mentioned as music by Dora Bright in The Sketch
13/9/1899.*
<u>Copy-edited score for piano and voice, includes scene for 'Un Jardin Indian',
stamped CH. SCHNEKLUD Paris 1910, 13 Rue des Abbesses, Bureau de Copie
de Musique (stage directions in French), at The Royal Academy of Dance.</u>

Dances
Valse – Mrs Knatchbull – Somerset Standard 11/1/1907.

The Dryad
A Pastoral Fantasy, Empire Theatre London. The Times 8/9/1908, p. 9.
*Published by Elkin & Co. Ltd 1909. A dance play in two tableaux first per-
formed by Dora Bright on 1/1/1907 at a small theatrical party at Babington
House reported in the Somerset Standard 11/1/1907. First performance at the
Playhouse 25/3/1907 reported by the Westminster Gazette 26/3/1907. Toured
with Adeline Genée in America, Australia and New Zealand** Reported in
The Stage Year Book 1908 as played at The Playhouse in 1907.* © C208598

27/5/1909 for piano. <u>Score for solo piano, Dora Bright's working hand-written copy of the manuscript, Tableau II only, includes stage directions for the dancers at The Royal Academy of Dance. Copy-edited score for piano with tableau I and II stamped CH. SCHNEKLUD Paris, 13 Rue des Abbesses, Bureau de Copie de Musique. Further published copy at The British Library. Published copy available from Boosey and Hawkes.</u>

The Faun
Ballet, 1910. Premiere: 3/10/1910, Empire Theatre London. The Times 10/10/1910, p. 12. *Reported in the Stage Year-Book 1910. First played at the Empire Theatre 10/10/1910 reported in the Globe 11/10/1910.*

The Portrait
A Dance-Play. Premiere: 24/11/1910, Prince of Wales's Theatre, London. See The Times 25/11/1910, p. 12. *First played at the Prince of Wales Theatre on 23/11/1910 reported in the Daily Telegraph and Courier 17/11/1910. © E259387 31/5/1911.*

Colinette
Chansonette from 'The Portrait' – Joseph Williams, USA 1911.
<u>Copy in The British Library. Copy in the Library of Congress, Washington DC, USA, M1621.B.</u>

The Abbé's Garden
Mimodrame *in 2 episodes – founded on an incident in Guy Maupassant's 'clair de lune',* World Premiere: 31/3/1911, Globe Theatre London. See The Times 21/3/1911, p. 11; see also The Times 1/4/11, p. 10.

Poor Pretty Columbine
Wordless dance play – music by Dora Bright – reported in The Stage Year Book – 1913 – played 3/6/1912 at the Kilburn Empire as reported in The Stage, 6/6/1912.

La Camargo
Miniature Ballet. Premiere: 27/5/1912. The Times 22/4/1912, p. 14. From Gavotte for orchestra, London: Elkin & Co., ca.1912. *First performance The Coliseum London 20/5/1912 reported in The Stage 25/4/1912. Performed at the New York Metropolitan Opera 3/12/1912. Toured with Adeline Genée in America, Australia and New Zealand** Snippet of music from Elkin & Co score in The Queen 28/9/1912. Set in the boudoir of Mlle Camargo in the Palace of Versailles 1730. © E286498 7/6/1912.*
<u>*Published printed piano solo version with Gavotte, Passepied, Sarabande and Flemish Dance at The British Library, London. Published piano solo copy*</u>

available from Boosey and Hawkes. Printed solo piano version of the Gavotte
in The Royal Academy of Music library.
Handwritten solo piano manuscript for Camargo ballet in Royal Academy of
Dance Adeline Genée archive:
1 Introduction (Corelli Sarabande)
2 (Handel March)
3 (Haydn Minuet)
4 Camargo Solo (Scarlatti Sonata)
5 Pas de Trois (Corelli Gigue)
6 Bridge (Rossini Marcia Muzicale from William Tell)
7 Teller Solo (Ballet Music from William Tell)
8 Pas de Quatre (Chopin Waltz op34 no. 1)
9 Polonaise (Liszt Polonaise no.2 in E)
10 (same as number 1 in short form)

The Wood Nymph
The Times 22/4/1912, p. 14.

In Haarlem There Dwelt
Music drama based on P. van der Meer, 1912. *First performed at The Three Arts*
Club Matinee at His Majesty's Theatre, London on 21/5/1912 – a Dutch Idyll
music drama in four pictures from a story by Pieter van de Meer – reported in
RAM Club news no. 36 May 1912. Played at His Majesty's Theatre on 21/1/1912
reported in Westminster Gazette 2/5/1912. Playhouse London on 22/1/1913 as
reported in The Stage Year Book 1914.

Monday's Child
Musical fancy – *children's ballet arranged for 2 pianos.* Premiere: 28/12/1912.
Court Theatre reported in The Times 16/12/1912, p. 10. *Based on the nursery*
rhyme 'Mondays child is fair of face'. Danced by the children dancers of RAM
at Babington House 19/7/1938 – Somerset Standard, 22/7/1938. Handwritten
working copy for two pianos at The Royal Academy of Dance.

The Colour of Life
(Captain Janssen)
The Times 31/1/1914, p. 11. *Played at the Coliseum by Mme Karina 2–28*
Feb 1914 – reported in 'The Art of Ballet' by Mark E. Perugini and The Era,
4/2/1914.
Dora Bright full orchestral score 'Danses des Couleurs' written for The Colour of
Life ballet (orchestrated by Henri Lucas), held at The Royal Academy of Dance
(includes copy of flyer from the Coliseum Theatre with Mme Karina on front):
Introduction – Tempo di Gavotte
1 Blanc
2 Vert

3 Violette
4 Gavotte
5 Theme and three variations
6 Rouge
7 Yellow and Black
8 Bleu
Finale

La Danse

Ballet music compiled and arranged by Dora Bright. ('An Authentic Record by Adeline Genée of Dancing and Dancers between the Years 1710 and 1845')**, 1914. The Musical Times, 4/4/1914, p. 6. The Globe 6/4/1914. *Performed at the New York Metropolitan Opera 17/12/1912. Toured with Adeline Genée in America, Australia and New Zealand** Includes works by Lully, Boccherini and Gluck with Gavotte Minuet and Chaconne – The Era 1/1/1913. The Era 8/4/1914 and Pall Mall Gazette 8/6/1914 reports the work as 7 tableau and Metropolitan Opera House outlines the ballet and music:*

> *Prelude – old pavanne and passacaille (J.F. Rebel)*
> *Tableau 1 – Passe-pied Lully dances – Triomphe de l'amour (passepied), Le menage de Mohere (Chaconne)*
> *Rameau's Rigaudon (Dora Bright)*
> *Tableau 2 – Gavotte in F (Padre Martini), Rigaudon (J.P. Rameau), Corelli Chaconne with variations (Dora Bright)*
> *Tableau 3 – Jean Baptiste Lully – Tambourin and Musette (J. P. Raneau), Colinette (Gretry) Old Breton air for strings, Don Giovanni: Serenade (Mozart)*
> *Tableau 4 – Les Petite Riens: Pas de Trois (Mozart), Minuet in A (Bocherrini), Paris and Helen: Gavotte in G (Gluck)*
> *Tableau 5 – La Valse – Fantasié on Waltz Themes (Strauss), Promotionen Waltz (Strauss), Who is Sylvia (Strauss), Das Fischermädchen (Meyerbeer), Du Bist Wie Eine Blume (Schumann), Lieder ohne Worte (Mendelssohn)*
> *Tableau 6 – Dances – Mazurka (Chopin), Valse (Chopin)*
> *Tableau 7 – Pas de Quatre – Coppélia: Ballade (Delibes)*

Adapted as a suite and played by Dora Bright at the Bournemouth Winter Gardens as reported in the Nottingham Evening Post 12/4/1928, relayed on the radio as reported in Hull Daily Mail 19/4/1928.

Debut de Valse

Music by Johann Strauss and Dora Bright at the Torquay Pavilion reported in the Pall Mall Gazette 8/6/1914.

The Princess and the Pea
Ballet pantomime after Hans Christian Andersen, 1915. The Times 28/6/1915, p. 3. *Played at the Haymarket 2/7/1915 (matinee) as reported in The Stage Year Book 1916 and The People 20/6/1915.*

Ballet Suite
Based on the fairy tale 'The Shoes That Were Danced to Pieces'. Premiere *in Bradford*: 4/11/1915. The Musical Times 1/1/1916, p. 48. *Shipley Times & Express 26/11/1915. 'Suite de Ballet' reported in the Newcastle Journal 30/7/1915.*

The Dancer's Adventure
Ballet. 1915. The Times 12/10/1915, p. 11. *Played at the Coliseum on 11/10/1915 with Adeline Genée reported in The Globe 29/9/1915.*

My Official Wife
Play 1916. Incidental music written for the play which appears to have never appeared. Reported in Clifton Society Journal 27/1/1916 with 4 Russian dances being premiered at 70 Ennismore Gardens, London. House concert in aid of the funds for 'British Prisoners of War and Interned Civilians in Germany'.

The Magic Pipe
One-act pantomime by Jules Delacre. The Times 7/6/1917, p. 3. *Performed at the Royalty Theatre 26/6/1917 reported in The Stage 7/6/1917. Sunday Mirror 10/6/1917 reports the work has the atmosphere of carnival time in the Latin quarter, Paris 1838.*

The Love Song
Ballet, 1932. The Times 30/1/1933, p. 8; 3/2/1933, p. 8.
This includes: Pavane – Minuet de la Cour – Passe Piéd – Galliard – Rigaudon. *Premiere at the Drury Lane Theatre 7/6/1932, gala charity matinee, by Adeline Genée in aid of the Hertford Hospital in Paris. Danced by Adeline Genée at the Coliseum reported in The Stage 2/2/1933. Televised on the London National Programme 11.00–11.30 15/3/1933 – The Scotsman. American premiere in aid of British War Relief Benefit at the Civic Opera House Chicago 3/11/1940 danced by Nina Stroganova.*

Ballet
Untitled, composed for the Guildhall School of Music. The Musical Times 1/4/1934, p. 357. *Specially written ballet music performed by the Guildhall School of Music 6/3/1934 – written in conjunction with Ben Frankell and Sydney Harrison, as reported in The Musical Times, April 1934, p. 357.*

My Lady's Minuet
Played at Babington House by the RAM dancers – Western Daily Press 26/7/1939.
Sung at Babington by Glynn Eastman and danced by Moira Tucker and Audrey Godfrey reported in the Western Daily Press 26/7/1939 as part of a concert to raise funds for the roof of Babington Church.

Incidental Music

Silas Ruthyn (previously referred to as Uncle Silas)
(Seymour Hicks and Laurence Irving after S. LeFanu), 1893. *Written specially for a performance of Silas Ruthyn played on 14/1/1895 at the Pleasure Garden Theatre in Folkstone reported in the Folkestone, Hythe, Sandygate and Cheriton Herald 12/1/1895. Played at the New Theatre Royal Lincoln, 15/3/1895.*

The Dream of Scrooge
(J.C. Buckstone after C. Dickens), 1901. *Reported in RAM Club news no. 1 1901, p. 10 to be played at the Vaudeville Theatre. London Daily News 9/9/1901. Played on BBC Radio Manchester 24/12/1928 21.35 by the Northern Wireless Orchestra – p. 811 of Radio Times 21/12/28. Music played on the radio by the Northern Radio Orchestra advertised in the Halifax Evening Courier 24/12/1928.*

The Hampton Club
(Seymour Hicks based on the French stage adaptation 'Suicide Club' by MM. Louzy-Eon and 'Armont' by Robert Louis Stevenson), 1909. *Cf. The Times 1/11/1909, p. 8.*

Garrick
Adaptation of the old story and the old play by Max Pemberton – incidental music by Dora Bright – played at the Coliseum 14/7/1913 as reported in The Stage Year Book 1914.

Songs

Whither?
Text by H.W. Longfellow, 1882. *The Musical World 1882. First published in 1882 by Shepherd and Kilner, 7 Grocers Hall Court, Poultry, London, E. C. Referred to in The Life and Works of Sir Edward German as 'I Heard a Brooklet Gushing', 2/1882.*
Copy in The British Library

The Task of the Flower
RAM Concert 7/7/1883 reported in the Illustrated Sporting and Dramatic News 14/7/1883 and Lichfield Mercury 20/7/1883.

The Song of the Shirt
(Thomas Hood) – RAM Concert 1884.

O Summer Storm
RAM Concert 1885. Sung at Mechanics Hall Frome, 25/1/1897 reported in Somerset Standard 28/1/1897.

My Lady Sweet Arise
(W. Shakespeare) – RAM Concert 1885.

Sigh No More Ladies
(W. Shakespeare) – RAM Concert 1886.

12 songs
(by Robert Herrick and William Shakespeare, among others), London: Novello and Co, 1889. *First published in 1896 reported in The Gloucester Journal 29/2/1896.*

1. To blossoms (RH) dedicated to A. J. Hipkins
2. To daisies (RH)
3. The primrose (RH)
4. To music (RH) *Sung at Mechanics Hall Frome, 25/1/1897 reported in Somerset Standard 28/1/1897*
5. Song (Anon)
6. Hark! Hark! the lark (WS) dedicated to W. Macfarren. *First played as Hark! The lark, at Shakespeare Society's meeting on 14/5/1886*
7. Who is Sylvia? (WS)
8. It was a lover and his lass (WS)
9. The maid's garland (H. Hailstone) dedicated to Christine Mackenzie
10. Finland love song (Thomas Moore) dedicated to Marie James*
11. The reaper and the flowers (H. Longfellow) dedicated to Mrs Whitehouse*
12. When all the world is young, *lad.* (Charles Kingsley) dedicated to Edward German
    10 & 11 played by Dora Bright and sung by Miss Mackenzie at Christ Church Boys School as reported in the Middlesex County Times 30/11/1889
    <u>*Copy in The British Library.*</u>

To Daffodils
Song. (Words by Robert Herrick) First performed at RAM concert 22/2/1884.
Song. London. Elkin & Co. 1903 St James Hall London The Globe, 14/6/1904 and
The Musical Times 1/7/1904, p. 467. Announced as new song in the Somerset
Standard 21/1/1899 and sung at local concert in Hemington, Somerset, by Mrs
Paget and Piano by Dora Bright.
Copy in The British Library. Copy in the Library of Congress, Washington DC,
USA, M1621.B.

The Splendid Tattered Flag
Swan & Co, 1888. Written by the Duchess of Somerset and set to music specially
written by Dora Bright for the benefit of and with all proceeds to the Transvaal
war fund reported in the Globe 26/2/1900. Suggested as her first theatrical
composition by The Sketch 11/12/1901. Prelude and incidental music reported
in The Globe 4/10/1901. Performed to the King and Queen at Sandringham as
reported in The Buxton Advertiser 7/12/1901.
Copy in The British Library.

There Sits a Bird
Song, London: Leonard. *Words by Thomas Ingoldsby. 1891 Pitz & Hatfield,*
London and Liepzig.
Copy in the Library of Congress, Washington DC, USA, M1621.B – available
to download as .pdf.

Dedication Song
To the marriage of Mr Herbert Gladstone and Miss D Paget reported in the
Somerset Standard 8/11/1901.

C'est Mon Ami
(music de la reine, Marie Antoinette) played at Babington House concert
8/1/1902 reported in Somerset Standard 10/1/1902.

Six songs from 'The Jungle Book'
Text by Rudyard Kipling, London: Elkin, ca.1903. Night song in the jungle.
1. Seal lullaby *E minor*
2. The mother seal's song *E major*
3. Tiger, tiger!
4. Road-song of the bandar-log
5. The song Toomai's mother sang to the baby.
Dedicated to Henry R Eyres. *First performed by Denis O'Sullivan (Baritone)*
at The Steinway Hall, London 14/10/1902 as reported in The Argonaut
13/10/1902. Reviewed in The Queen 27/6/1903. Heard for the first time with
orchestra at Bath Pump Rooms 9/5/1936 with Dora Bright present.

Copy in the Royal College of Music library (edition 1 – high voice, edition 2 – low voice). Signed copy in the Boston City Library, USA. Published copies available from Boosey and Hawkes and Musicroom.com. Copy in the Library of Congress, Washington DC, USA, M1621.B

The Ballad of the Red Deer in Eb and F
Song. *(Words by F. H)* London: Elkin & Co, 1904. *Reviewed in The Musical Times 1/4/1904.*
No. 1 in E flat for low voice and piano
No. 2 in F for high voice and piano
Copy in The British Library. Copy in Royal College of Music Library. Published copy available from Boosey & Hawkes. Copy in the Library of Congress, Washington DC, USA, M1621.W. 7-page song.

Star of My Night
13/6/1904 – St James Hall London. The Globe 14/6/1904 and The Musical Times 1/7/1904, p. 467.

Messmates
('He gave us all a goodbye cheerily')
Song (*Baritone solo with male voice obbligato*), text by Henry Newbolt, London: Elkin, ca.1907. *First reported sung at the Bechstein Hall by Mt Bispham, 19/1/1907 reported in the Westminster Gazette 20/1/1907.*
Copy in Royal Academy of Music Library and The British Library. Copy in the Library of Congress, Washington DC, USA, M1621.B. Published copy available from Boosey and Hawkes.

A Child's Garden of Verses
Six songs, 1908. *First heard at a recital in the Broadwood Rooms on 22/1/1908 – recorded in RAM Club News no.24 May 1908 and reported in the London Daily News 23/1/1908. Songs 5 and 6 lost.*
1. It is very nice to think the world is full of meat and drink
2. Every night my prayers I say
3. In winter I get up at night
4. Marching song

I Know a Lady Sweet and Kind
Song, text by Robert Herrick, 1913 © *E317166 16/8/1913 Chappell & Co. Ltd. London*
Mentioned in The Times Obituary to Dora Bright 23/11/1951.
Copy in The British Library. Copy in the Library of Congress, Washington DC, USA, M1621.B.

The Orchard Rhymes

13 Nursery Rhymes with actions. Written with Ethel Mary Boyce, London: Novello, 1917. *Advertised in The Musical Times 1/5/1917, p. 233 – School Songs book 260. 2 pieces by Dora Bright, The Rose is Red (no. 3) and Monday's Child (no. 11) – see The Musical Advertiser 1/7/1917, p. 333. © 1917 for both. Also 'Girls and Boys' and 'Ring-a-Ring o'Roses' included by Dora Bright. Copy in The British Library. Copy in the Library of Congress, Washington DC, USA, M1993.B78 O6 (piano acc.).*

'Hame Hame Hame' and 'The Rose is Red'

See 'The Orchard Rhymes' with Ethel Boyce, in the School Music Review (no. 308) advertised in The Musical Times 1/2/1918, p. 90.

Ring-a-Ring o'Roses

(in collaboration with Ethel Mary Boyce), London: Novello and Co, 1922. *Copy in The British Library.*

Sing a Song of Sixpence

(in collaboration with Ethel Mary Boyce), London: Novello and Co, 1922. *Copy in The British Library.*

The Donkey

Song. Text by G. K. Chesterton. 1936. Dedicated to Harold Williams. *Copy in The British Library. Copy in the Library of Congress, Washington DC, USA, M1621.B Published copy available from Boosey and Hawkes.*

Orchestral Works

Concert piece (*Concertstücke*)

For piano and orchestra in C sharp minor, 1885. Premiere: RAM Concert at St James Hall, 3/7/1885, Musical Times 1/8/1885, p. 479.

Variations on an original Theme of Sir George Alexander Macfarren for piano and orchestra

Also in a version for two pianos, Edwin Ashdown 1888. Dedicated to W. Macfarren. *Theme reported as written specially for Dora Bright by G. A. Macfarren in The Queen 24/11/1894 as the last theme he wrote. Copy in The Royal Academy of Music Library, The British Library has 4 hand version. Published and available from Hildegard Publishing edited by Sophie Fuller.*

Concerto for Piano and Orchestra No. 1 in A minor

1888. Played Crystal Palace 1891. *First played at RAM concert 24/7/1888 in St James Hall reported in the London Daily News 25/7/1888. Played at Prom Concert Covent Garden 26/9/1888 reported in the London Evening Standard 27/7/1888. Played in Dresden on 8/10/1889 for the Dresden Philharmonic Society reported in The Queen 5/10/1889. Reported in the Sheffield Independent 2/4/1891. Crystal Palace programmes held in Bodleian Library Collection (Mus. 318 d.28). Well reviewed in The Times 30/3/1891 and played at the Crystal Palace where the Western Daily Press 18/1/1899 suggest 'the work had been fully revised and in parts re-written by her'. Also played in Leipzig by Dora Bright and Dr Reinecke in a 4-hand version reported in the Shepton Mallet Journal 1/3/1895.*
<u>Copies of score and 2 piano version – valerielangfield.co.uk. CD version SOMMCD 273. Copy at The Royal Academy of Music.</u>

Fantasia for Piano and Orchestra in G minor

1890 Daily Telegraph & Reporter (London) 24/10/1890 reports 'The new work thus first introduced to public notice, though called a Fantasia is more of a concerto somewhat freely constructed, played in Dresden and Koln (18/10/1890) recently'. Daily Telegraph & Reporter (London) 31/10 1890 further report on Die Zeitung article relating to the Dora Bright concerts in Dresden and Koln, stating 'a pianoforte concerto, full of original and beautiful ideas, excellent workmanship, and very praiseworthy instrumentation, was received in the warmest manner'. The Queen 25/4/1891 reports upcoming visits to Dresden, Koln and St Petersburg – states 'works include concerto in A minor, Fantasia in G minor, suite for violin and pianoforte, album of songs, several duets for two pianofortes, some pieces for flute, etc. She is engaged on an orchestral suite (three of five movements written) and a quartet for piano and strings'.

Spanish Dance Suite for Orchestra

1891 – Prelude, Liebesleid, Seguidilla, Romance, Finale – played Cologne 10/1891 (Sophie Fuller PhD Thesis).

Fantasia for Piano and Orchestra in No. 2 in G major

1892 – G major first movement in 4/4 sonata form with cadenza leading to a short 6/8 serenata in the tonic minor and finally a rondo in G major in 2/4 time. Sheffield Independent 3/3/1892 reports 'Dora Bright's Fantasia will be one of the novelties of the forthcoming season of the Philharmonic Society, is in the key of G, and is in one movement, although practically it is that of a condensed concerto. It was written on the return of Dora Bright from Germany last October, so that it is the young composer's latest work'. First performance and snippets (p. 17) of themes in Philharmonic Society programme 5th Concert 11/5/1892 at St. James Hall London. This was mis-advertised and mis-reported as being in G minor in many papers and the original programme, before and shortly after the concert. The Times 13/5/1892 correctly ascribes it as being in G major and the snippets published in the programme show G major for the first and last movements.

Orchestral Ouverture
The Times of 26/12/1893 reports the work was played at a recent RAM concert. Also mentioned as Orchestral Entr'act in London Daily News 21/10/1893, also Western Daily Press 30/10/1893.

Love Song for Orchestra
London: Edwin Ashdown, 1897. *Leibesleid first performed at the Henry Wood Queens Hall Promenade Concert 6/3/1896 advertised in the Morning Post 2/3/1896.*

Variations for Piano and Orchestra in F major
Paris 1910. *Played first time in the UK on BBC Radio 8/4/1937 6.40pm. Radio Times, p. 705, suggests written in Paris in 1912.*
Copy in the collection of The Royal Academy of Music, London. Copies of score at valerielangfield.co.uk. CD version SOMMCD 273

Concertstück for Six Drums and Orchestra
The Musical Times 1/5/1915, p. 305. *Premier at Harrogate concert as reported the Yorkshire Post & Leeds Intelligence 6/4/1915.*

Suite of 4 Russian Dances for Orchestra
First performed in London 21/1/1916 as reported in the Clifton Society Journal 27/1/1916, reported as written as part of a dramatised version of 'My Official Wife' as yet unperformed. Played by the BBC Theatre Orchestra in w/e 20/1/1939 as reported in the Somerset Standard 20/1/1939.

Suite Bretonne
For flute and orchestra, 1917. The Times 3/8/1917, p. 9 and 25/8/1917, p. 9, *played at Promenade Series No.25 22/9/1917. Reported in The Globe 4/8/1917 as being part of the 1917 promenade series. Three movements reported in Freemans Journal, 24/9/1917 and Liverpool Daily Post 25/9/1917 as, 1. Lyric in minor key, 2. Chanson Varie, 3. Angelus and Dance.*

Vienna for Orchestra
The Times 23/4/1927, p. 8. *Performed at 68th Halle Season Concert 18/3/1926 – see concertprogrammes.org.uk*

Suite of 18th-Century Dances for Piano and Orchestra
Undated (1907–1918 most likely)

Handwritten working piano solo copy with single line indicating orchestral
accompaniment at The Royal Academy of Dance (timings indicate work no
longer than 14 minutes):
Introduction
Passepied
Minuet de la Lour
Galliarde
Rigaudon (d'apres Lulli).

Chamber Music

Air and Variations for String Quartet
1887. The Times 10/5/1887, p. 12. *Dora Bright wins the Charles Lucas medal****
for the composition – Illustrated London News 4/8/1/888. Written specifically
for and played as part of the 5th season of the Westminster Orchestra Society.
As reported in The Era, 7/12/1889.

String Quartet
1888. *The Times 26/12/1893 suggests played at RAM concert in that year.*

2 Sketches (Trifles)
For flute with pianoforte accompaniment. Performed in Swansea on 22/8/1889
as reported in The Musical Times 1/9/1889.

Suite of 5 Pieces for Violin and Piano
Dedicated to J. T. Carrodus. Edwin Ashdown Ltd., 1891
Copy in The British Library
alternatively
Suite for Violin & Piano (Suite of Five Pieces)
London: Edwin Ashdown, year unknown.
First played at Princes Hall 30/4/1890 as reported in The Queen 3/5/1890 –
consisting of Prelude, Scherzino, Scotch air and variations, Romance and Moto
Perpetuo. The Times 26/12/1893 suggests played at concert in Hampstead in
that year. Reported in The Musical Times 1/5/1890, p. 297 as an original work
by Dora Bright played on 23/4/1890 in the Princes Hall together with some
songs.

Romanza and Seguidilla
For flute and piano. *Published by Rudall Carter & Co, 1891. Played at Stanley*
Hall Hampstead, reported in the Hampstead and Highgate Express 2/5/1891.
Dedicated to the Welsh flute player, Frederic Griffiths, a student of The Royal
Academy and Principal flute of the Royal Italian Opera Orchestra in London.

Copy in The British Library. Published copy available from juneemersonwind-music.com

Piano Quartet in D major
1892. *Musical News 16/6/1894, p. 564. The Times 26/12/1893 suggests played at Mr Dannreuther concert in that year. Played in Hanover Germany, October 1892 as reported in Western Morning News 20/10/1892. Reported in The Graphic 24/3/1894.*
alternatively
Quartet for Piano and Strings
(viola, violin and violincello) – Allegro Maestoso in D major, air with eight variations – 1 in 2/4, 2 in 6/4, 2 in 2/4, 4 scherzino 6/8, 5 vivace 2/4, 6 in 2/4 tonic major, 7 in 4/4, 8 in 3/4 leggierissimo. Specially written for Madame Serruy's 2nd Matinee on 10/2/1894 – reported in the Norfolk News 17/2/1894.

Sketches a la Russe
Flute, cor-anglais, harp and piano. Played at Wigmore Hall with Dora Bright at the piano. Reported in The Era 15/10/1924.

Work for two solo instruments and piano
1924 (premier). The Times 6/10/1924, p. 10.

Two pieces
(two pieces for cello (or violin) and piano), London: Elkin & Co., ca.1934.
Including:
No.1 Das Fischermädchen, a melody by Meyerbeer.
Copy held in The British Library
No. 2 Polka à la Strauss
Copyright outlined in Library of Congress Catalogue of Copyright 29/5/1934.
Copy in The Royal College of Music library. Recording by Catherine Wilmers – features on ASV recording of Women composers. Copy held in The British Library.

Piano Works

Sonata in G
Played from manuscript at RAM concert 1/7/1882, as reported in The Musical World 8/7/1882.

Sonata in Eb
Played from manuscript at RAM concert 11/11/1882, as reported in The Musical World 18/11/1882.

Two Sketches
F# minor and A for piano – first performed at RAM concert on 6/10/1883.
London: *Webb & Co,* 1884. Dedicated to W. Macfarren – *The Atheneum 16/8/1884, p. 219.*
<u>*Copy in The British Library.*</u>

Two Sketches
For flute with pianoforte accompaniment – The Musical Times 1/1/1889.

Three Sketches
Reported in Manchester Courier and Lancashire General Advertiser 13/1/1894 to be played at Gentleman's concerts 15/1/1894. (Perhaps the Two Sketches from the 1883 RAM concert with a new addition.)

Theme and Variations in F sharp *minor* for two pianos
1886. The Musical Times 1/8/1886, p. 480. *Theme and Eighteen variations in F # minor on an original theme for 2 pianos – Brighton Gazette 13/7/1886.*

Suite in G minor
RAM Concert 19/11/1886 played at the Musical Artists Society, Willis Rooms, London and reported in The Queen 2/4/1887, also The Era 9/4/1887 reports of a Scherzetto and Barcarolle as part of the work. Sheffield Daily Telegraph 27/10/1887 reports work as Prelude, Romance, Scherzetto, Barcarolle, Finale-presto. The Musical Times 1/12/1886, p. 719, records the work played at St James Hall on 19/11/1886.

Variations on a Theme of Purcell
For 2 piano. RAM Concert 1887 reported in The Queen 25/6/1888.

Variations in Eb
(on a theme by J. E. German) – performed at RAM concert 15/10/1887.

Variations on an original Theme of Sir George Alexander Macfarren for two pianos in G minor
(Variations on an original theme by Sir George Alexander Macfarren for two pianos), 1888. *First reported played at the St James Hall 17/2/1888 in the London Evening Standard 18/2/1888.*
<u>*(new edition: Bryn Mawr, PA: Hildegard Publ. 2000, ed. V. Sophie Fuller) 1894 edition Edwin Ashdown and 1937 edition Edwin Ashdown held in The British Library.*</u>

Duet for 2 Pianos
The Musical News 1/7/1891, p. 392; 10/7/1891, p. 384.

Piano Quintet
1891 – *The Atheneum 29/4/1893, p. 549.*

Three Pieces for Piano
London: Edwin Ashdown, 1895. Musical Times 1/3/1895, p. 170. *Reviewed in*
The Queen 2/2/1895:
  1.   Berceuse – dedicated to Mrs Graham *G minor*
  2.   Love song: Liebesleid Duettino – dedicated to Lady Katherine
       Thynne *Bb major*
  3.   Tarantella *G minor*
Copies of Berceuse Duettino and Tarrantella in The British Library. Full copy of
all three items in Cambridge University Library – non-borrowable (Mus.24.62)

Humouresque
Played by Ethel Leginska at the Aelioan Hall on 6/5/1909 reported in the
Morning Post 7/5/1909.

Romanza for piano
Dedicated to Ethel Boyce. London: Edwin Ashdown, ca.1922. *Single work pub-*
lished 1889.
Copy in The British Library.

Scherzetto for piano
London: Edwin Ashdown, ca.1922.

Romanza and Scherzetto
Published as the pair in 1922.
Reported in The Queen 23/2/1889 as being in Eb and Bb respectively. Organ
version of Romanza played on 19/3/1922 in Runcorn as reported in the Runcorn
Weekly News 24/3/1922. © E544395 and E544396 respectively 10/8/1922.
Copy in The British Library.

Arrangements and Transcriptions

Neu Wien
Johann Strauss. New Viennese Waltz piano transcription/arrangement by
Dora Bright, London: Elkin & Co., ca.1924. *Recorded on HMV 12' 78rpm no*
G-C2505. Hull Daily Mail 7/4/1924 notes 'the waltz of Johann Strauss has
been freely arranged for the piano by Dora Bright and is published at 3s. It is
full of bright and sparkling tunes assisted by an insistent and pleasing rhythm'.
© E582327 5/2/1924.
Copy in The British Library.

Siciliano and Gigue from the Suite in D minor

Thomas A. Arne. Piano transcription by Dora Bright, London: Elkin & Co., 1948.
Copy in The Royal Academy of Music Library and Library of Congress, Washington DC, USA (missing – not on shelf). Copy in The British Library © EF10238 28/7/1948.

Un Soireé de Vienne

First performed at the Halle in Manchester as reported in the Sheffield Daily Telegraph 7/12/1925. Specially written for the Halle series. Performed on BBC radio 7/1/1926.

Other

Melody

Played on the organ at the wedding of Miss Nancy Parish to John Paget at St Margaret's Westminster as reported in the Shepton Mallet Journal 24/11/1944.

Works Removed

Concerto for Piano and Orchestra No. 2 in D minor

1892
Sophie Fuller PhD footnote – Who's Who (1913/15) and International Who's Who (1918) outlines Piano Concerto no. 2, performed in Cologne, 1892.
Who's Who incorrectly ascribe the Cologne performance as a Piano Concerto – this was most likely the Fantasia no. 2 in G major as written for the Philharmonic Society, played 11/5/1892 and subsequently performed in Cologne, and then alongside the Piano Quartet in D major in Hanover as reported in the Western Morning News 20/10/1892. The Philharmonic 5th concert programme 11/5/1892, p. 17, describes the Fantasia in the form of a 'condensed concerto'. Both the Fantasia (G major and G minor) are described as similar to a 'condensed concerto'. There are no references in any musical magazine or newspaper of any concert, which included a Piano Concerto in D minor. Nor is there any other mention of a second piano concerto in any other literature or research, other than in those outlines of Dora Bright's work, post the (incorrect) Who's Who entry.

Location of Works

Other than those identified above, the following link also identifies known versions through the WorldCat internet site:

Bright, Dora [WorldCat Identities]

Endnotes

* Sung at Christ Church Boys School (Ealing?) by Miss MacKenzie as reported in The Middlesex County Times 30/11/1889.

** Wikipedia on Adeline Genée.

***Lucas Prize awarded and based on the best composition written on a subject provided by the examiners 2 months prior to the award. Dora Bright wins the silver medal against 9 other students.

© copyright catalogue entries from the Library of Congress copyright collection.

References

This new catalogue above supersedes all other previous listings.

Initial references used in the development of this catalogue are listed below. However, it should be noted that there are a number of websites which have brief outlines of Dora Bright's life and works and appear to be mainly copied from the Wikipedia site short list of works.

https://en.wikipedia.org/wiki/DoraBright

https://mugi.hfmt-hamburg.de

https://www.trubcher.com/blog/dora-bright

'Women Composers during the British Musical Renaissance, 1880–1918' – Sophie Fuller, PhD Thesis, Kings College London, 1998, ISNI 0000 0001 2460 2952.

Appendix 2: Dora Bright Family Tree

Bad Durkheim
Henry Hirsch
(Micholls)
1728–1815

?
Grenendla
Mapthali
1741–1820

Southampton
Charles Dibdin
1745–1814

?
Harriet Pitt
1748–1814

Bayreuth
Isaac Bright
1763–1849

Norfolk
Ann Micholls
1775–1847

Morocco
Moses C.
Delara
1825–?

Sarah Delara
?

London
Thomas John
Dibdin
1771–1841

London
Ann Nancy
Hillier
1770–1828

Kent
Henry
Coveney
1790–?

London
Ellen Coveney
1822–?

Sheffield
Selim Bright
1799–1891

Gibraltar
Estella de Lara
1804–1878

Lancashire
Charles Alexander
Dibdin Pitt
1815–1866

Maurice,
Henry, Edward
*

Sheffield
Horatio Bright
1829–1906

Buxton
Michael
Octavius Bright
1833–1901

Buxton
Augustus Bright
1830–1880

Manchester
Katherine
Coveney Pitt
1844–1906

Buxton
Maurice Delara
Bright
1826–1902

Sheffield
Dora Estella
Bright
1862–1951

* Sons of Isaac included in text. There are no reports of the six daughters.

Appendix 3: Music by Maurice Delara Bright (1825–1902)

The list of works is derived from searches of the internet, library archives and news reports during and after the composer's lifetime.

The Quadrilles – The Emperor Fountain (Piano & Cornet) – Coole & Tirney London 1852 – British Library and Bibliotèque National de France.

L'énfant de France – Boosey & Co 1858 20 Military Band Parts – British Library.

Napoléon et Eugénie Quadrille – J. Heinz 1856 – British Library and Bibliotèque National de France.

The Prince Royal of England (Pas Redouble) – J. Heinz – Bibliotèque National De France.

Défilé (Napoleon 1ˢᵗ e sà memoire immortelle) – Signed autograph copy October 1858 – Bibliotèque National De France.

The Wellington March – reported in the *Morning Chronicle*, 25 February 1856.

Le Canrobert March – reported in the *Morning Post*, 14 February 1859.

Grand Divertissément – reported in *The Jersey Independent and Daily Telegraph*, 23 July 1859.

Grand March – Grand Duke of Hesse – reported in *The Richmond and Ripon Chronicle*, 3 September 1859.

Retrâite (dedicated to the Duke of Magenta) – reported in *The Richmond and Ripon Chronicle*, 3 September 1859.

Galop "Victoria" – Performed at Windsor Castle in front of Queen Victoria on 15 July 1881 by the Royal Artillery Band (Memoirs of the Royal Artillery Band, Henry Farmer, 1904, Boosey and Co.).

Appendix 4: Royal Academy of Music Prizes[*]

The prizes outlined below are those presented to Dora Bright during her period at the Royal Academy of Music 1881–1888. They are detailed in the order achieved.

Certificates of Merit (7/1882), Bronze (7/1882) and Silver Medals (7/1883)
Awarded at the annual July examinations, to the most deserving pupils who have been studying throughout the three preceding terms.

The Lucas Prize (7/1884)
A silver medal, from a design by T. Woolner, R.A. will be competed for annually, in July, by composers who shall have been studying in the Academy throughout the three consecutive preceding terms, and it will be awarded to the one who shall compose the best work of which the subject shall be named by the Committee two months before the date of the competition.

Potter Exhibition (12/1884)
The 'Potter Exhibition' has been founded, by subscription, as a Testimonial to the Late Cipriani Potter (Principal of the Institution from 1832 to 1859), which will be contended for annually in December. It is open to competition, by female and male candidates, in alternate years, who shall be pupils of the Academy, and have studied not less than two years in the Institution.

The amount of the Exhibition is £12 (£1,500 today), which will be appropriated towards the cost of a year's instruction in the academy.

---

[*] Definitions of prizes from the Royal Academy of Music Concert Book: 1824–1879.

Sterndale Bennett Scholarship (5/1885)

A scholarship has been founded by subscription, as a testimonial to Sir William Sterndale Bennett (Principal of the Royal Academy of Music from 1866 to 1875), and be contended for biennially in April. The scholarship is open for competition in any branch of music, between the ages of fourteen and twenty-one years.

The competitor must be a British-born subject, and will have to pass an examination in general education, previously to entering the musical competition. The subjects for examination will comprise orthography, English grammar, elementary arithmetic, rudiments of geography and English history; candidates above 18, any foreign language of their own choice.

The successful candidate is entitled to two years' free education in the Royal Academy of Music. Certificate of birth must be produced.

Lady Goldsmid Scholarship (1886)

The scholarship entitles the holder to free musical education for two years in the Royal Academy of Music. It was competed for by female pianists, being British-born subjects, between the ages of sixteen and twenty-one years, and was awarded to the one judged to show the greatest promise as a player – preference being given where there is also a talent for composition, or other sign of musical aptitude. Certificate of birth must be produced.

Appendix 5: Dedicated Works

Works dedicated to others

Romanza and Seguidilla – to the Welsh flute player, Frederic Griffiths, a student of the Royal Academy and Principal flute of the Royal Italian Opera Orchestra in London.

Suite of 5 pieces for violin and piano – to J. T. Carrodus (Cousin Ada's husband)

Romanza and Scherzetto for piano (1889) – to Ethel Boyce

There Sits a Bird – to Mrs John Leach Barrett

To Daffodils – to Mr David Bispham

The Donkey – to Harold Williams

Berceuse – to Mrs Graham

Liebesleid – to Lady Katherine Thynne

Tarantella – to Lady Katherine Thynne

Two Sketches – to Walter Macfarren

Variations on an Original Theme of Sir G. A. Macfarren for Piano and Orchestra – to Walter Macfarren

Works dedicated to Dora Bright

W. Macfarren – *12 Studies for Pianoforte in Style and Technique* – 2nd set.

W. Macfarren – *Suite de Pieces in Eb Major* – dedicated to Dora Bright, Ethel Boyce and Edith Young

Edward German – *Polish Dance*

M. Moszkowski – *Klavierstucke No. 1 op.80* – *Piece Romantique*

Rev. C. Wills (Principal of Portishead College) – *The Reaper and the Flowers*

Appendix 6: Recorded Works

Neu Wien op.342 – Gramophone GC2505 played by Mark Hambourg – B side Delibes Coppelia Waltz.

Polka à la Strauss for Cello and Piano – Catherine Wilmers, CD QS 6245, 2000 ASV Ltd., https://intothelightradio.org/audio/ITL158_1.mp3

'Romance & Seguidilla', https://soundcloud.com/rosflute/dora-bright-romance-seguidilla-extract

Piano Concerto No 1. in A Minor & Variations for Piano and Orchestra – SOMM Recording, SOMMCD 273, 2019.

Notes

Preface

1. *Somerset Standard*, 20 November 1951.
2. *The Times*, 29 November 1951.

Introduction

1. *Sheffield Daily Telegraph*, 7 July 1905.
2. Sir Thomas Beecham, 'The Position of Women in Music', in *Vogue's First Reader* (New York: Conde Nast Publications Inc., 1942).
3. *The Stage*, 25 September 1919.
4. J. A. Fuller-Maitland, *English Music in the XIX Century* (London: Grant Richards, 1902).
5. *The Times*, 27 August 1958.
6. C. Brush, 'A Study of the Composers and Music of the English Renaissance and their Influence upon the Compositional Style of Ralph V. Williams' (Master of Music research paper, Ball State University, Muncie, Indiana, 2012).
7. S. Fuller, 'Women Composers during the British Musical Renaissance 1880–1918' (PhD thesis, Kings College, University of London, 1998).

Chapter 1

1. Adelina De Lara, *Finale* (London: Burke Publishing Co, 1915).
2. Percy M. Young, *Keyboard Musicians of the World* (London: Abelard-Shuman, 1967).
3. De Lara, *Finale*.
4. Ibid.
5. Ibid.
6. Letter from J. B. McEwen to Charles Edward Howell, Monday, 21 April 1919.
7. *The Times*, 11 September 1919.
8. *The Daily Sketch*, 13 November 1919.
9. *The Musical Times*, December 1928.
10. Ethel Smyth, *A Final Burning of Boats* (London: Longman, Green & Co, 1929).

11. Vincent James Byrne, 'The Life and Works of Dorothy Howell' (Master of Arts thesis, Department of Music, University of Birmingham, 2015).

Chapter 2

1. Armin Krausz, 'Philip and Isaac Bright (d. 1849) in 1790', in *Sheffield Jewry: Commentary on a Community* (Ramat-Gan: Bar-Ilan University; Sheffield: Naor Publications, 1980).
2. *Jewish Chronicle and Hebrew Observer*, 30 July 1858, p. 260.
3. Dora Bright, 'My Early Years', unpublished memoir.
4. Chris Hobbs, 'The Bright Family', http://chrishobbs.com/horatiobrightfamily.htm
5. Eric Lipson, *The Brights of Market Place*, Transactions of the Hunter Archaeological Society, Vol. 6 (London: Hunter Archaeological Society, 1947).
6. Krausz, 'Philip and Isaac Bright'.
7. Lipson, *The Brights of Market Place*.
8. Krausz, 'Philip and Isaac Bright'.
9. Lipson, *The Brights of Market Place*.
10. Derbyshire Archives reference D258/19/1/19.
11. *Doncaster Gazette*, 3 September 1841.
12. *Jewish Chronicle and Hebrew Observer*, 30 July 1858, p. 260.
13. *The Morning Chronicle*, 2 September 1848.
14. *The Express* (London), 2 September 1848.
15. Lipson, *The Brights of Market Place*.
16. Hobbs, 'The Bright Family'.
17. N. Bradley, 'Sheffield Characters: Horatio Bright of Lydgate Hall', *The Sheffield Spectator*, August/September 1966.
18. Lipson, *The Brights of Market Place*.
19. *Sheffield Daily Telegraph*, 7 April 1856.
20. *The Sheffield Independent*, 4 July 1857.
21. *The Sheffield Independent*, 26 January 1861.
22. *The Sheffield Independent*, 27 April 1861.
23. *The Sheffield Independent*, 25 June 1854.
24. *Sheffield Daily News and Advertiser*, 27 July 1859.
25. *The Telegraph*, 24 December 1890.
26. *The Sheffield Independent*, 5 February 1906.
27. N. Bradley, 'Sheffield Characters: Horatio Bright of Lydgate Hall', *The Sheffield Spectator*, August/September 1966.
28. *Sheffield Daily Telegraph*, 27 April 1906.
29. Ibid.
30. Lipson, *The Brights of Market Place*.
31. *The Buxton Herald*, 2 September 1858.
32. Ibid.
33. Ibid.
34. *London Evening Standard*, 22 February 1867.
35. *Northampton Mercury*, 10 November 1866.
36. *London Evening Standard*, 22 February 1867.
37. *Northampton Mercury*, 3 November 1867.
38. *The Sheffield Independent*, 5 August 1871.
39. *Manchester Times*, 14 February 1874.
40. Belle Vue prison records, 1874.
41. *The Sheffield Independent*, 9 May 1882.
42. Supplement to the *Sheffield and Rotherham Independent*, 25 October 1856.

43. *Leamington Spa Courier*, 30 October 1852.
44. *Sheffield Daily Telegraph*, 3 July 1856.
45. *The Sheffield Independent*, 4 October 1856.
46. Hobbs, 'The Bright Family'.
47. Guarnerius alongside Stradivardi was one of the two most celebrated violin makers of all time. The violin was sold after Augustus's death at a price of £4 13s (£4,500 today).
48. *The Hampshire Telegraph*, 28 March 1891.
49. *Sunday World* (Dublin), 14 July 1895 and *The Bolton Evening News*, 15 July 1895.

Chapter 3

1. *Sheffield Daily Telegraph*, 24 December 1872.
2. *Sheffield Daily Telegraph*, 16 March 1867.
3. *Sheffield Daily Telegraph*, 28 May 1859.
4. *Sheffield Daily Telegraph*, 8 April 1865.
5. *The Sheffield Independent*, 26 April 1865.
6. *Sheffield Daily Telegraph*, 9 August 1871.
7. *Sheffield Daily Telegraph*, 23 July 1873.
8. *Weekly Dispatch* (London), 9 December 1866.
9. *Sheffield Daily Telegraph*, 20 May 1859.
10. *Morning Post*, 23 August 1871.
11. *Sheffield Daily Telegraph*, 15 December 1881.
12. *Sheffield Daily Telegraph*, 28 May 1859.
13. *Sheffield Daily Telegraph*, 11 March 1861.
14. *Sheffield Daily Telegraph*, 13 April 1861.
15. *The Stage*, 30 March 1902.
16. *Sheffield Daily Telegraph*, 19 October 1860.
17. *The Sheffield Independent*, 27 October 1860.
18. *The Sheffield Independent*, 30 October 1860.
19. *The Stage*, 30 March 1902.
20. *The Cardiff Times*, 14 June 1861.
21. *The Era*, 11 May 1879.
22. *Sheffield Daily Telegraph*, 11 January 1868.
23. Hilary Jane Wilson, 'The Challenge of Nineteenth Century Theatre in Sheffield' (PhD School of English Language, Literature and Linguistics, University of Sheffield, 2014).
24. Dora Bright, 'My Early Years', unpublished memoir.
25. *The Sheffield Independent*, 27 May 1868.
26. *The Sheffield Independent*, 16 December 1876.
27. *Sheffield Daily Telegraph*, 6 December 1877.
28. *The Sheffield Independent* & *Sheffield Daily Telegraph*, 2 November 1880.
29. Last Will and Testament of Dora Estella Knatchbull, 10 February 1918.
30. Sophie Fuller, 'Women Composers during the British Musical Renaissance 1880–1918' (PhD thesis, Kings College, University of London, 1998); *Sheffield Daily Telegraph*, 30 November 1867.
31. *The Sheffield Independent*, 23 August 1881.
32. *Oxford Journal*, 25 August 1883.
33. *The Stage*, 12 March 1886.
34. *The Stage*, 31 October 1895.
35. *Newcastle Journal*, 25 March 1916.
36. *The Stage*, 16 May 1929.
37. Last Will and Testament of Dora Estella Knatchbull, 10 February 1918.

38. *The Stage*, 9 April 1931.
39. *The Stage*, 22 March 1934.
40. *The Stage*, 24 June 1937.
41. *The Stage*, 22 January 1942
42. *The Stage*, 13 July 1961.
43. *The Era*, 17 May 1874.
44. *The Era*, 31 March 1878.
45. *Exeter and Plymouth Gazette Daily Telegram*, 5 October 1878.
46. Ibid.
47. *Yorkshire Post and Leeds Intelligencer*, 30 November 1878.
48. *The Era*, 11 May 1879.
49. *The Era*, 12 December 1880.
50. *The Sheffield Independent*, 9 August 1881.
51. C. C. Bright, 'Grandfather's Little Actress', *Era Almanack* (London), January 1879.
52. *The Sheffield Independent*, 17 September 1881.
53. *The Stage*, 12 August 1881.
54. *The Era*, 21 January 1882.
55. Ibid.
56. *The Sheffield Independent*, 12 August 1882.
57. *The Stage*, 8 December 1882.
58. *The Era*, 2 January 1886.
59. *The Stage*, 20 March 1902.
60. *Lloyds Weekly Newspaper*, 30 March 1902.
61. *The Era*, 6 January 1906.

Chapter 4

1. Mrs. [Sarah] Ellis, *The Daughters of England: Their Position in Society, Character and Responsibilities*, Philosophical and Historical Perspectives Vol. 4, Issue 2 (London and Paris: Fisher, Son, & Co., 1842), pp. 97–98.
2. *St James's Gazette*, 16 December 1884.
3. *St James's Gazette*, 14 April 1886.
4. *Sheffield Evening Telegraph*, 9 June 1887.
5. *Pall Mall Gazette*, 16 July 1888.
6. Brian Rees, *A Musical Peacemaker: The Life and Work of Sir Edward German* (Kensal Press, 1986).
7. Ibid.
8. Ibid.
9. Chertsey Museum – Ethel Boyce letter CHYMS.2463.030.
10. Rees, *A Musical Peacemaker*.
1. Paula Gillett, *Musical Women in England 1870–1914* (London: St. Martin's Press).
12. *Islington Gazette*, 31 January 1882.
13. Ibid.
14. *The Musical World*, 25 February 1882.
15. *St James's Gazette*, 17 October 1882.
16. Royal Academy programmes, 27 June 1883, 7 July 1883, 6 October 1883 and 26 October 1883.
17. *The Musical Times*, 1 August 1883.
18. *The Era*, 17 November 1883.
19. *Croydon Guardian and Surrey County Gazette*, 1 March 1884.
20. *Buxton Herald*, 26 July 1884.

21. *Buxton Advertiser*, 2 August 1884.

22. *The Musical Times*, 1 August 1885.

23. *The Graphic*, 11 July 1885.

24. *Dundee Evening Telegraph*, 9 April 1886.

25. *Buxton Herald*, 15 September 1886; *Nottinghamshire Guardian*, 15 August 1886; *St James's Gazette*, 27 October 1886.

26. *Buxton Herald*, 14 April 1886.

27. *Brighton Gazette*, 13 July 1886.

28. *Liverpool Mercury*, 23 May 1887.

29. *The Globe*, 10 May 1887.

30. *St James's Gazette*, 16 May 1887.

31. *Sheffield Evening Telegraph*, 9 June 1887.

32. *Sheffield Daily Telegraph*, 20 October 1887.

33. *Sheffield Daily Telegraph*, 27 October 1887.

34. *The Era*, 25 February 1888.

35. *The Era*, 28 July 1888.

36. *Sheffield Daily Telegraph*, 12 February 1889.

37. *The Queen*, 23 February 1889.

38. *Sheffield Daily Telegraph*, 12 February 1889.

39. *London Daily News*, 31 January 1889.

40. *The Musical Times*, 1 April 1889.

41. *The Queen*, 30 March 1889.

42. *The Musical Times*, 1 May 1889, p. 283. George Alexander Macfarren (1813–1887) was a composer and musicologist of some note in the nineteenth century. His brother Walter Macfarren (1826–1905) was also a composer of some note and a pianoforte teacher at the Royal Academy of Music.

43. *Pall Mall Gazette*, 28 March 1889.

44. *The Monthly Musical Record*, 1 April 1889.

45. *The Sydney Mail and New South Wales Advertiser*, 20 July 1889.

46. Application FO611/15, Findmypast.co.uk

47. *The Queen*, 5 October 1889.

48. *The Queen*, 18 October 1890.

49. *Daily Telegraph and Report* (London), 31 October 1890.

50. *The Queen*, 25 April 1891.

51. *Daily Telegraph and Courier* (London), 24 October 1890.

52. *Sheffield Daily Telegraph*, 6 November 1890.

53. *The Gentlewoman*, 25 June 1892.

54. *Aberdeen Evening Express*, 29 October 1892.

55. *Croydon Advertiser and East Surrey Reporter*, 7 February 1889.

56. *Saturday Review of Politics, Literature, Science and Art*, vol. 71, 1891.

57. *Sheffield Daily Telegraph*, 17 October 1889, *Huddersfield Daily Chronicle*, 19 October 1889, *Leicester Chronicle*, 19 October 1889, *Leicester Journal*, 25 October 1889.

58. Paula Gillett, *Musical Women in England 1870–1914: Encroaching on All Man's Privileges* (London: Macmillan, 2000).

59. *The Musical Times*, 1 June 1889.

60. *St James's Gazette*, 31 December 1891.

Chapter 5

1. http://www.thepeerage.com/p14836.htm#i148359

2. *The Sun* (London), 4 December 1847.

3. *Western Gazette*, 8 December 1871.
4. *Bath Chronicle and Weekly Gazette*, 5 September 1878.
5. London Electoral Registers 1885, 1888, 1892.
6. *Sporting Gazette*, 28 July 1883.
7. Violet Powell, *The Departure Platform* (London: William Heinemann, 1998).
8. *The Gentlewoman*, 2 April 1892.
9. *The Times*, 4 December 1951.
10. *Somerset Standard*, 10 March 1894.
11. *The Times*, 4 December 1951.
12. *Clifton Society*, 21 January 1897.
13. Letter from Ethel Boyce to Harland Chaldecott, postmarked 19 January 1897. Chertsey Museum: Harland Chaldecott Papers (D 2463/87).
14. *Somerset Standard*, 6 January 1894.
15. *Somerset Standard*, 13 January 1894.
16. Letter from Bright to Francesco Berger, 8 August 1891. Philharmonic Society Papers (BL Loan 48.13/5).
17. *St James Gazette*, 28 December 1891.
18. *Sheffield Daily Telegraph*, 3 March 1892.
19. *The Queen*, 19 March 1892.
20. *Sheffield Daily Telegraph*, 3 March 1892 as above.
21. *The Queen*, 7 May 1892.
22. *Morning Post*, 9 May 1892.
23. *The Globe*, 12 May 1892.
24. *The Times*, 13 May 1892.
25. *The Queen*, 21 May 1892.
26. J. P. Wearing, *The London Stage 1890–1899: A Calendar of Plays and Players* (Metuchen, NJ: The Scarecrow Press, 1976), p. 287.
27. Sophie Fuller, 'Women Composers during the British Musical Renaissance 1880–1918' (PhD thesis, Kings College, University of London, 1998).
28. *Clifton Society*, 10 January 1895.
29. *Somerset Standard*, 26 January 1895.
30. Ibid.
31. *Shepton Mallet Journal*, 22 January 1897.
32. *Wells Journal*, 28 December 1899.
33. *Shepton Mallet Journal*, 22 January 1897.
34. *Musical News*, 3 June 1893.
35. *Westminster Gazette*, 13 April 1893.
36. *The Times*, 14 April 1893, 20 April 1893, 27 April 1893.
37. *The Times*, 27 April 1893.
38. *Western Morning News*, 20 October 1892.
39. *Norfolk News*, 17 April 1894.
40. *London Evening Standard*, 31 October 1895.
41. *The Times*, 21 October 1895.
42. *The Times*, 12 November 1895.
43. *London Evening Standard*, 12 November 1895.
44. *London Evening Standard*, 30 November 1895.
45. Ibid.
46. *The Era*, 14 December 1895.
47. Dora Bright, 'My Early Years', unpublished memoir.
48. *The Queen*, 24 November 1894.
49. Roz Trubger, 'Forgotten Composers' (2014), bfs.org.uk.
50. *Somerset Standard*, 9 February 1900.

Chapter 6

1. Violet Powell, *The Departure Platform* (London: William Heinemann Ltd, 1998).
2. *Somerset Standard*, 23 March 1900.
3. *Somerset Standard*, 10 August 1900.
4. *Somerset Standard*, 23 March 1900.
5. Evangeline Holland, 'Edwardian Promenade – An Edwardian Music Primer' (Blog), 14 October 2014.
6. *The Globe*, 4 October 1901.
7. Bill Pertwee, *By Royal Command* (Newton Abbot, Devon: David & Charles, 1981).
8. *The Sketch*, 11 December 1901.
9. *Somerset Standard*, 8 November 1901.
10. *The Queen*, 29 August 1903.
11. *Shepton Mallet Journal*, 31 October 1902.
12. *Le Monde* (Paris), 11 October 1903.
13. Leo Trevor, 'Recollections of the Chatsworth Theatricals', *The Pall Mall Magazine*, November 1903, vol. 31.
14. *Sheffield Daily Telegraph*, 6 February 1903.
15. *Westminster Gazette*, 30 January 1903.
16. *Dundee Evening Telegraph*, 30 October 1903.
17. *The Gentlewoman*, 7 November 1903.
18. *Hull Daily Mail*, 16 November 1903.
19. *London Evening Standard*, 6 January 1904.
20. *Sheffield Daily Telegraph*, 8 January 1904.
21. *The Queen*, 10 September 1904.
22. *Truth*, 28 April 1909.
23. Ivor Guest, *Adeline Genée: A lifetime of ballet under six reigns; based on the personal reminiscences of Dame Adeline Genée-Isitt, D.B.E.* (London: A. and C. Black, 1958).
24. *Yorkshire Post* and *Leeds Intelligencer*, 3 March 1903.
25. *The Graphic*, 28 March 1903.
26. *London Daily News*, 10 February 1903.
27. Sir Henry Coward, *Reminiscences of Henry Coward* (London: J. Curwen & Sons, 1919).
28. *Truth*, 12 March 1903.
29. *Leeds Mercury*, 16 September 1903.
30. *The Times*, 5 May 1951.
31. *London Daily News*, 18 February 1905.
32. *London Daily News*, 23 March 1905.
33. *Shepton Mallett Journal*, 31 March 1905.
34. *Westminster Gazette*, 5 April 1905.
35. *The Monthly Musical Record*, 1 May 1905, p. 98.
36. *The Musical Times*, 1 January 1905.
37. *Morning Post*, 31 March 1906.
38. *London Daily News*, 2 May 1906.
39. *The Times*, 27 November 1907.
40. *The Times*, 12 December 1907.
41. *Somerset Standard*, 19 December 1902.
42. *Somerset Standard*, 30 September 1904.
43. *Somerset Standard*, 11 January 1907.
44. *The Musical Times*, 1 July 1903.
45. *Somerset Standard*, 11 October 1907.
46. Dora Bright, 'My Early Years', unpublished autobiography.
47. Ibid.

48. *Manchester Courier and Lancashire General Advisor*, 14 September 1907.
49. *London Evening Standard*, 20 February 1908.
50. *The Queen*, 26 October 1912.
51. Hugh Carey, *Duet for Two Voices* (Cambridge: Cambridge University Press, 1979).
52. Ibid.

Chapter 7

1. *The Era*, 16 March 1907.
2. *Westminster Gazette*, 26 March 1907.
3. *East Anglian Daily Times*, 5 June 1909.
4. Ivor Guest, *Adeline Genée: A lifetime of ballet under six reigns; based on the personal reminiscences of Dame Adeline Genée-Isitt, D.B.E.* (London: A. and C. Black, 1958).
5. *The Times*, 8 September 1908.
6. *The Billboard*, 26 September 1908.
7. Guest, *Adeline Genée*.
8. Ibid.
9. *The New York Evening Sun*, 5 May 1911.
10. Guest, *Adeline Genée*.
11. Ibid.
12. *The Era*, 1 April 1914.
13. *The Tatler and Bystander* – Self profile Adeline Genée by Adeline Genée, 25 February 1948.
14. Guest, *Adeline Genée*.
15. Ibid.
16. *The Tatler and Bystander*, 25 February 1948.
17. *Somerset Standard*, 26 May 1911.
18. *Somerset Standard*, 11 August 1911.
19. *Daily Telegraph and Courier* (London), 22 May 1909.
20. *The Globe*, 11 October 1910.
21. *The Times*, 11 October 1910.
22. *Music Hall and Theatre Review*, 13 October 1910.
23. Guest, *Adeline Genée*.
24. *The Times*, 21 December 1912.
25. *Cheltenham Looker-On*, 24 August 1912; *The Queen*, 28 September 1912.
26. *The Era*, 26 April 1914.
27. *Pall Mall Gazette*, 25 March 1914.
28. Ted Shawn, 'The History of the Art of Dancing – part 3', *Denishawn Magazine*, Spring 1925.
29. *Westminster Gazette*, 7 April 1914.
30. Ibid.
31. *The Times*, 7 April 1914.
32. *The People*, 20 June 1915.
33. *The Times*, 28 June 1915.
34. *The Times*, 1 January 1916.
35. Guest, *Adeline Genée*.
36. Ibid.
37. *The Tatler and Bystander*, 25 February 1948.
38. *The Times*, 1 November 1909.
39. *The Globe*, 25 November 1910.
40. *The Stage*, 23 March 1911.

41. *John Bull*, 25 March 1911.
42. *The Referee*, 2 April 1911.
43. *The Referee*, 19 May 1912.
44. *The Stage*, 23 May 1912.
45. *Sheffield Daily Telegraph*, 24 January 1913.
46. *Yorkshire Post and Leeds Intelligencer*, 28 June 1917.
47. *Westminster Gazette*, 23 June 1917.
48. *Kinematograph Weekly*, 1 May 1919.
49. Sophie Fuller, 'Discovering Music: Early 20th Century', The Society of Women Musicians, https://www.bl.uk/20th-century-music/articles/the-society-of-women-musicians.
50. Laura Seddon, 'The Instrumental Music of British Women Composers in the Early Twentieth Century' (Unpublished Doctoral thesis, City University London, 2011).
51. *Birmingham Daily Gazette*, 23 March 1906.
52. *Cambridge Chronicle and Journal*, 19 March 1890.
53. *London Daily News*, 23 January 1908.
54. *The Times*, 23 November 1951.
55. *The Globe*, 28 June 1916.
56. *Clifton Society*, 27 January 1916.
57. *Somerset Standard*, 20 January 1939.
58. *Yorkshire Post and Intelligencer*, 6 April 1915.
59. *Liverpool Daily Post*, 25 September 1917.
60. Letter from Ethel Boyce to Harland Chaldecott. Chertsey Museum: Harland Chaldecott Papers [CHYMS.2463.054].
61. Mrs. W. Knatchbull, Last Will and Testament, 10 February 1918.
62. Ibid.

Chapter 8

1. *Somerset Standard*, 9 July 1920.
2. Robert Benchley, *20,000 Leagues under the Sea; or, David Copperfield* (New York: Henry Holt & Co., 1928).
3. The Very Rev William R. Inge, *Diary of a Dean* (New York: Macmillan Press, 1950).
4. Letter from Ethel Boyce to Harland Chaldecott. Chertsey Museum: Harland Chaldecott Papers [CHYMS.2463.086].
5. George A. Birmingham, *Pleasant Places* (Kingswood, Surrey: Windmill Press, 1934).
6. *Somerset Standard*, 12 January 1940.
7. *Somerset Guardian and Radstock Observer*, 9 September 1932; *Somerset Standard*, 9 September 1932.
8. *Somerset Standard*, 11 August 1939.
9. *Country Life*, 16 April 1943.
10. *Western Daily Press*, 14 January 1922.
11. 'Letters of Ralph Vaughan Williams to Dora Knatchbull', https://vaughanwilliamsfoundation.org/letter/letter-from-ralph-vaughan-williams-to-dora-knatchbull/
12. *Somerset Standard*, 7 November 1919.
13. *Somerset Standard*, 17 June 1927.
14. *Somerset Standard*, 26 November 1936.
15. *Somerset Standard*, 24 December 1937.
16. *Somerset Standard*, 7 January 1938.
17. *Somerset Guardian and Radstock Observer*, 21 January 1938.
18. Ibid.

19. *Somerset Guardian and Radstock Observer*, 22 July 1938.
20. *Somerset Standard*, 21 July 1939.
21. *Somerset Standard*, 28 July 1939.
22. *Aberdeen Press and Journal*, 7 November 1924.
23. *Radio Times* Issue 705, 4–10 April 1937.
24. *Somerset Guardian and Radstock Observer*, 14 April 1939.
25. *The Stage*, 28 April 1932.
26. *The Stage*, 2 February 1933.
27. Television advertising from *The Scotsman*, 15 March 1933.
28. *Somerset Standard*, 20 November 1936.
29. *Bath Chronicle and Weekly Gazette*, 22 April 1939.
30. *The Times*, 25 January 1926.
31. *Radio Times*, 8 April 1937.
32. Violet Powell, *The Departure Platform* (London: William Heinemann Ltd, 1998).

Chapter 9

1. *Somerset Standard*, 1 May 1942.
2. *Somerset Standard*, 11 September 1942.
3. Sophie Fuller, 'Women Composers during the British Musical Renaissance 1880–1918' (PhD thesis, Kings College, University of London, 1998).
4. *Musical Opinion*, November 1941, pp. 37–38.
5. *Musical Opinion*, March 1942, pp. 198–99.
6. Adelina De Lara, *Finale* (London: Burke Publishing Co., 1915).
7. *Shepton Mallet Journal*, 24 November 1944.
8. *Somerset Standard*, 23 November 1951.
9. *The Musical Times*, January 1952.
10. *The Stage*, 22 November 1951.
11. *The Times*, 29 November 1951, Adeline Genée archive L18 – Royal Academy of Dance.
11. *Somerset Standard*, 20 November 1951.
13. *Somerset Guardian and Radstock Observer*, 16 May 1952.
14. Violet Powell, *The Departure Platform* (London: William Heinemann Ltd, 1998).
15. Susan W. Albert, *The Tale of Applebeck Orchard* (New York: Berkley Prime Crime, 2009).

Chapter 10

1. Michael Dervan, 'Classical Music Still Lags Behind on Gender Policy', *The Irish Times*, 13 February 2019.
2. Crystal A. Frost, 'How Female Classical Composers are Encouraging Gender Equality', Grammy.com, 8 April 2020, https://www.grammy.com/news/how-female-classical-composers-are-encouraging-gender-equality.
3. Gabriella Di Laccio, 'Equality & Diversity in Concert Halls: 100 Orchestras Worldwide' (Donne Charitable Foundation, 2020).
4. Marcia J. Citron, *Gender and the Musical Canon* (Cambridge: CUP Archive, 1993).
5. Emily Gunton, 'Bang the Drum for Change: Why Do Orchestras Have So Few Female Percussionists?' *The Guardian*, 8 March 2021.
6. Ibid.
7. Ian Youngs, 'Pop Music's Growing Gender Gap Revealed in the Collaboration Age', *BBC News*, 19 February 2019, https://www.bbc.co.uk/news/entertainment-arts-47232677.

8. Paula Gillett, *Musical Women in England 1870–1914: Encroaching on All Man's Privileges* (London: Macmillan, 2000), pp. 110–11.
9. Sandra Canosa, 'Modern Feminism: The Role of Women in Music', *Highbrow Magazine*, 4 April 2014),
www.highbrowmagazine.com/3879-modern-feminism-role-women-music
10. https://www.rollingstone.com/music/music-country/
taylor-swift-music-is-art-and-art-should-be-paid-for-244144/

Chapter 11

1. *The Musical Times*, 1 March 1888.
2. *The Queen*, 24 November 1894.
3. *The Musical Times*, 1 January 1897.
4. *The Queen*, 4 April 1891.
5. 'Lady Instrumentalists: Miss Dora Bright', *The Strand Musical Magazine* 3 (1896), p. 157.
6. SOMMCD 273 Piano Concertos by Dora Bright and Ruth Gipps, SOMM Recordings, 2019.
7. George Bernard Shaw, *Music in London 1890–1894*, rev ed. (London: Constable 1932), p. 160.
8. *London Evening Standard*, 27 September 1888.
9. *The Globe*, 27 September 1888.
10. *Illustrated Sporting and Dramatic News*, 29 September 1888.
11. *The Musical World*, 28 July 1888.
12. *Hampstead & Highgate Express*, 2 May 1891.
13. *The Queen*, 3 May 1890.
14. *The Sheffield Independent*, 4 February 1891.
15. *Norfolk News*, 17 February 1894.
16. *Lloyds Weekly Newspaper*, 7 July 1897.
17. *The Musical Times*, 1 April 1897.
18. *The Queen*, 2 February 1895.
19. *London Daily News*, 24 June 1895.
20. *The Musical Times*, 1 March 1885.
21. *The Sketch*, 13 September 1899.
22. *Dundee Evening Telegraph*, 30 October 1903.
23. *Hull Daily Mail*, 16 November 1903.
24. *The Musical Times*, 1 April 1904.
25. *The Times*, 8 September 1908.
26. *The Times*, 11 October 1910.
27. *The Globe*, 25 November 1910.
28. *The Times*, 1 April 1911.
29. *The Stage*, 23 May 1912.
30. *The Stage*, 6 June 1912.
31. *Cheltenham Examiner*, 9 January 1913.
32. Synopsis from the programme to the premiere of the work in the USA at the Boston Opera House, 16 November 1912.
33. *Daily Citizen* (Manchester), 7 July 1913.
34. *The Era*, 4 February 1914.
35. *The Times*, 7 April 1914.
36. J. T. Grein, 'The World of the Theatre', *The Illustrated London News*, 1 January 1927.
37. *The Times*, 25 November 1926.
38. *The Sphere*, 15 June 1935.

References

Albert, S. (2009) *The Tale of Applebeck Orchard*. New York: Berkley Prime Crime.

Beecham, Sir Thomas (1942) The Position of Women in Music. In *Vogue's First Reader*. New York: Conde Nast Publications Inc.

Benchley, R. (1928) *20,000 Leagues under the Sea; or, David Copperfield*. New York: Henry Holt & Co.

Bernard Shaw, G. (1932) *Music in London 1890–1894*, rev. ed. London: Constable.

Birmingham, G. A. (1934) *Pleasant Places*. Kingswood, Surrey: Windmill Press.

Bright, D. (n.d.) My Early Years. Unpublished memoir.

Brush, C. (2012) A Study of the Composers and Music of the English Renaissance and their Influence upon the Compositional Style of Ralph V. Williams. Master of Music research paper, Ball State University, Muncie, Indiana.

Byrne, V. J. (2015) The Life and Works of Dorothy Howell. Master of Arts thesis, Department of Music, University of Birmingham.

Canosa, S. (2014) Modern Feminism: The Role of Women in Music. *Highbrow Magazine*, April 4. www.highbrowmagazine.com/3879-modern-feminism-role-women-music

Carey, H. (1979) *Duet for Two Voices*. Cambridge: Cambridge University Press.

Citron, M. J. (1993) *Gender and the Musical Canon*. Cambridge: CUP Archive.

Coward, Henry (1919) *Reminiscences of Henry Coward*. London: J. Curwen & Sons.

De Laccio, G. (2020) Equality & Diversity in Concert Halls: 100 Orchestras Worldwide. Donne Charitable Foundation.

De Lara, A. (1915) *Finale*. London: Burke Publishing Co.

Dervan, M. (2019) Classical Music Still Lags Behind on Gender Policy. *The Irish Times*, 13 February.

Ellis, S. S. (1842) *The Daughters of England: Their Position in Society, Character and Responsibilities*. London and Paris: Fisher, Son, & Co.

Fuller, S. (n.d.) Discovering Music: Early 20th Century. The Society of Women Musicians. https://www.bl.uk/20th-century-music/articles/the-society-of-women-musicians

Fuller, S. (1998) Women Composers during the British Musical Renaissance 1880–1918. PhD thesis, Kings College, University of London.

Fuller-Maitland, J. A. (1902) *English Music in the XIXth Century*. London: Grant Richards.

Gillett, P. (2000) *Musical Women in England 1870–1914: Encroaching on All Man's Privileges*. London: Macmillan. https://doi.org/10.1057/9780312299347

Grein, J. T. (1927) The World of the Theatre. *The Illustrated London News*, 1 January 1927.

Guest, I. (1958) *Adeline Genée: A lifetime of ballet under six reigns; based on the personal reminiscences of Dame Adeline Genée-Isitt, D.B.E.* London: A. and C. Black.

Inge, The Very Rev William R. (1950) *Diary of a Dean*. New York: Macmillan Press.

Krausz, A. (1980) *Sheffield Jewry: Commentary on a Community*. Ramat-Gan: Bar-Ilan University; Sheffield: Naor Publications.

Lipson, E. (1947) *The Brights of Market Place*. Transactions of the Hunter Archaeological Society, Vol. 6. London: Hunter Archaeological Society.

Pertwee, B. (1981) *By Royal Command*. Newton Abbot, Devon: David & Charles.

Powell, V. (1998) *The Departure Platform*. London: William Heinemann Ltd.

Rees, B. (1986) *A Musical Peacemaker: The Life and Work of Sir Edward German*. n.p.: Kensal Press.

Seddon, L. (2011) The Instrumental Music of British Women Composers in the Early Twentieth Century. Unpublished Doctoral thesis, City University London.

Shawn, T. (1925) The History of the Art of Dancing – part 3. *Denishawn Magazine*, Spring.

Smyth, E. (1929) *A Final Burning of Boats*. London: Longman, Green & Co.

Trevor, L. (1903) Recollections of the Chatsworth Theatricals. *The Pall Mall Magazine*, May 1893–September 1914; November 1903.

Wearing, J. P. (1976) *The London Stage 1890–1899: A Calendar of Plays and Players*. Metuchen, NJ: The Scarecrow Press.

Wilson, H. J. (2014) The Challenge of Nineteenth Century Theatre in Sheffield. PhD thesis, School of English Language, Literature and Linguistics, University of Sheffield.

Young, P. M. (1967) *Keyboard Musicians of the World*. London: Abelard-Shuman.

Youngs, I. (2019) Pop Music's Growing Gender Gap Revealed in the Collaboration Age. *BBC News*. https://www.bbc.co.uk/news/entertainment-arts-47232677

Index

www.ingramcontent.com/pod-product-compliance
Lightning Source LLC
Chambersburg PA
CBHW040408110426
42812CB00011B/2486